14.95

Indexed in Essay &
General Literature

19 - 19

DATE DUE

DEC 5 1990			

DEMCO 38-296

D0090081

A list of books in the series appears at the end of this volume.

THE CHALLENGE
OF FEMINIST BIOGRAPHY

The CHALLENGE *of* FEMINIST BIOGRAPHY

Writing the Lives of Modern American Women

EDITED BY
Sara Alpern, Joyce Antler,
Elisabeth Israels Perry, and
Ingrid Winther Scobie

UNIVERSITY OF ILLINOIS PRESS
Urbana and Chicago

Contents

μ

Introduction

AT THE FIRST SOUTHERN CONFERENCE on Women's History in Spartanburg, South Carolina, in June 1988, the editors of this volume participated in a panel called "Biographies of Women in Public Life: Challenges and Results." We were all biographers of twentieth-century American women. Three of us had published a biography the previous year; the fourth was on the verge of finishing her manuscript. All of us had worked on our projects for over ten years, years that represented periods of intense personal, intellectual, and professional growth for us. By sharing the key features of that experience with others, we hoped to bring an important chapter of our lives to a formal close.

The panel attracted a large and enthusiastic audience, and many listeners stayed afterward to ask questions or tell about their own experiences. Stimulated and excited by their response, the four of us headed for a reception and shelter from the summer sun. As we walked, more stories about our adventures as biographers—funny stories, ironic stories, some sad and even chastening—poured out. At the same time, we continued to explore critical issues of approach, strategy, and meaning in the writing of women's lives in the modern era. We began to realize two things. First, the conference session had not given us enough time to do justice to all the issues we wanted to raise, and, second, other biographers might be eager to contribute to a forum on these issues. It was our good fortune that Carole Appel, women's studies editor at the University of Illinois Press, who was also attending the conference, found us at that moment and shared our enthusiasm for such a project.

We came to see our anthology as a workshop in print that would inform and encourage those interested in the writing and reading of biography and especially in the biographical construction of modern women's lives. Because we were especially interested in the intersection of biography and society's larger sense of the past, we hoped that the essays would touch on the relationship between biography and history, particularly women's history. For this reason, we invited contributions from biographers who considered themselves historians and whose biographies, which had to be already or nearly published, offered a fresh, and feminist, perspective on larger political and cultural issues in history. We gave them freedom to write essays along whatever lines they wished, offering few restrictions or guidelines. We wanted all the essays to be personal, open, and honest.

Not everyone we approached accepted our invitation. Some could not meet our deadlines. Others had not yet finished their books or had not yet developed a critical perspective on their experiences as biographers. Despite these disappointments, the ten essays we include here more than fulfill our original intent. Scholars are rarely asked to articulate how their work evolves, at least not in print, and thus the process by which they construct their work often remains private or is shared with only a few friends and colleagues. And yet our panel at Spartanburg made it clear that others in the field wanted and needed to know what we had learned. All of the essays in this anthology share that knowledge in self-revelatory and often dramatic ways. They tell some gripping tales—of near misses and surprising discoveries in the quest for documents; of the significant evidence we found that others had overlooked, dismissed, or misinterpreted; of the major and sometimes painful shifts in interpretation or approach we felt forced to make as our projects matured; of the often complex ramifications of our encounters with subjects' relatives or colleagues (or, in Ingrid Winther Scobie's case, with the subject herself); and of the intense effects our projects had on our personal lives and relationships. Because our research and writing problems varied, we all felt these moments differently and thus speak about them with diverse voices.

And yet, because we also shared a common vision and experience of feminist biography, we speak with a collective voice as well. We were all individual women writing about other individual women during a highly self-conscious period in American women's lives. In the 1960s a long-dormant feminist movement revived, raising our consciousness as women and forcing us to ask new and disturbing questions about gender relations and the organization of our private and public lives. A few years later the women's studies movement began to establish itself as an academic field, giving us an intellectual community that nurtured our work. It also helped us, as historians, to develop a new, female-centered perspective on all historical subjects and, in our quest for subjects, to turn toward women.

We did not all decide to write a woman's life because of modern feminism and the women's studies movement. For some of us, our work derived from a fascination with the genre of biography or with particular subjects as the *dramatis personae* of history. For others, large questions about history or women's history drew us toward a particular woman in whose life multiple strands seemed to merge. However different our original motivations, once we had begun our work the women's movement added a special edge to it. As we passed through our own life transitions, we began almost inevitably to identify with and compare ourselves to our female subjects. As we tried to pull together the pieces of their lives and to relate those lives to larger issues and questions in women's history, we felt compelled to sort out the connection between their lives and the personal, political, or ideological issues of our own epoch.

As a result of that common experience, we touch on common themes in our essays. We discuss how feminist scholarship led us to approach women's lives in ways that are different from those of traditional biographers. We try to pinpoint the hallmarks of feminist biography and discuss the methodological and conceptual tools appropriate to writing the lives of women from a feminist perspective. Our essays, then, are individual "autobiographies" of our biographies and of ourselves. While providing guides to the theory and practice of feminist biography, they capture important turning points in the intellectual development of academic women from the beginning of the modern women's movement to the end of the 1980s.

When the authors of these essays began work on their biographies, few biographers were considering feminist issues. In 1979, for example, the Biographical Research Center at the University of Hawaii began planning a conference on "new directions in biography." In the process, the center surveyed over four hundred biographers to find out what they thought those directions might be. The respondents' sole comment relevant to women was to hope that there would be treatment of more women subjects in the future. No respondent suggested the usefulness of feminist perspectives on the writing of women's lives, and the volume of essays summarizing the results of the conference made no mention of feminist issues.[1]

In addition, the historical profession tended to dismiss biography as a genre. Like many contemporary literary critics, some modern historians continued to show a lack of regard for biography.[2] During the 1960s and 1970s, when the "new social history" came into its own, esteem for biography fell even further. In its earliest days biography had been at the center of the modern women's history movement. In order to rescue from historical oblivion the women who had been agents of change or articulate critics and leaders of their culture and society, the first generation of modern women's historians had spent years restoring to the record the deeds and accomplishments of "notable" women. But in the mid-1970s, such work, by that time called "compensatory," moved out to the margins.[3]

A later development dimmed even further the prospects for biographers of some twentieth-century women in public life. The intense political atmosphere of the 1970s divided and confused scholars about the validity of some historical subjects. As Bonnie G. Smith writes, "By the late 1970s, historians had devised tests of loyalty to gender, race, and class. As in the nineteenth century, the prominent woman caused consternation among scholars to whom oppression was the principle theme of the history of woman; her historic visibility either undermined that theme or testified to her lack of feminist or other virtues."[4] The elite backgrounds of some of our subjects, or their absorption by cultural, social, or personal goals other than those of the women's movement, led some scholars to question their significance to contemporary historical scholarship. Writing our biographies during the struggle to ratify the Equal Rights Amendment (ERA) exacerbated this situation. Some of our subjects' opposition to the ERA further compromised their feminist credentials to other scholars, who, along with us, were in the middle of the ratification struggle.

Over time, perspectives in the profession expanded. Historians began to understand better the protective impulses that had led some Progressives to oppose the ERA for as long as they did. They also began to recognize, and even appreciate, the variety of ways in which modern women expressed their concerns about women's issues. As a result, the meanings of feminism were no longer limited to those of the contemporary women's movement.[5] Thus, although a number of us felt isolated in the early years of our biographical work, by the 1980s we began to find the profession more interested in and supportive of our efforts.

In 1988, the historian Gerda Lerner called attention to the rising interest in the genre of biography in a survey of current work in United States women's history. After reviewing the explosion in monographs in the field that had taken place between 1980 and 1987, she commented that, in the concomitant explosion in doctoral dissertations, the most popular approach was biographical. She urged, however, that potential practitioners of the genre apply a more feminist approach to women's lives, using the new feminist scholarship in literature, psychology, and anthropology. Such an approach would allow biographers to use life-cycle analysis or to address topics most biographies seldom touch on, such as how women's private and public lives intersect, the impact of mother-daughter relationships, or the "familial and female friendship support networks that sustained women's public activities." Lerner also called for a fuller analysis of "the mental products of women's lives, their ideas, their writings, and their discourse." She concluded by asserting that the "biographical field within women's history remains one of the most promising and challenging for the researcher."[6]

A renewed interest in biography has also spread to the general public. Biography and women's studies sections in bookstores now brim with books chronicling the lives of women: according to one account, nearly two hundred biographies of women have been written since 1970. These books are regularly reviewed in the *New York Times* and other media, some of which have devoted front-page attention to the phenomenon of women's biography.[7] As one *Newsweek* article put it, America has entered a "golden age" of women and biography: "You can now buy biographies of women who paint, women who write fiction, women who write poems; biographies of actors, singers, dancers; biographies of journalists and photographers; biographies of fliers and psychiatrists; biographies of minority women and lesbians, something for everyone."[8] Today we can say that biography, once a "men's club," has been radically changed by the flood of attention now paid to women's lives.

In the 1990s, the writing of women's biographies should assume still new directions. Over the previous two decades, women's biographies, following the general contours of women's history research, have focused on white, primarily middle-class women. The essays in this anthology reflect that early focus of the field. However, efforts of women's historians to develop more adequate multiracial and multicultural perspectives have begun to influence the choice of biographical subjects. In addition to recently published biographies of women of color, other studies now in process or recently completed as doctoral dissertations point the way to more inclusive feminist biographical treatments.[9]

How has changing the gender of the subject changed the nature and practice of the biographical craft? First and foremost, a different type of person is now receiving biographical treatment. Not all of our subjects achieved the kind of celebrity or lasting fame that many male biographical subjects enjoyed. This was due not to a lack of achievement on their part but more to the failure of historians to pay attention to their kind of achievement. Feminist biographers are not only restoring "invisible" women to the record but enlarging our perspective of the record. Barbara Tuchman called biography a "prism of history" that encompasses "the universal in the particular."[10] When the particular becomes female, the universal can no longer be male. As Lois Rudnick writes in her essay, "Women's lives have rarely fit the model of the normative biographical hero-type. As feminist biographers have carved out a major domain within the genre, we have not only uncovered and restored 'lost' women, many of whom were not heroic in the traditional sense, but we have also called into question the masculinist grounds on which biography has conventionally been defined and accepted." Thus Rudnick contends that Mabel Dodge Luhan, writer, patron, and salon hostess, should not be dismissed as "mere" muse or catalyst but be regarded herself as an individual creative force.

Much the same can be said of others among our subjects, all of whom have suffered from some form of historical neglect, marginalization, or misinterpretation. Although some of our subjects have appeared in recent biographical surveys such as *Notable American Women,* many of them have never attracted major biographical attention. This is true of Belle Moskowitz, Molly Dewson, and Helen Gahagan Douglas, who played significant but not always highly visible roles in American political life, and of Lucy Sprague Mitchell, a prominent figure in progressive education in the early twentieth century. The same is also true of Jessie Daniel Ames, who dedicated her life to the fight against racism; of Freda Kirchwey, editor, owner, and publisher of *The Nation*, who shaped public opinion for almost forty years; and of the labor activist Mary Heaton Vorse, whose reports on major strikes and unions made her a foremost American labor journalist. As biographers of these women, we wanted to move their stories from footnote or passing reference to the center of the historical narrative.

Some of our other subjects, like Mabel Dodge Luhan, had been dismissed as minor figures or had been evaluated negatively. Even Florence Kelley, who was so important that the U.S. Supreme Court justice Felix Frankfurter believed she had "probably the largest single share in shaping the social history of the United States during the first thirty years of this century," had received no comprehensive study of her life and work, although two brief biographies, written in 1953 and 1966, do exist. The exception is Emma Goldman, who has received considerable scholarly attention. In fact, Alice Wexler saw her work "as one of humanizing a mythic figure." Most of our contributors, however, have focused more keenly than earlier biographers on their subjects' lives and careers as women and have expanded the concept of historical significance to include and validate their work as women.

There is a second major way in which changing the gender of the subject changes biography. When the subject is female, gender moves to the center of the analysis. Feminists contend that women's lives differ from men's, often in profound ways. Because society tends to value male models of achievement and behavior more than it values female models, a woman's gender may exercise greater constraints on the way her life evolves. Failing to consider this difference distorts, if not falsifies, any account of a woman's life. This is true even when a woman is unaware of or inarticulate about the effects of gender on her life. No matter how "free" of gender-specific conditions a woman may think she is, these conditions nonetheless affect her. In addition, of course, other aspects of her identity—class, race, religion, ethnicity, sexuality, region—also play critical roles.

The gender consciousness a feminist biographer brings to a female subject can enrich biographies of male subjects as well. Few biographies of men highlight gender issues in men's lives. They generally focus instead on a man's preparation for and fulfillment of his life course in the public arena. A heightened gender consciousness would help biographers explore the constraints by which society forces men into certain molds of behavior. It would not ignore, or dismiss as irrelevant, a man's private life or the nature of his family and work relations with individuals of both sexes. Finally, a gender consciousness in men's biographies would lead to a greater recognition of the tensions men often feel, but seldom publicly acknowledge, between their private and public selves. In summary, there can and ought to be "feminist" biographies of men that involve an awareness of gender constraints and issues in all aspects of men's lives.

When assessing female biography, some feminist commentators look beyond gender constraints, arguing that women share in a female "culture" that arises from their common biological or life-cycle experiences and from the values and ideas about women that are current in a particular time or place. Again, distinctions must be drawn, for not all women respond in the same way to either the gender-specific conditions or the aspects of a female culture that surround them. Some women press at the boundaries of constraints or reject being identified with female culture, others accept the constraints, operating comfortably and creatively within them or using them to reap advantages from society. No matter how feminist biographers sort out the complexities of any one individual woman's response, they accept as a given that gender will always, in some way, be central to an understanding of a woman's life, even if that woman is not particularly conscious of that centrality or even denies it.

This perspective on the centrality of gender has had a broad impact on the way we, as feminist biographers, have written our subjects' lives. As the essays in this volume show, the expression of this perspective took somewhat different forms for each of us. Again, however, common themes emerge. For some writers, the tension that often develops for women between their private and public selves proved a useful emphasis. Sara Alpern, for example, in discussing Freda Kirchwey's merging of her personal life into *The Nation* after her son Jeffrey's death, shows how Kirchwey and *The Nation* became one. Susan Ware initially treated Molly Dewson as an exemplar of a political style and era but eventually realized that, because the person "you share your bed with and how you pay the bills do have an impact on events beyond the household," Dewson's relationship to her lover, Polly Porter, had to become a key part, if not the centerpiece, of her biography. While

Ware notes that her insight about the importance of the private applies to men and women, she believes that women achievers tend more often than men to make decisions and sacrifices on the basis of personal needs.

In emphasizing the private, others of us have stressed the impact of ordinary daily lives and female experiences on our subjects' public achievements. Some wonderful discoveries came out of this emphasis. Joyce Antler reveals that she received access to the previously closed diaries of Lucy Sprague Mitchell's husband, Wesley Clair Mitchell, because the husband's biographer believed that the personal information contained in the diaries was irrelevant to his own study of Wesley. These diaries proved invaluable to Antler's reconstruction of essential aspects of Lucy's life.[11] During later stages of writing, Ingrid Winther Scobie unexpectedly gained access to fifty years of personal correspondence between Helen Gahagan Douglas and her husband, Melvyn. These letters dramatically changed the way Scobie was able to interpret Helen's public life. The interrelationship between the private and the public also informs Elisabeth Israels Perry's work. Her analysis of Belle Moskowitz's relationship to her political mentor, Alfred E. Smith, hinges on an understanding of Moskowitz's self-image as wife and mother. This image runs as a leitmotif throughout Moskowitz's adult career, affecting even the publicity she wrote for Smith in his 1928 presidential race.

A focus on the female life-cycle experience is yet another aspect of the feminist biographers' consciousness of gender. This focus enables them to develop fuller portrayals of women, to do what Carolyn Heilbrun calls "reinventing the narrative of women's lives" by shifting attention away from the "marriage plot" to a consideration of all stages of the life cycle, including mature adulthood and old age.[12] Joyce Antler focuses on this dynamic when she writes of feminism "as life process"—an attempt by women "to mold their destinies in the world and achieve autonomy" through successive stages of the life cycle—and explains that Lucy Mitchell's seventies and eighties were among the most fruitful decades of her life, the period Mitchell herself described as becoming "more so," or more herself.

Several authors note the importance of female friendships during their subjects' major life transitions. For some subjects, like Molly Dewson, a friendship with one woman could be the central experience that determined important life decisions. For others, friendships with a variety of women formed the core of a growing personal life as well as of expanding political judgments. The radical older women whom Dee Garrison interviewed during the course of her research on Mary Heaton Vorse—Vorse's "insurgent" friends—taught Garrison the enduring meaning of her subject's life work. For us as well as our subjects, networks of female friends and allies have been critical to our personal and professional growth.

For most of us, because we were women writing about women, our heightened consciousness of the role of gender meant an especially close relationship with our subjects. Such a relationship is not unique to feminist biography, for most biographers enter into dialogues with their subjects, even when the subjects are long dead. As one commentator observes, "any biography uneasily shelters an autobiography within it," and this autobiography inevitably alters the biographer's material.[13] But, when the biographer is a woman writing about another woman, what further dimensions are added?

For many feminist biographers the connection between writer and subject becomes highly personal. Kathryn Kish Sklar, for example, relates that her work process developed in three layers, the first laid by nonbiographical questions, the next following a "social science approach to biography," and the final acknowledging a "personal relationship between the author and her subject." This final layer became so enveloping that, as she coped with changes occurring in her own life, images of death dogged her. For other authors the personal attachment to subjects was present from the beginning and intensified according to the various stages of life transition at which the authors found themselves. Writers in the collection talk about their own experiences of getting married or divorced, becoming widowed, experiencing the death of siblings and parents, giving birth, raising children, and also separating from children who were growing up and becoming adults. Several authors point out how deeply entwined the process of writing biography became in their family's lives. Sara Alpern's son, for example, once referred to her biographical subject as his sister. Dee Garrison's friends sometimes speak of her subject as though she were a "dead relative."

The close interaction that developed between our subjects' and our own experiences helped us deal not only with our own problems but with life-cycle issues in our subjects' lives. But several risks were involved. We had to struggle through various stages of identification and rejection in order to achieve the distance necessary for a critical stance.

We had to resolve issues concerning our subjects' need for privacy. A woman's struggles sometimes to fuse, sometimes to sever, the private and public dimensions of her life is one of feminist biography's most important themes. But, in unraveling the strands of that struggle, because of our personal involvement in our subjects' lives we also felt more conflicted about revelations that violated their privacy. One of our essayists tells of a dream in which she appeared as a mugger. Others worry that the very act of appropriating another's life infringes on the subject's privacy, perhaps even violating her identity.

Expressing fears that we may be invading subjects' privacy or revealing the depth of our attachment to subjects are among the ways that some contributors to this volume recognize and seem to reject the standard of objective truth as the sine qua non of biography. In her essay, Lois Rudnick observes that the "distanced, authorial voice that provides the illusion that the life actually was as it is presented" has been integral to the myth of the heroic individual so characteristic of much biographical writing. She suggests that perhaps it is feminist biographers' sensitivity to the varied ways in which women have been socially constructed that has allowed them to unmask the "once-presumed objectivity of biography."

To recognize the subjectivity of biography means that biographers can reveal their attachments and detachments even while maintaining a critical, scholarly stance. Dee Garrison writes of solving her "dilemma of subjectivity" by becoming aware, and thus critical, of her own personal concerns. Such a process allows biographers to admit that perhaps they made mistakes, as Jacquelyn Dowd Hall does in her essay. Because the project of self-discovery is open-ended, she explains, "Second readings . . . come with the territory of feminist biography." She writes, "We have challenged the illusion of objectivity and given up the arrogance of believing that we can, once and for all, get our foremothers right. . . . only by telling new stories and telling our stories anew can we glimpse the truths that emerge not once and for all but all in their own good time." This emphasis on attachment and re-visioning suggests that writing a woman's life requires an active, not a neutral, voice from the biographer. Inherent in that voice is the willingness to learn from the specificity of a subject's life, to acknowledge and express her complexities, contradictions, and tensions. These essays talk about the ways in which our subjects continued to surprise and very often to disappoint us, for the life and the persona turned out to be infinitely more complicated than we could have imagined. We learned how hard it was for any of our subjects to lead lives that we would have considered totally admirable, for they, like us, could never fully escape the culture in which they lived.

Many of the practical problems biographers face intersect with those of every historian. All historians have to make hard decisions about the reconstruction, selection, and inclusion of events or the analysis of motive and cause. But biographers, in reconstructing an individual's life, face special challenges, not the least of which is the wide preparation they need to understand a person's often multiple realms of activity.

Many other issues challenge biographers. How should a biography be structured: according to strict chronology, by combining thematic and chronological approaches, or by using even more unusual formats? How, in the absence of intimate diaries, does the biographer get to know a subject from the inside? If an important fact is lacking, what options does the biographer have to fill the gap? How can the complex interaction of subject, family, and historical context be unraveled? When are the subject's own memoirs trustworthy? For example, when Alice Wexler used Emma Goldman's autobiography as a source of information, she tried "to use it more as an account of how Goldman remembered her past than as a story of how she actually lived it." When confronted with memoirs that present changing "selves" to the world, how does the biographer distinguish among them? Finally, there are serious ethical questions to resolve about revealing a subject's secrets, and serious consequences in doing so for relations between the biographer and a subject's heirs. These are not easy questions, and our essayists all touch on how they came to grips with them.

Biographies of women pose additional problems unique to the genre. These essays discuss our struggles to find sufficient and reliable documentation and our frustration with the lack of secondary sources in our still very young field of women's history. Faced with the lack of sources, some of us used photographs and other nonliterary materials, including domestic memorabilia. We used oral evidence, the testimony of children, relatives, and friends of our subjects. Again, all historians who use oral evidence must resolve dilemmas about the reliability, accuracy, and motives of witnesses. But biographers of women face special problems. Some children, we found, blanked out everything negative about their mothers, others everything favorable. Because society still expects mothers to be more responsible for domestic life than fathers, might children judge mothers more harshly than fathers? If so, how does the biographer weigh their testimony?

In communicating our own experiences and discoveries in trying to answer these and related questions, our goal was not to set down rigid guidelines about how such questions should be answered or to force a template onto women's biographies. We wanted, rather, to contribute to the ongoing discussion of the nature and practice of feminist biography and to assist and encourage others in their own projects. We also wanted to draw attention to the role feminist biography ought to play in our discipline. Although biography, by focusing on one person, may exaggerate the importance of individuals in history,[14] we would argue that feminist biography not only expands our knowledge about women's lives but alters the frameworks within which we interpret historical experience. Writing the lives of the women in this book, for example, has led the contributors to reconceptualize many facets of twentieth-century political life, including the advent of the welfare state, the processes of formal and informal education, labor history, and the history of racism and of the avant garde, among other major topics.

For all of us, then, the engagement with biography has been significant in several important ways. It has helped us illuminate the lives of vanished or obscured individual women, our own experience, and the broadest reaches of women's history and of historical change in general. We offer this anthology both to celebrate and ensure the continuing development of the genre.

NOTES

We thank the history department of Texas A&M University for the financial support that enabled us to coordinate the final stages of this book and express our appreciation to Daisy Jones and Linda Strube for their help with the index. Special thanks go to Carole Appel and Terry Sears of the University of Illinois Press for their enthusiastic support of our book. We are also grateful to Megan Marshall, Susan Quinn, Lois Rudnick, and Judith Tick, members of Joyce Antler's writers' group in Boston, for their comments on several drafts of this introduction.

1. See Anthony M. Friedson, ed., *New Directions in Biography* (Honolulu: University of Hawaii Press, 1981), ix–x, xvi–xvii, 96.

2. On the views of literary critics toward literary biographies, see David Novarr, *The Lines of Life: Theories of Biography, 1880–1970* (West Lafayette, Ind.: Purdue University Press, 1986), or Miles F. Shore, who comments on how biography, located "somewhere between literature and history," is "regarded with misgivings" by both fields ("Biography in the 1980s: A Psychological Perspective," *Journal of Interdisciplinary History* 12/1 [Spring 1981]: 89–113).

3. See that ambitious biographical project of the first generation of modern women's historians, *Notable American Women* (Edward T. James et al., 3 vols., [Cambridge, Mass.: Harvard University Press, 1971], and vol. 4, *The Modern Period*, Barbara Sicherman and Carol Hurd Green, eds., 1980). While this publication completed a part of the early "compensatory" task, it had, of course, hardly exhausted women as biographical topics. Nonetheless, the historian of women Gerda Lerner afterward urged historians to go beyond the history of "luminaries" to examine a broader range of women's experiences. See her collection of pathbreaking essays, *The Majority Finds Its Past* (New York: Oxford University Press, 1979).

4. Bonnie G. Smith, "The Contribution of Women to Modern Historiography in Great Britain, France, and the United States, 1750–1940," *American Historical Review* 89/3 (June 1984): 727.

5. Among the works helpful in this regard were Nancy Cott's discussion of postsuffrage feminist politics, *The Grounding of Modern Feminism* (New Haven, Conn.: Yale University Press, 1987) and Joan Hoff-Wilson's anthology of essays on the ERA, *Rights of Passage: The Past and Future of the ERA* (Bloomington: Indiana University Press, 1986). See also Karen Offen's illuminating article, "Defining Feminism: A Comparative Historical Approach," *Signs: A Journal of Women in Culture and Society* 14/1 (Autumn 1988): 119–57; and Joan Wallach Scott's *Gender and the Politics of History* (New York: Columbia University Press, 1988).

6. See Lerner, "Priorities and Challenges in Women's History Research," *Perspectives,* Newsletter of the American Historical Association, April 1988, 17–20.

7. *Boston Globe,* October 14, 1984, pp. 1, 26.

8. *Newsweek,* November 6, 1989, p. 78.

9. See, for example, Jacqueline Ann Rouse, *Lugenia Burns Hope, Black Southern Reformer* (Athens: University of Georgia Press, 1989); Sara L. Lightfoot, *Balm in Gilead: Journey of a Healer* (Reading, Mass.: Addison-Wesley, 1988).

10. Barbara Tuchman, "Biography as a Prism of History," in Marc Pachter, ed., *Telling Lives: The Biographer's Art* (Philadelphia: University of Pennsylvania Press, 1981), 133–47.

11. Recently another historian made creative use of a woman's diary that others had dismissed as filled only with domestic trivia. See Laurel Thatcher Ulrich's Pulitzer Prize-winning book, *A Midwife's Tale: The Life of Martha Ballard, Based on Her Diary, 1785-1812* (New York: Alfred A. Knopf, 1990).

12. Carolyn Heilbrun, *Writing a Woman's Life* (New York: W. W. Norton, 1988), 51, 89–95, 131.

13. Paul Murray Kendall, *The Art of Biography* (London: George Allen & Unwin, 1965), x.

14. See David Brion Davis's caveat in "Recent Directions in American Cultural History," *American Historical Review* 73/3 (February 1968). While pointing out that biography runs "the risk of exaggerating the historical importance of individuals," he observed further that biography can also provide "a concreteness and sense of historical development that most studies of culture lack. And by showing how cultural tensions and contradictions may be internalized, struggled with, and resolved within actual individuals, it offers the most promising key to the synthesis of culture and history" (704–5).

KATHRYN KISH SKLAR

Coming to Terms with Florence Kelley: The Tale of a Reluctant Biographer

Everything about Florence Kelley (1859–1932) seems to be larger than life. Her father, William Darrah Kelley, was a U.S. congressman from Philadelphia who served fifteen consecutive terms between 1860 and 1890 and helped draft the Fifteenth Amendment, which extended voting rights to former slaves. Kelley's maternal great-aunt, Sarah Pugh, with whom she spent much of her childhood, was Lucretia Mott's best friend. As a Quaker and longtime member of the Executive Committee of the Pennsylvania Anti-Slavery Society, Pugh wrote the official remonstrance against the exclusion of women delegates from the 1840 London World's Anti-Slavery Convention.

Kelley graduated from Cornell in 1882 at the age of twenty-three. Her honors thesis, "On Some Changes in the Legal Status of the Child since Blackstone," published that year, remains for legal historians today an important harbinger of the Progressive era. Other highlights of her life include her years in Zurich, Switzerland, where she studied public policy, underwent conversion to socialism, began translating the writings of Engels and Marx and other works of "scientific socialism," and, in 1884, married a Polish-Jewish socialist medical student, Lazare Wischnewetsky. Beginning in 1885, she gave birth to three children in three years. Moving to New York, she and Lazare were expelled from the Socialist Labor party in 1887 after Florence attacked the party's lukewarm reception of the writings of Marx and Engels. She then became an expert critic of the methods of social inquiry utilized by the state boards of labor statistics, the most important policy agencies affecting working women and children in the late 1880s. In 1890 Lazare began hitting her, and in 1891 she left him to start a new life with her children in Chicago.

Exemplifying the mutual support that the social settlement movement offered women reformers, Jane Addams and others at Hull-House welcomed Kelley. The children boarded with the family of Henry Demarest Lloyd. Thereafter Kelley's children lived with her only sporadically. Nicholas ("Ko"), aged seven, Margaret, aged six, and John, aged five, remained emotionally close to their mother but lived with her friends or at boarding schools. Kelley struggled to work them into what became a frenetic schedule of reform activity but could not see them as much as she wished. Their visits to Hull-House meant that the children developed strong bonds with the band of women reformers there. Ko later wrote, "I was blessed with the best bringing-up and educating of anybody that I have known of my time."[1]

At Hull-House Kelley's reform career took off—especially after her appointment as chief factory inspector of Illinois to enforce a path-breaking eight-hour law for women wage earners that she had helped draft. Having gained national prominence, she left Chicago in 1899 to become general secretary of the newly founded National Consumers' League (NCL), a position she held until her death. She lived at Lillian Wald's Henry Street Settlement but she traveled widely, nurturing the development of sixty-four local leagues by 1904 and creating in the NCL and its locals the most powerful advocate for labor legislation for women and children. The NCL fought some of the same battles for working men as they did for working women, arguing successfully, for example, before the U.S. Supreme Court in 1917 on behalf of a ten-hour law for men to match the law for women that it had defended in 1908. When, after World War I, the tide of opinion turned against Kelley's state-building efforts, right-wing attacks called her "Moscow's chief conspirator," but many of the policies she advocated were adopted by state and federal governments in the 1930s.

———

"Biography is not taxonomy with the specimen to be reclassified according to the latest findings—it is the story of one life as seen by another, with both always growing and changing."
—Elinor Langer, *Josephine Herbst* (1983)

People sometimes ask me, "Do you *like* Florence Kelley?"—a simple question to which I have no simple answer. Usually I say, "I respect her," sparing the questioner a fuller and more genuine response. I do love researching and writing about her. I love struggling with her monumental historical significance. I love discovering how to do justice to her life story. And in many ways I also love her. But *like* her? No. For me, as for her contemporaries, she is too demanding, too formidable, too uncompromising, too passionate, too charismatic to be merely liked. I doubt that she was "liked" by anyone who knew her. Kelley inspired stronger feelings. Devotion, courage, and collective action among those who responded to her positively; fear, hostility, and opposition among those who did not. Newton Baker, with whom she worked closely during World War I, captured this intensity when he said, "Everyone was brave from the moment she walked into the room."[2]

This essay gives me a welcome opportunity to write about my relationship with this compelling person. I have lived with her now for ten years. Our relationship is as mature as it is likely to become—a bit one-sided, but enormously rewarding—and I can now look back on it and observe its stages of development. These stages are at once unique and commonplace. They derive from my very particular goals as a biographer and a feminist, but they also reflect a process that many other writers share.

I am a reluctant biographer. In fact, in the first stage of our relationship I rejected Kelley. I intended to write about the group of women reformers who clustered around two major social settlements—Hull-

House in Chicago, founded by Jane Addams in 1889, and Henry Street on Manhattan's Lower East Side, founded by Lillian Wald in 1895. My question was (and is): "Why were women so central to the creation of the welfare state in the United States?" Thus I began this project with an interest in the history of the relationship between women and public power, not an attraction to an individual. In fact, having already written one biography, I was determined to try something different.

For more than a year I avoided facing up to the colossus who stood astride the two groups I was studying. Two conclusions gradually compelled me to redefine my task, however. First, I decided that the groups I was studying could not adequately be understood without a scholarly biography of Kelley. The brief 1953 biography by her protégé Josephine Goldmark lacked footnotes and served more as a primary source than a scholarly analysis. Supplementing this was Dorothy Rose Blumberg's *Florence Kelley: The Making of a Social Pioneer*. Published by Kelley's grandson Augustus Kelley in 1966, the book focused primarily on Kelley's correspondence with Friedrich Engels and stopped soon after 1899 when the mature stage of Kelley's career began. In addition to realizing that a biography of Kelley was a necessary preliminary to our understanding of her contemporaries, I also came to feel that a study of her life would be the most effective vehicle for analyzing them.

Once those realizations sank in, there was no turning back. The task of writing about Kelley would be demanding, I knew. An immense amount of research lay before me, and I concentrated on strategies that eventually produced dozens of drawers of annotated files and notes. At first I wondered at my good fortune—I was learning so much and enjoying the process so much. But this wonder gave way to sober realism as serious obstacles began to present themselves. First, the daunting scale of the project emerged. This scale discouraged dissertation writers and nontenured scholars who needed to publish fairly quickly and could not count on multiple years of research support. I had tenure, but could I expect to conquer the mountain of research awaiting me?

Second, Kelley's years of study in Zurich, Switzerland, and her translation of the writings of Engels and Marx required sophisticated German language skills. I had lived in Germany and knew the language well enough to realize that I had to know it better before I could analyze this stage of her life. How could I avoid getting bogged down in German?

Third, as I became increasingly aware of the unpopularity of her ideas among my friends and colleagues in women's history—especially her life work of protective labor legislation for women and children—I began to wonder whether I would ever be able to bridge the gap between her political commitments and those of late twentieth-century feminists. The ERA struggle in which I and other historians of women were then enmeshed placed us among her historical opponents. Could I work creatively within this contradiction?

These were three good reasons why I might have moved on to more genial topics. But each seemed a challenge that I wanted to meet. I was tenured, I felt fortified for the coming combat with German, and this was not the first time that I had found unpopular ideas appealing. About two years into my research I stopped wondering why no one else was writing about Kelley and began applying for grants.

If rejecting Kelley characterized the first stage of my work, over-commitment to her was the chief attribute of the second. The scale of the research demanded heroic efforts, and the challenge of presenting Kelley's ideas to my colleagues required a rigorous speaking schedule. My children, aged sixteen and twenty-one, were living with their father in New York City, so my transition from single motherhood to single personhood was timely.

One reason historians of women have succeeded in transforming large areas of the discipline of history is the missionary zeal with which they approach their work. They write for today, but they also write for the eternities. A group without a history is a group without an identity. By creating a history of women, historians do more than re-construct the past in new ways. They transform the possibilities in women's present and future.

This in part explains why historians of women work so hard. Added to this responsibility for women's future, however, is the sheer fun of investigating women's past—its poetry, its dignity, its unpredictability. My own commitment combines these two motivations with a third—the ability of women's history to illuminate the interaction between women and social structures that are dominated by men. This inter-action lay at the heart of my question about the centrality of women in the shaping of modern welfare policies in the United States. If I could answer that question I felt I could shed new light on how women fit into American political life.

So at first my attitude toward Florence Kelley was not very personal; I saw her primarily as a vehicle for significant social analysis. Though in my own time she was not well known, her contemporaries shared my convictions about her centrality to social change, and this gave me all the encouragement I needed. Especially helpful were Felix Frankfurter's comments in 1954: "[She] had probably the largest single share in shaping the social history of the United States during the first thirty years of this century. . . . During that period hers was no doubt a powerful if not decisive role in securing legislation for the removal of the most glaring abuses of our hectic industrialization following the Civil War. But we owe her an even deeper and more enduring debt for the continuing process she so largely helped to initiate, by which social legislation is promoted and eventually gets on the statute books."[3] Like Frankfurter, I was sure that my story lay in the larger social patterns, not in the unique individual.

First I searched for those patterns in Kelley's writings, compiled her astounding bibliography, which between 1882 and 1932 totaled two books and about four hundred other items, including both popular and scholarly articles, edited books, pamphlets, book reviews, and conference reports. In 1909, a typical year at the height of her productivity, she wrote at least fourteen articles. Some were published in professional periodicals like *Survey*, where she was an editor, or *Annals of the American Academy of Political and Social Science*, some in middle-class magazines like *Outlook*, and some in women's magazines like the *Ladies' Home Journal*. Those in the first category were well documented with informative tables; the rest were forcefully argued moral positions. Combined, the articles embraced a wide range of topics, the vast majority of which were hardy perennials in Kelley's repertoire—the need for consumers to exert a moral influence over conditions in which goods were produced for them; condemnation of child labor and the inadequate wages of working women; and energetic support for factory inspection and the U.S. Children's Bureau. Themes and timings in her orchestration of ideas and social forces began to emerge. Even her extensive German publications between 1887 and 1900 began to seem part of a larger whole.

Fellowship support enabled me to build on this bibliographic work with two years of archival research between 1981 and 1983, during which the bulk of my research was accomplished. A partial listing of the archives I visited conveys the peripatetic demands of those years.

I began with the largest collections—in Washington D.C., the Manuscript Division of the Library of Congress and the National Archives, which respectively house the National Consumers' League Papers and those of the U.S. Children's Bureau and the U.S. Women's Bureau, along with a multitude of other relevant collections; then to New York for the Tamiment Collection at New York University; the mammoth Kelley collection at the New York Public Library; the Charity Organization Society Papers at Columbia University; and the Josephine Shaw Lowell Papers at the New-York Historical Society. The Arthur and Elizabeth Schlesinger Library in the History of American Women, the Sophia Smith Collection at Smith College in Northampton, Massachusetts, the W. E. B. Du Bois Papers at the University of Massachusetts, Amherst, and Cornell's Industrial Relations Library contained dozens of pertinent collections. After an interlude in Maine, where I unexpectedly encountered Kelley's own library, I mined the Midwest. In Chicago the Newberry Library, the Chicago Historical Society, and the University of Illinois occupied me for the better part of a year. Nearby Rockford College, the Illinois State Archives in Springfield, the State Historical Society of Wisconsin, the Social Welfare Archives at the University of Minnesota, and the Western Reserve Historical Society of Cleveland were also essential. Back in California, my institutional home, I found archival gold in the Bancroft Library at Berkeley, the Henry Huntington Library in San Marino, and the Katherine Edson Papers at the University of California at Los Angeles. A multitude of smaller archives responded to my requests by mail.

Not surprisingly, these years on the road deepened my relationship with Florence Kelley. As I lavished my financial resources as well as my time and energy on her, her life gradually encompassed my own. "Mom who?" my daughter once said in response to her brother's inquiry about my whereabouts. Like Kelley herself, I was finding it hard to do justice to my personal responsibilities and at the same time push ahead with burgeoning professional obligations.

Bell Gale Chevigny, the biographer of Margaret Fuller, has written astutely about the process of personal identification whereby biographers gain authority and autonomy in their own lives by writing about surrogate mothers who struggled for authority and autonomy. Her chief idea deserves repetition here: the main challenge of that process lies in recognizing the necessity for distance between the self and the subject when symbiosis with the subject is a daily goal. Chevigny's insight arose from a personal crisis resulting from too close a merger with Fuller during a public talk.[4]

My own experience confirms her perception. It too was shaped by crisis, not from too close an identification but from too great a commitment. Florence Kelley became a mother who guided me through the political, social, and economic mysteries of American history during the critical decades of transformation between 1880 and 1930. Her gifts to me were great, and I responded by submerging my life in hers.

The high point of this process, perhaps, was the summer of 1982, when, as a summer fellow at the Smithsonian's Woodrow Wilson International Center for Scholars, I had the good fortune to employ four research assistants, one provided by the center, two hired with my own funds, and one volunteer—a college-bound descendant of Louis Brandeis who heard I was working on Florence Kelley and wanted to learn more about her family's heritage of social reform. They were wonderful assistants and soon caught my contagion of total dedication to the task at hand. Their help meant that I could work intensely in the Manuscript Division of the Library of Congress from the time its doors opened at 9:00 A.M. until they closed at 5:00 P.M., then work equally hard at the National Archives from 5:30 to 10:00 P.M. I scrutinized the archival folders and flagged the items to be photocopied; they stood in line at the copier machine, fed it coins, returned items to the proper folder, folders to the proper place in their boxes, wrote the citation on the reproduced items, and carried them to our office at the Wilson Center. At the center they organized and cataloged new file folders for the bundles of photocopied material we collected each day and filled the file drawers.

As I walked to the Library of Congress, my day began with a trip to a bank to seek, in exchange for paper currency, $100 worth of dimes for the insatiable photocopy machines. Since banks did not have to provide such coins for noncommercial customers, and since tellers became annoyed with my repeated requests, I tried to find a new teller each day, whose surprise at my request usually overrode her memory of the noncommercial rule.

Each morning that mile walk from my rented apartment to the Library of Congress took me past the haunting and hopeless gaze of unemployed black men. At night on my bus ride home the graphic talk of African-American women who cleaned federal office buildings in the evening jolted me out of my archival compulsions. Forming their own community and ignoring me, these spirited women argued and conferred about problems plaguing their lives—money needed for a child's medical expenses, the trials of an unemployed son, an ailing back. Half-knowing, but not caring, that I was ignoring important aspects of my own life, my encounter with the present narrowed to brief but extremely intense exposures to the tragic realities of racism in Washington, D.C., and to daily reminders of the persistence of social injustices that Kelley had combated eighty years earlier.

On my first day in Washington, May 1, my spirits had been lifted by participating in a "Poor People's March" that moved from a park through downtown to the Capitol lawn. My son and two of his friends came from New York to welcome me to the East and join the march. I carried a sign: "Don't Let Them Kid You, The Money Is There!" A month later, however, the hopelessness of the Reagan administration's policies, the wasted lives I encountered on my morning walk, and the sorrows I overheard each night on the bus weighed heavily on my spirits. These present-day miseries gradually fused with the documents I scanned daily in the archives, documents that condemned the nation's inaction in the face of economic injustice but believed that a brighter day was dawning. Perhaps I was exhausted beyond the point of realizing my need for rest. Perhaps I was subconsciously mourning the loss of my shared life with my children, who were now pursuing their own lives. Certainly I had allowed myself to become absorbed to a psychologically dangerous degree into Florence Kelley's life and its continuing ramifications in the present.

These causes produced a remarkable effect. I began to experience the upper half of my body within the confines of a pine coffin. I saw and felt the coffin kinesthetically (though not in a tactile way) for about two weeks. At the time, I explained it primarily as a manifestation of my transition from active mothering to the parenting of adult children. Kelley's painful separation from her children probably heightened my own sadness. "I miss the chicks with a perennial heartache," she wrote her mother during her first weeks at Hull-House when she boarded Ko, Margaret, and John with Henry and Jessie Lloyd.[5] Her grief at Margaret's death from a heart attack during her first week at Smith College in 1905 doubtlessly drew me closer to my own grief. I too missed the day-to-day physical reality of my children's presence. For the first time in twenty-three years I was not only absent from them but also from the home we had shared and the mementos of our lives together.

Death was not alien to me. My brother and grandmother had recently died. New England gravestone carvings dating between 1660 and 1860 were one of my favorite hobbies, and I had taught a course on "American Attitudes toward Death, 1630 to the Present." I accepted this symbolic encounter with death as a recognition of my own mortality, and hence as a sign of my psychological health. If I weren't so strong, I reasoned, I'd not be able to create such a vivid imagining of death. As a feminist and as a woman I expected myself to be in touch with basic life forces and found a perverse pleasure in my extraordinary experience. With close friends I complained about the stupidity of the psychoanalytic profession, their inhuman metaphor of an "empty nest," and their bizarre notion that women who had other purposes in their lives would not mourn the loss of their children so intensely. My children's composure was especially gratifying. As I passed through this valley, they counseled me, concerned but not afraid—"this makes sense; it's you; accept it; call us often."

Since then I have concluded that my weird, "out of body" experience derived primarily from my absorption in Kelley's life. It never occurred to me to reduce my seven-day work schedule; Sundays were for cataloging. The coffin faded in the archives, when I became totally immersed in her life, so it didn't actually impede my work. It emerged when I tried to reenter my own life—especially at the end of the day, or at gatherings unrelated to my research. Lying in bed the kinesthetic effect was so strong that I feared I might actually visualize and then achieve a cardiac arrest, so I took to sleeping on the living room floor.

Friends tell me that the closest equivalent to this biographical overdose can be found among actors and actresses. They too submerge their lives into others. They too sometimes go so far that it becomes a spiritual or psychic journey. Shirley MacLaine's antics make a crazy kind of sense to me now. The stage fright that tormented Laurence Olivier so horribly at the peak of his career may have expressed a war between his own psyche and the fictive characters that constantly possessed him.[6] Like gifted actors and actresses, all historians who relate strongly to the lives they study run the same risk of forsaking the familiar terrain of their own lives. We, however, are less likely to talk about it.

If I had it to do over again I'm not sure I'd do anything differently.

Clearly I was working too far beyond the point of exhaustion, but I did get the work done and that was my first priority. My attitude toward the coffin, then and now, was to accept it as part of my experience—as a woman and as a historian. Nevertheless, a few months later this adventure led me to take a day off. I flew to Maine to visit Florence Kelley's summer home. No archive beckoned me there. I wanted to experience the same calm that she derived from her summer retreat—to see it and explore the reasons why she and her generation of women reformers sought this seasonal renewal.

My trip necessitated some detective work. Did the house still exist? Who owned it? Having answered these questions I flew to Bangor, rented a car, and expected to return to Boston the same day. The clear beauty of the November day complemented my mood of anticipation, drawing me into the experience and easing my drive to Penobscot Bay. The house owners had kindly connected me with a caretaker who led the way on dirt roads lined with grasping thickets. I could never have found my way unaided. Arriving at the house in its clearing on the bay, I was grateful for the glimpse it gave me into Florence Kelley's leisure, and I happily consented to a tour of the cottage. The owners' earlier remark that some of her books still remained there had slipped my mind, since I assumed that a few summer novels were not very weighty compared to the papers I had canvassed. So imagine my astonishment when I encountered a full wall of her personal library covering about sixty square feet.

Speechless with wonder, I browsed through the most accessible shelves. How, I finally asked myself and the caretaker, could such a thing happen? Fifty years after her death, here was her professional library—just as she had left it. Calling the owner, I asked permission to stay until I had cataloged the collection. An academic himself, he understood my amazement, encouraged me to stay, telling me more about the history of the place. When he bought the property in the 1950s, the roof was totally caved in, protecting the wall of books, and a band of porcupines had taken over the hearth. He and his family left the books untouched when they renovated. I could stay on—but there was no heat and no plumbing. With frequent trips to the local store, working evenings by candlelight in gloves in which I had cut out the fingertips, I made cards for about four hundred items in three days and nights; those with marginal comments took much more time to record. Stoking the fire was my chief diversion. Items that I saw for the first time included Kelley's factory inspector reports for Illinois from the mid-1890s and her subscriptions to *Die Neue Zeit* and other periodicals. A calm settled over me far greater than any I had imagined seeking. Contingencies in Kelley's life and in mine combined to connect us through these enduring artifacts. No archaeologist discovering her weight in Sumerian goldware could have been happier.

Some of Kelley's original furnishings remained in the house—her wicker chaise lounge, her bed. These I found uncomfortable, perhaps because they so vividly evoked her presence. Each evening I greeted the dusk with a walk through pasture and woods to Penobscot Bay, whose waters were visible from the knoll where the house stood, but my maximum use of daylight kept me housebound till twilight. I recognized spots recorded in family pictures—where John, Kelley's youngest child, had kept his boat; where a grape arbor once flourished. A herd of sheep grazed in the pasture by day, placing added risks in my path after dark, so I didn't linger. Back in the house I worked each night until the pain in my eyes grew too great to continue.

I know that I will not penetrate all the mysteries in Florence Kelley's life, but those days with her library established a closeness between us that time has not diminished. This nonarchival research had begun in New York City months earlier. There I had explored the physical surroundings of her life by residing briefly at the Henry Street Settlement, where she lived from 1899 to 1926. I couldn't identify her room, but Lillian Wald's comfortable parlor and the handsome dining room helped me picture her collective life with other reformers. I had also visited the Charities Building—still standing at Park Avenue and Twenty-second Street—where Kelley ran the national headquarters of the National Consumers' League. There a brief but sharp encounter with an arrogant upper-middle-class woman who worked for today's equivalent of the Charity Organization Society plunged me back into nineteenth-century class relations. Treating my request for archives like an appeal for charity, this woman gave me a visceral understanding of why Kelley worked for legislative rather than charitable solutions to social problems.

Interviews with family members also gave me insights into Kelley's life that couldn't have come from archives. Her daughter-in-law, Augusta, born into the Maverick family in Texas, kindly shared her memories of Nicholas's imperious mother. It was easy for me to imagine Kelley stopping by her son's townhouse near Stuyvesant Park, for after

Nicholas's death it had become a part of Friends Seminary, where my own son attended high school, and I had often visited. Augustus Kelley, son of Augusta and Nicholas, the publisher to whom historians of the United States are indebted for his reprinting of economic and social classics, received me on his sickbed in Little Compton, Rhode Island. The family's contact with Little Compton had begun in the 1890s when Ko regularly joined the Henry Demarest Lloyd family there. Gus regaled me with stories about "granny," whom he obviously loved very much and sought to imitate in his own life. His sister, Florence Kelley, formerly chief judge of New York City's family court, also received me warmly in her Little Compton home.

In Washington I had been extremely fortunate to interview and speak several times with Clara Mortenson Beyer, Kelley's most knowledgeable surviving protégé. The daughter of an immigrant dairy farmer in California, Clara Mortenson had graduated from the University of California and started a Ph.D. in economics at Barnard when she met Kelley around 1916. The older woman succeeded in attracting her away from academics with the offer of a job on the Washington, D.C., Minimum Wage Board, where Mortenson worked with Elizabeth Brandeis. Instrumental in the passage of the Fair Labor Standards Act, Clara Mortenson became the chief power at the Bureau of Labor Standards, where she wrote and enforced the regulations for a wide range of labor legislation. She remained for many years a source of constant encouragement and inspiration for historians of women writing about the political legacy of women and Progressive reform.

In Washington I also learned about the organizational aftermath of Kelley's death from Mary Dublin Keyserling, who took Kelley's place as general secretary of the National Consumers' League in the mid-1930s. Neither of us could have predicted then that our relationship with Tom Dublin would turn us into kin five years later, but we enjoyed one another's company very much. Now when Mary visits our home in northern Susquehanna County, Pennsylvania, she and I delight in discovering items in my research files that bear her signature. Like many historians of women, I cannot easily say where my research ends and my personal life begins.

In more ways than one my study of Kelley has become a way of life. The final stage—writing—has been the most rewarding and the most frustrating. There is too much to say. With the first draft completed, thanks to fellowships, I have the equivalent of two large volumes. These would have been appropriate for a nineteenth-century audience, but they need to be rewritten to hold the shorter attention span of twentieth-century readers.

In their books' "acknowledgments" scholars thank archivists who aided their research and colleagues whose comments improved the final product—both groups to whom I am deeply indebted—but they often omit the ongoing process of conferences and meetings that did so much to shape their ideas. In my case this debt is quite large. It began with my first invitation to speak about Kelley at Indiana University in 1980 and reached its fullest fruition with the thoughts that went into the preparation of this essay.

Like most historians I know, I accept speaking and writing invitations because the deadline sounds too distant ever to become real, because I'm flattered to be asked, and because I use such occasions to force myself to develop ideas about topics important to my ongoing work. Meetings of the Berkshire Conference of Women Historians have been especially valuable in this regard. Affording me a lead time of over a year to prepare my thoughts, and the opportunity to construct a panel of scholars on related topics, the Berkshire Conference has been a perfect arena to test my notions about how women's political culture in the United States resembled or differed from women's political culture in England, France, and Germany. Meetings of the Organization of American Historians have offered me valuable opportunities to test ideas about the connections between men's and women's political culture in the United States. Colleagues and students at the many institutions at which I spoke about Kelley between 1980 and 1992 have helped shape my work by generously sharing their thoughts about it. Special occasions have rendered special service. For example, I had not adequately realized the significance of Florence Kelley's peace activism in the 1914–19 war until I prepared and delivered a paper at an international conference on women and peace.

Written publications that might at first glance appear to be diversions also opened important learning opportunities. Editing Florence Kelley's autobiography in 1983 first focused my attention on the closing years of her career after 1925. An article on the statutory regulation of women's working hours confirmed my conviction that protective labor legislation was more than a sexist ploy to keep women in their place. Editing a book on the social survey movement helped me put one of

Kelley's early achievements, *Hull-House Maps and Papers* (1895), into historical perspective.[7]

But from my present vantage point one occasion seems especially pivotal—my trial run for this essay, delivered at Barnard's Women's Center in the fall of 1988. Almost nothing here survives intact from that trial effort, but by giving me permission to assess my work process, it set me thinking along lines that have grown increasingly fruitful. In the first two stages of this project I approached the past as a social scientist, asking questions that could be duplicated by others, who, with the same interaction with the same sources, would draw the same conclusions. In this way I developed a sturdy conceptual framework for explaining the power of women's political culture in the United States between 1890 and 1930.

I still believe in this framework, and I still want to use Florence Kelley's life to analyze a fundamental transformation in American history, but while working on this essay I have realized that I must also leave a unique imprint on this story—must shape it with the tools of the artist and the humanist as well as with those of the social scientist.

My exhaustive and exhausting first draft of the book is a social scientist's story. Its systematic view of the evidence proves my case—women were central to the creation of early social and labor legislation in the United States because of a combination of factors related to the history of women's political culture, on the one hand, and to men's political culture on the other. I used to feel that analyzing the complex interaction between these overlapping political cultures was sufficient, but I have come to understand that this is not enough. I can't leave the story there; it is at once too much and not enough. An inherent part of the biographer's art was missing—in viewing Kelley as a colossus that could explain her era, I had explained the era at the expense of the person. I had not fully claimed the person as my own. Like her contemporaries, I had found her too daunting and had been too polite.

What was I afraid of? Giving my personal imprint to a story and somehow thereby fatally diminishing it? How silly. My time and Kelley's were meant for each other—both knew rapid social transformation, war, and callous retrenchment. Claiming the colossus as my own would not necessarily diminish her. And it could make her more real—both to me and my readers. I am not the same person who set out to write about Kelley ten years ago. Why should she remain the same person?

As I look back on my work process, sedimentary metaphors seem to describe most accurately how it has changed over time. The first layer or groundwork was laid by nonbiographical questions. The next layer took a social science approach to biography. The final layer recognized a personal relationship between the author and her subject. Each was shaped by the preceding phase, invisible though it might be beneath the current strategy.

Jane Gallop has written about "challenging the split between public and private which keeps our lives out of our knowledge."[8] My original intentions did not embrace such a merger, but in retrospect it seems inevitable. As a student of change I should have expected that my intentions would change.

One possible difference between a feminist work process and that of a nonfeminist biographer might be the degree to which a feminist biographer is willing to connect her work with the vulnerabilities and struggles associated with her own life. In the process of working on Kelley's life, I have separated from my own life as the mother of young children, encountered death, dealt with the anxieties of resource depletion, remarried, and moved across a continent. These changes involved struggle. But in the process I also grew more confirmed in myself as a person, and in subtle and not-so-subtle ways I am sure that Florence Kelley helped.

NOTES

The photograph of Florence Kelley, ca. 1905 at age forty-five, is used courtesy of the Kelley Family Papers, Butler Library, Columbia University, New York. I am grateful to Constance Coiner, Thomas Dublin, Anne Firor Scott, William R. Taylor, and SUNY Binghamton graduate students in History 511, fall 1989, for their helpful comments on earlier drafts of this essay. I thank Constance Coiner for calling to my attention the Elinor Langer quotation that begins this essay (*Josephine Herbst: The Story She Could Never Tell* [Boston: Little Brown, 1983], 13).

1. Nicholas Kelley, "Early Days at Hull House," *Social Service Review* 28/4 (December 1954): 424.

2. Newton Baker, "Remarks about Mrs. Kelley on Memorial Meeting of March 16, 1932," papers of the National Consumers' League, Library of Congress, 11.

3. Felix Frankfurter, Foreword to Josephine Goldmark, *Impatient Crusader: Florence Kelley's Life Story* (Urbana: University of Illinois Press, 1953),v.

4. Bell Gale Chevigny, "Daughters Writing: Toward a Theory of Women's Biography," in Carol Ascher, Louis DeSalvo, and Sara Ruddick, eds., *Between Women: Biographers, Novelists, Critics, Teachers and Artists Write about Their Work on Women* (Boston: Beacon Press, 1984), 356–79.

5. Florence Kelley to Caroline Kelley, n.p., n.d. [Hull-House, 1892], Kelley Family Papers, New York Public Library.

6. On this theme, see Brian Bates, *The Way of the Actor: A New Path to Personal Knowledge and Power* (London: Century, Hutchinson, 1986); and Joseph R. Roach, *The Player's Passion: Studies in the Science of Acting* (Newark, N.J.: University of Delaware Press, 1985).

7. Kathryn Kish Sklar, ed., *The Autobiography of Florence Kelley: Notes of Sixty Years* (Chicago: Charles Kerr, 1986); Sklar, " 'The greater Part of the Petitioners are Female': The Reduction of Women's Working Hours in the Paid Labor Force, 1840–1917," in Gary Cross, ed., *Worktime and Industrialization: An International History* (Philadelphia: Temple University Press, 1988), 103–33; Sklar, "*Hull-House Maps and Papers:* Social Science as Women's Work in the 1890s," in Martin Bulmer, Kevin Bales, and K. K. Sklar, eds., *The Social Survey Movement in Historical Perspective* (Cambridge: Cambridge University Press, 1990).

8. Jane Gallop, *Thinking through the Body* (New York: Columbia University Press, 1988), 4. I am grateful to Constance Coiner for calling this quotation to my attention.

ALICE WEXLER

Emma Goldman and the Anxiety of Biography

Eмма GOLDMAN (1869–1940), born in Kovno, Lithuania, grew up in a precariously petit-bourgeois, deeply patriarchal Jewish family in a world bounded by Russian anti-Semitism, a growing revolutionary movement against Czarism, and the first stirrings of Russian feminism. After attending *Realschule* in Konigsberg, she moved with her family to Petersburg in 1881. Here she also attended school until her parents' straitened circumstances forced her to find factory work. In 1885 she emigrated with an older half-sister to Rochester, New York, where she was radicalized by the harsh conditions of industrial capitalism and by the Haymarket tragedy of 1886–87. Within a few years, Goldman emerged as one of the most charismatic and controversial figures of international anarchism, a branch of the radical movement committed to antiparliamentary, decentralized, libertarian forms of socialism. Goldman's iconoclastic anarchist vision owed much to the communist anarchism of Peter Kropotkin, which she attempted to integrate with the individualism of Nietzsche, Stirner, and Ibsen. In her lectures, in two books—*Anarchism and Other Essays* (1912) and *The Social Significance of the Modern Drama* (1914)—and in *Mother Earth,* the monthly "little magazine" she published between 1906 and 1918, Goldman advanced her startlingly modern ideas on a wide range of topics, including free love, libertarian education, the "new woman," homosexuality, parent-child relations, and the uses of art to foment revolution. She particularly urged women to free themselves from the tyranny of bourgeois sexual morality and puritanical public opinion. At the age of thirty-nine, she threw herself into a tumultuous nine-year love affair with a Chicago doctor ten years younger than she, Dr. Ben L. Reitman, who campaigned with her as her manager.

Throughout her career, Goldman was harassed by police and frequently arrested, at first because of her association with Alexander Berkman, who had attempted to assassinate the antilabor steel magnate Henry Clay Frick during the Homestead strike of 1892. She served three prison terms, including one year for allegedly "inciting to riot" during a hunger demonstration, two weeks for advocating birth control, and two years for opposing the draft during World War I. Deported with Berkman in 1919 to the Soviet Union, Goldman soon turned against the Bolsheviks on account of their persecution of non-Communists and the growing centralization and repressiveness of the regime. Along with Berkman, she voluntarily left Russia in late 1921 to become an ardent anti-Soviet agitator. Her autobiographical 1923 book, *My Disillusionment in Russia,* offered a compelling portrait of the chaos and devastation of the civil war years, which she attributed largely to the centralizing, authoritarian policies of the Bolsheviks. In exile Goldman also wrote *Living My Life,* published to critical acclaim in 1931. During the Spanish civil war she served as agent and publicist in England for the Spanish anarcho-syndicalists, traveling three times to Barcelona to visit her comrades. Their militant resistance to fascism and their experiments with agricultural and industrial collectives fulfilled her dreams of libertarian revolution. Embittered by the defeat of the anarchists, and later of the Republic, she traveled to Toronto in the spring of 1939 to raise money for Spanish and other refugees from fascism. After her death in May 1940, she was buried near the Haymarket martyrs in Chicago, in the country she still considered her home.

─────────────────

At a 1990 American Historical Association panel on biography, Elinor Langer commented on how the woman she had been when she began her biography of the writer Josephine Herbst was not the same as the one who completed the work. Her feelings about Herbst had changed, from grateful admiration to a sense of disappointment and distance. Since writing a life often takes a decade or more, this problem may be endemic to the project of biography.

In looking back over the more than ten years I spent thinking and writing about Emma Goldman, I cannot help pondering how much my own thought changed, in part as a result of the work on Goldman, but also in response to contacts within various feminist and intellectual communities, to the political climate of the Reagan years, and to the changing discourse of feminism itself. This essay, written over a period of two years, represents several phases of rethinking about Goldman; it is meant less as a continuous argument than as a series of separate reflections: an effort to situate the biography in the places and moments in which it was written.

I first began to think of writing about Emma Goldman in 1975, when I was teaching U.S. women's history at Sonoma State College in northern California. At that time a filmmaker friend of mine, David Schickele, fell in love with *Living My Life* and proposed we make a film documentary about her.[1] We sent out preliminary inquiries about grants and received a few favorable replies, but David was compelled to take on another project so we put this one on hold. In the meantime, I too had become possessed by Emma Goldman and had decided to go ahead, first with a series of articles, and finally a biography.

I had always wanted to write biography, ever since the age of eleven, when I interviewed Aline Mosby, the United Press International correspondent in Moscow, and wrote a profile of her for the school newspaper. A few years later I met Fawn Brodie, a tall, rather formidable woman whose famous biography of Joseph Smith had led to her excommunication from the Mormon church, in which members of her family were distinguished elders. My parents had become friends with her and her husband, and when I met her she was working on a life of Sir Richard Burton, the nineteenth-century British author, explorer, and sexual adventurer. When I was in college, she began her controversial intimate biography of Thomas Jefferson and would tell us stories of her adventures in the archives. Biography from that time on always seemed to me a romantic venture, even a way of doing what my psychoanalyst father did—analyze lives—without having to become a therapist with patients who telephoned in the middle of the night. Fawn did not think of herself as a feminist. She liked socializing with the Los Angeles psychoanalysts—mostly men—and her psychoanalytic views were fairly orthodox. Yet her emphasis on the emotional, private, even unconscious dimensions of her male subjects' lives always seemed to me a hidden feminist subtext, a resistance to heroic myths of masculinity that more conventional male biographers put forth. Since I had grown up in the cold war Eisenhower era, in a family where my meek, university-educated mother stayed home to take care of her children, Fawn Brodie symbolized an exciting world of possibilities.

In the graduate history program at Indiana University, biography was scorned as a form of belles-lettres, but I did attempt several short biographical projects, writing essays and papers on such figures as the seventeenth-century Mexican poet Sor Juana Inés de la Cruz, Father Coughlin, and Ivan Illich. Despite a concentration on Latin American history, I seriously considered doing a biography of Mabel Dodge Luhan for my dissertation, a choice shaped in part by the emerging women's movement. But my advisor scotched the proposal, particularly since a biography of Mabel Dodge was already in progress (by Emily Hahn). But even after I had given up that topic, I still dreamed of writing a woman's life.

A few years later Emma Goldman captured my imagination. The militance of the 1960s, and especially the movement against the war in Vietnam, had heightened the appeal of the historical anarchists. With their antiwar legacy, their tactics of direct action, and their critique of hierarchy, domination, and power, they spoke to us as our contemporaries. With the flowering of feminism in the early 1970s, Emma Goldman in particular became a new heroine. Her outspoken sexual radicalism and her brief brush with Freud in Vienna (echoes of my own family's involvement with psychoanalysis) further enhanced her appeal for me. Moreover, I could identify with her background as an

East European Jewish immigrant, since my grandparents were also Russian Jews who had come to America in the late nineteenth century.

Most important of all was her contrast with my mother. Emma Goldman was forceful, assertive, bold and daring, while my mother, though very intelligent and well read, had become increasingly timid and dependent. Now she seemed more insubstantial than ever as the hereditary neurological illness that had killed her father and brothers—Huntington's disease—gradually consumed her as well, while my sister and I struggled with the knowledge that we were both at risk for the same awful illness. In Emma Goldman, I am certain I was seeking an alternative mother to take her place, a woman whose strength and courage in overcoming obstacles could inspire me as well. "We think back through our mothers if we are women," wrote Virginia Woolf. And since thinking back through my own shipwrecked mother was fraught with anxiety, and even terror, thinking back through Emma Goldman seemed especially attractive. I much preferred to ponder gender than think about genetics; gender roles could be changed, while genetic legacy seemed inexorable and absolute. Actually the risk of Huntington's disease gave a special urgency to the biography project, for I felt that if I didn't start now, I might never have the chance. Fawn Brodie encouraged me, my students at Sonoma got involved with research on Goldman, and the National Endowment for the Humanities provided generous support. I decided to begin.

From early in my research, I recognized Goldman's 1931 autobiography as a major ally, obstacle, and rival. *Living My Life* resembled a sprawling nineteenth-century novel—the opening paragraphs in fact recall *Sister Carrie,* and it is worth noting that Goldman was corresponding with Theodore Dreiser at the time she began the memoir. (In retrospect, I may have underestimated the importance of such literary models for the autobiography, which a more intertextual approach might illuminate.) Goldman had written it at a moment when the anarchist movement to which she had dedicated her life had been decimated everywhere (except in Spain, though she was not aware of it then), when she felt that everything meaningful to her lay in ashes. It was as if the tremendous length and dizzying detail were meant to provide a solid bulwark against the emptiness and insecurity of her life at that moment.

This enormous text of nearly a thousand pages had defined the

Emma Goldman legend for decades. She was probably known more from that autobiography than from any of her other writings, at least until Richard Drinnon's 1961 biography, *Rebel in Paradise,* and later editions of her letters and essays.[2] But even Drinnon's biography, and that of Alix Kates Shulman, *To the Barricades,* written for young people, essentially followed Goldman's own heroic self-presentation in the memoir, downplaying evidence of inner tensions to portray her as an exhuberant larger-than-life heroine.[3] Yet for all her bravado, Goldman had also been frank about her doubts and contradictions, which she saw as gender-related. Contrasting herself with her male comrades, she described a deeply conflicted self. "I was not hewn of one piece, like Sasha or other heroic figures," she said. "I had long realized that I was woven of many skeins, conflicting in shade and texture. To the end of my days I should be torn between the yearning for a personal life and the need of giving all of my ideal" (LML, p. 153). In another particularly poignant passage, Goldman recounted how, in 1915, when she was forty-six, the artist Robert Henri had wanted to paint her portrait, "to depict 'the real Emma Goldman.' 'But which is the real one?' I asked; 'I have never been able to unearth her' " (LML, p. 529).

These were irresistible challenges to a biographer, invitations to probe Goldman's intimate, interior life. Yet until the great avalanche of Goldman's love letters to her "Great, Grand Passion," the spectacular hobo-turned-physician, Dr. Ben L. Reitman, became available— when Reitman's relatives donated most of them to the library at the University of Illinois at Chicago in the early 1970s—one could find little intimate information about Goldman apart from her letters to Alexander Berkman at the International Institute of Social History in Amsterdam. The letters to Reitman were a wonderful new resource, but they began only in 1908, when Emma was nearly thirty-nine years old, long after her formative early years. For her life from 1869 to 1908, the evidence was fragmentary.

In writing *Emma Goldman in America,* which covers Goldman's life until her deportation at the end of 1919, I too, like other biographers, found myself turning to the autobiography more than I had intended, particularly for information about her childhood and adolescence.[4] Occasionally it was possible, even for her earliest years, to find some confirmation of autobiographical claims. For example, a persistent theme of the early part of the memoir is Emma's account of her father's rejection, his preference for his sons and his disappointment that she had been born a girl. I wanted to find out whether this feeling had some basis in her father's behavior, if there was evidence of his rejection other than Emma's own memory. There was. A great-niece also recalled that Abraham Goldman seemed to treat this daughter more harshly than his other children or his nieces and nephews, with whom he had been very gentle. Moreover, I discovered a copy of Abraham's will in Rochester, New York, in which he had shown his preferences in the legacies he left: a thousand dollars along with his gold watch and fur overcoat to his youngest son, the doctor, a thousand dollars in trust to the older son, a machinist, and three hundred dollars cash to Emma, though, of all his children, she had the fewest resources.

But this kind of evidence surfaced rarely. For the most part, when I felt compelled to use the autobiography as a source of information, I tried to use it more as an account of how Goldman remembered her past than as a story of how she actually lived it. In describing her conversion to anarchism, for example, I tried to make clear that I was describing a memory, not an actual event. "Many years later (no contemporary accounts have survived), Emma spoke of her conversion to anarchism not as an active, reasoned choice, but rather as an epiphany" (LML, p. 36).

In the second volume of the biography, I tried to address *Living My Life* less as a source of information than as an event in Emma Goldman's life, a construction more than a recollection. I wanted to show how she attempted to create a new kind of female hero who was outspoken both in her sexuality and her politics. I also hoped to trace the ways in which she created this identity, in part by rewriting Frank Harris's *My Life and Loves* and Peter Kropotkin's *Memoirs of a Revolutionist* as a woman's story, a female epic. Still, at times I probably approached the autobiography more as a prosecuting attorney than as a sympathetic critic. Despite my desire to treat the autobiography as a literary work, I found myself constantly questioning Goldman's veracity. For example, since she often drew unflattering portraits of her fellow anarchists, some of whom were known outside the movement mainly through her portrayal, it seemed necessary to indicate where her accusations might be especially unfair or misleading. One such case was her insinuation that Abraham Isaak, the editor of a Chicago anarchist paper, had inadvertently inspired the McKinley assassination in Buffalo in 1901. Goldman told how Isaak had become suspicious of a young man hanging about anarchist circles talking loosely of violence.

Thinking the man might be a police spy, Isaak placed a warning in his paper, urging his comrades to exercise caution. In her autobiography, Goldman suggested that this warning might have inspired the assassin, Leon Czolgosz, to prove his sincerity by attempting an act of "propaganda of the deed" (LML, p. 309). She also suggested that Isaak had unwittingly caused her arrest and near extradition by telling a reporter she had introduced him to Czolgosz. Such accusations were difficult to prove or disprove, yet Goldman's inclusion of these charges in her memoir gave them a tremendous weight and aura of credibility, thereby condemning Isaak (who had died long before the autobiography appeared) in the annals of anarchism.

Many other individuals suffered Goldman's withering portrayals. She cast several of her former lovers as petulant, possessive drunks, showed Ben Reitman as a former police spy, thief, and buffoon, and even presented her beloved Alexander Berkman as insensitive and arrogant, dependent on her without appreciating her sacrifices. Like many autobiographies, *Living My Life* was also an act of settling accounts, especially against the men Goldman felt had injured her in various ways, but also against some of her women comrades, such as Voltairine de Cleyre, whom Goldman portrayed as narrow and unforgiving. Since many people read the *Life* for its insights into the anarchist movement, it seemed necessary to consider Goldman's claims in light of other types of evidence.

Were I writing today, however, I would accord less weight to considerations of "factuality" or "fairness," and I would emphasize the feminist implications of Goldman's own construction of herself as multiple and contradictory, "woven of many skeins, conflicting in shade and texture." Indeed, her self-description accords with recent feminist theorizing about the female subject, which has questioned the idea of the unified self, positing instead, as Teresa de Lauretis has put it, the female subject as a site of differences that are not only sexual, racial, economic, or cultural, but often all of these together and often in tension with one another. As de Lauretis elaborates, "a multiple, shifting, and often self-contradictory identity, a subject that is not divided in, but rather at odds with, language; an identity made up of heterogeneous and heteronomous representations of gender, race, and class, and often indeed across languages and cultures; an identity that one decides to reclaim from a history of multiple assimilations, and that one insists on as a strategy."[5] Such a formulation, I believe, suggests fruitful ways of approaching *Living My Life,* which was written self-consciously from the perspectives of a multiple outsider in the United States—a Jew, an East European immigrant, a woman and an anarchist, precariously petit-bourgeois by birth, one who identified with the working class and invented herself as an American. (Being white and heterosexual, Goldman could claim certain aspects of insider identity as well.)

Goldman's metaphor of the autobiographer as an actor, rehearsing—and performing—a variety of roles, also suggests other critical approaches to her highly theatrical style. Certainly she regarded the autobiography as a dramatization rather than an exploration of her life, yet another dramatic performance in a lifetime of performances on a variety of public stages. As Sue-Ellen Case has observed, "The inclusion of broad social, political and community work in the category of theater creates new perspectives on women and performance that reverse patriarchal evaluations of such projects."[6] Goldman clearly regarded her own political activism as a form of theater. Moreover, the theater was for her a powerful site for political and cultural transformation, as witnessed by her lifelong involvement with actors and directors, her promotion of the pre–World War I Little Theater movement in the United States, and her lectures and essays on the modern drama. Placing *Living My Life* within a female performing tradition, as well as an autobiographical one, might further illuminate the ways in which Goldman worked to construct herself as a public figure.

The theatrical dimension of Goldman's subjectivity also emerges clearly in her letters, which differed considerably depending upon her correspondent and her mood of the moment. Letters written within days of each other, or even on the same day, often presented contradictory self-portraits. Some of them, including her steamiest love letters, suggested her use of literary models and her characteristic excess and extravagance. The most dramatic letters were those she wrote to Dr. Ben L. Reitman, her lover between 1908 and 1917. During this period she wrote hundreds of passionate and angry letters to Reitman, ostensibly revealing her fantasies and vulnerabilities more nakedly than in any of her other writings.

But even her letters to Ben posed problems of interpretation, for they often shifted back and forth between soliloquies of mental torment and brisk discussions of lectures and arrangements. I found myself questioning her self-presentation, irritated by what sometimes seemed her manipulativeness and calculation. Was she really as miserable as she claimed? And how was it possible to reconcile her anguished laments with the tremendous energy and accomplishments of those years? Viewed from a different perspective, however, such literary performances might be seen as yet another expression of that theatricality and extravagance which worked to such good effect on the lecture podium. Perhaps the letters, too, were a kind of performance, in which she dramatized herself as the suffering martyred mother or as the unhappy heroine of the romantic and sentimental novels she had read as an adolescent. Although she often alluded to the differences between her optimistic, uncompromising public persona and the self she experienced privately as needy, uncertain, and depressed, her letters suggested that even this private self engaged in forms of role-playing and play-acting, that some of her most personal and impassioned love letters were also shaped by literary conventions, performances enacted for an audience of one.

Just how such practices related to Emma Goldman's sense of female identity is a question that leads away from biography toward the wider history of gender construction.[7] Certainly, working with Goldman's letters and her autobiography made me conscious of my own need for feminist theory to make sense of her extravagant language and her expressions of divided, conflicted subjectivity. Although some of this theory calls into question the very notion of biography, based, as it has been, on notions of a coherent, bounded, transcendent self unfolding inexorably through linear time, it also suggests new ways of thinking about female subjectivity and the construction of identity that have already begun to transform the genre of biography itself.

If dealing with Goldman's theatrical self-presentation posed one kind of problem, Russia, and Goldman's anticommunism, posed another. Actually, when I first began writing, I did not intend to cover her years in exile. The prospect of researching her experience in Russia during the civil war of 1918–21, and in the Spanish civil war of 1936–39, seemed too daunting, the controversies too embedded in cold war politics and Left polemics. Both these subjects boasted an immense historiography, and stepping into it felt like entering a minefield.

Nonetheless, soon after the publication of *Emma Goldman in America* in 1984, I decided to complete the biography. In part, immersion in Goldman's correspondence after 1919—which was necessary even for writing about her American years—had deepened my interest in continuing the work. The richness of the sources for her later years in comparison to their thinness for the earlier period made the project extremely appealing: there were almost daily letters from early 1922 until her death in 1940. In addition, the Reagan campaign against the Nicaraguan revolution, on the one hand, and the beginnings of glasnost and perestroika in the Soviet Union, on the other, also deepened my desire to pursue Goldman's analysis of Russia and "the Bolshevik myth." Although Goldman's left-wing critique of Communism certainly came from a different direction than that of more conservative critics, her insistence on the inevitable, inherent, monolithic totalitarianism of Soviet Russia echoed disturbingly in the 1980s.

For one who was not a Soviet specialist, placing Goldman's views within a historical context proved extremely difficult, especially since the reforms under Gorbachev had opened up many formerly closed questions about the Soviet past within the Soviet Union itself. Historical controversies raged not only in scholarly journals but also in the popular press, mostly about the Stalinist 1930s, but edging back toward the 1920s as well.

Western scholars joined the debates, which always had implications for present-day politics. Stephen F. Cohen's *Rethinking the Soviet Experience* provided a useful orientation to the field of Western Sovietology, as did his "Sovieticus" columns in *The Nation*.[8] I found particularly compelling Cohen's critique of the "totalitarianism school," which viewed the Soviet Union as a vast totalitarian state ruling over a passive, frozen society. Cohen also challenged what he called "the continuity thesis": the idea that one could draw a straight line from Bolshevism to Stalinism, or indeed from Marxism to Stalinism, as many anti-Soviet (and some pro-Soviet) commentators in the West contended. Apart from Cohen, the work of other political scientists and historians helped illuminate the catastrophic Soviet years of 1920 and 1921, for example, Paul Avrich, E. H. Carr, William Henry Chamberlin, Moshe Lewin, Sheila Fitzpatrick, Victor Daniels, and Beatrice Farnsworth.

The more I read of these scholars, however, the less compelling I found Goldman's narrative of a revolution completely defeated, corrupted, and turned into tyranny by the spring of 1921. To Goldman, everything that followed was an uninterrupted story of persecution, oppression, slavery, and terror carried out by a tyrannical Communist party solely bent on power and control. Even gender seemed to disappear as a category of concern for Goldman, who mentioned the tribulations of Soviet women in passing while ignoring or denying their advances. For the catastrophic state of the country in 1920 and 1921, Goldman firmly blamed Bolshevik ideology, the "Bolshevik idea." She dismissed the Western military intervention, the civil war, and the Allied blockade as cynical excuses offered by the Bolsheviks to justify their evils.

In her assessment of the failure of the Russian Revolution, of course, Goldman was not alone. For most anarchists, anti-Leninism and anticommunism (that communism represented by the Soviet Union) had become central articles of political faith by the early 1920s, in part because of her own and Berkman's influence. Much of Goldman's energy in the 1920s and 1930s was devoted to writing and campaigning against the Communists and trying to expose the "Bolshevik myth," which she felt had captured the imagination of the entire world. Though she refused to ally herself with conservative groups in the West and even remained apart from most socialists—whose polemics against the Communists were as fierce as those of the anarchists—Goldman published her articles in the capitalist press and was sometimes cited by conservative anticommunists to support their own quite different aims. Ultimately, she found herself increasingly embraced by anticommunist liberals, with diminished energies for reconceptualizing anarchism, a project that the Russian Revolution had made ever more urgent. While she remained an anarchist, she came to doubt the desirability of social revolution and at times argued for a more gradual process of educating individuals, who would serve as a vanguard to inspire the masses.

Goldman's single-minded anticommunism and the elitist, antidemocratic strains in her thought created for me an emotional knot in the biographical process, a deepened sense of ambivalence. Her one-dimensional accounts of Russia, considered alongside those of her contemporaries and of later scholars, seemed very problematical, flattening what even she herself, while actually inside Russia, described as an enormously complex and contradictory panorama. I found myself losing some of the sympathy I had felt for her while writing about her earlier years. And yet I felt unsure of how to position myself as biographer with respect to debates over the Soviet Union in the 1920s, including those between anarchists and Communists, and with respect to Soviet historiography of that era.

In the end I took a stance rather critical of Goldman, placing her arguments within the context of a picture of the Soviet 1920s that was more open and fluid than her portrait allowed. Within this frame I tried to show how she constructed her particular, partial vision to present a uniformly negative portrait, which, I suggested, may have contributed to a growing anticommunist consensus in the West. Whatever tentativeness I felt in this interpretation I more or less suppressed in the final version of the book, leaving out what Liz Stanley has called the "labour process" of the biography in the supposed interest of succinctness and seamless narrative.[9]

Emma Goldman in Exile was published in June 1989.[10] Three months later, in November, the Berlin Wall came crashing down, and the people everywhere in Eastern Europe began rising up against repressive Stalinist regimes to demand freedom and democratic rights. Now Ronald Reagan's "evil empire" rhetoric was coming to seem a faint memory. The overwhelming defeat of Marxism and Communism precipitated a profound crisis within the Western Left, and it certainly made me ask myself whether I had overstated the case against Emma Goldman. Some of Goldman's formulations appeared increasingly prescient in light of recent events. Could she have been right after all, if so many Russians, as well as Poles, Czechs, Hungarians, and others were denouncing not only Stalinism but the very foundations of socialist rule?

Looking back at the biography across the great divide of 1989 has made me realize how deeply my response to Goldman's encounter with Russia was shaped by the atmosphere of the 1980s. On the one hand, new scholarship on the Soviet 1920s as a possible model for a non-Stalinist socialism made Goldman's attack on that era seem determinist and dogmatic. On the other hand, Reagan's demonization of the Soviet Union and militant anticommunist foreign policy created a milieu in which it was perhaps too easy to downplay the differences between Goldman's radical critique of state socialism and the criticisms of liberals and conservatives. While I felt that her obsession with Communism drained away her energy for rebuilding anarchism, my own obsession with her anticommunism may have led me to underestimate the strengths of her critique and to exaggerate her influence on anti-Soviet opinion in the West.

In any case, as new archives are opened and we learn more about the civil war period in Russia, we will certainly be in a better position to relate Goldman's critique to other assessments. As we learn more about the history of anarchism, especially the Russian anarchists, it should be possible to see Goldman more fully as part of a political movement whose history is just now being written. Situating Goldman within the fiercely contested, constantly changing terrain of Russian history may become easier as Soviet historiography moves beyond the borders of ancient, emotional cold war polemics.

However, it seems to me likely that new interpretations of Emma Goldman will emerge not from the discovery of new archival materials but from new theoretical perspectives, particularly feminist perspectives, which will change the contexts in which we try to situate her, the kinds of questions we may ask about her, and, perhaps also, the narrative forms in which we try to answer them. Perhaps even an anarchist feminist form, in writing or possibly in film or theater, may offer new accounts of Emma Goldman whose outlines we cannot yet imagine.

In the course of writing *Emma Goldman in Exile,* I often asked myself why I was spending so much time on a woman about whom I felt so ambivalent. I always felt myself struggling for empathy with her. I wanted to like her more than I did. Certainly the emotional dynamics of writing this book were more complex than those of the first volume, in part because I had come to know and like a number of Emma's friends and admirers, including many younger anarchists, and I worried about their response to my deepening criticism. In fact, publication of the book ended my communication with some of them and elicited hostile responses from others, an outcome that was extremely painful. Nonetheless, I believe I was able to use my own mixed feelings toward Goldman to understand the frequently divided responses of her comrades, to grasp something of Emma's difficulties with intimacy, the ways in which she distanced people from her even while trying desperately to bring them closer.

To a considerable extent, I think what kept me going was her accessibility, or what I thought was her accessibility. With her mountains of personal, intimate letters and her massive autobiography, I thought I could get to know her well. Bell Gale Chevigny's essay about her efforts to write a biographical study of Margaret Fuller speaks to this issue. In this essay, "Daughters Writing: Toward a Theory of Women's Biography," Chevigny suggested that women writing about women are likely to be drawn toward subjects that symbolically recreate "their internalized relations with their mothers and that offer them an opportunity to recreate those relations." Whether the subjects are famous women whose histories are distorted or unknown women whose histories have been neglected, "the act of daughters writing about them is likely to be, on some level, an act of retrieval that is experienced as rescue." During the biographical process, Chevigny continues, author and subject in effect become "surrogate mothers in that they offer one another 'maternal' nurture. . . . Ideally then, as biographers, we recreate 'mothers' from whom we can integrate and separate more effectively than from our biological mothers." Such efforts, she felt, "were rooted not only in my desire for vicarious self-knowledge but also in a desire to know a precursor in ways I could not know my own mother." In a culture that privileges the knowledge of men over that of women, "we approach the lives of our mothers (and foremothers) with few and arbitrary tools. More crucially here, it is a psychological issue. Bars to our knowledge of ourselves and our knowledge of our mothers are psychologically linked. . . . I am convinced that when, as daughters writing, we are moved to study a foremother, we are grappling with some aspect of this ignorance which is so costly to ourselves."[11]

Chevigny may overstate the case, yet her thesis speaks to my own motivation. I am certain that the labyrinth of secrets in my own family while I was growing up, including the secret of Huntington's disease, deepened my attraction to a woman seemingly willing to lay bare her heart. I am sure it was no coincidence that I was first attracted to Goldman as my mother lay dying; ironically, my mother died on May 14—the same day that Goldman died nearly forty years earlier—as if to dramatize the symbolic connection. No doubt this loss intensified my motivation to study another woman whom I could engage with, argue with, possibly even "rescue" in a way that I could not do with my mother.

In the end, of course, I did not "rescue" Emma Goldman. Unlike many feminist biographers of women writing for the first time about little-known figures or correcting negative distortions of famous ones, I found myself in the uncomfortable position of criticizing a heroic figure who was already considered a role model. The satisfactions of this endeavor were distinctly mixed. At times I felt ashamed, as if I had somehow betrayed a heroine, though Emma Goldman continues to inspire a wide range of feminist activists and artists, including playwrights, actors, musicians, and filmmakers. I wondered whether I might have felt more empathy with her had I been more of an activist myself, more able to share the disillusions of a woman who had staked her entire life on a political movement that endured a steady succession of defeats.

Unlike Alix Kates Shulman, who found in Emma Goldman a great teacher and mentor, I felt closer to the experience of Elinor Langer, who gradually fell out of love with her subject. While I had never had any desire to diminish Goldman and saw my project as one of humanizing a mythic figure, I did experience a slight feeling of disappointment. Was this feeling the realistic recognition of limitations that my earlier infatuated gaze had overlooked? Was it perhaps the reenactment of earlier disappointments with my mother, displaced onto Emma Goldman? Did I underestimate the tremendous obstacles Goldman faced as a woman, out of a failure of feminist identification?

I have not yet arrived at the distance from the biography needed for a more detached perspective. But certainly Emma Goldman remains for me a powerful presence, a point of reference, both politically and personally. She has taken up permanent residence in my life as part of a feminist network of the imagination, an alter-ego, an/Other/Mother with whom I continue to argue and identify. Through her I have come to see the world in different ways, though not always the ways she would have chosen. I have also come to see myself in a new light, not always the light I would have liked. She has shaped the architecture of my life as much, or more, than I have shaped hers. Although I no longer dream of unearthing "the real Emma Goldman," as she herself once hoped to do, I do dream of returning one day to her life with new questions and contexts. It is strange, perhaps, to think of a published text as a work-in-progress, but that is how I think of the biography I have written: as part of a dialogue that still continues.

NOTES

The photograph of Emma Goldman appears courtesy of the National Archives, 165-WW-164B-5. I wish to thank the editors, especially Sara Alpern, for their suggestions and their patience with the many revisions of this essay. I am also grateful to members of the Focused Research Project in Gender Theory at the University of California, Riverside, and to members of the Los

Angeles Biography Group, particularly Ellen DuBois and Robert Rosenstone, for provocative discussions that helped shape my thinking about feminist theory and about the biographical process.

1. Emma Goldman, *Living My Life* (New York: Alfred A. Knopf, 1931) (later cited in the text as LML).

2. Richard Drinnon, *Rebel in Paradise* (Chicago: University of Chicago Press, 1961).

3. Alix Kates Shulman, *To the Barricades: The Anarchist Life of Emma Goldman* (New York: Thomas Y. Crowell, 1971).

4. Alice Wexler, *Emma Goldman in America* (New York: Beacon Press, 1984). This book was originally published by Pantheon Books under the title *Emma Goldman: An Intimate Life.*

5. Teresa de Lauretis, "Issues, Terms and Contexts," in *Feminist Studies/ Critical Studies,* ed. Teresa de Lauretis (Bloomington: Indiana University Press, 1985), 9.

6. Sue-Ellen Case, *Feminism and Theatre* (New York: Methuen, 1988), 54–55.

7. See, for example, Judith Butler's notion of gender as a performative act, something one does rather than what one is. Judith Butler, *Gender Trouble: Feminism and the Subversion of Identity* (New York: Routledge, 1990).

8. Stephen F. Cohen, *Rethinking the Soviet Experience: Politics and History since 1917* (New York: Oxford University Press, 1985).

9. Liz Stanley, "Moments of Writing: Is There a Feminist Auto/biography?" *Gender and History* (Spring 1990): 62.

10. Alice Wexler, *Emma Goldman in Exile: From the Russian Revolution to the Spanish Civil War* (Boston: Beacon Press, 1989).

11. Bell Gale Chevigny, "Daughters Writing: Toward a Theory of Women's Biography," in *Between Women,* ed. Carol Ascher, Louise DeSalvo, and Sara Ruddick (Boston: Beacon Press, 1984), 375.

SUSAN WARE

Unlocking the Porter-Dewson Partnership: A Challenge for the Feminist Biographer

MOLLY DEWSON (1874–1962), Democratic politician, feminist, and social reformer, is best known for her contributions to the New Deal in the 1930s. Born Mary Williams Dewson in Quincy, Massachusetts, but always known as Molly, she graduated from Wellesley College in 1897. In her early career she ran a parole department for delinquent girls, worked for the minimum wage in Massachusetts in 1912, and participated in the suffrage movement. She and her partner, Polly Porter, with whom she shared her life for more than fifty years, ran a dairy farm in central Massachusetts and volunteered for duty in France with the American Red Cross in World War I. From then on, the partners alternated their time between Greenwich Village and Castine, Maine, where they had a summer home. From 1919 to 1924

Dewson worked as Florence Kelley's chief specialist on the minimum wage at the National Consumers' League. After a brief stint as the civic secretary of the Women's City Club, Dewson became president of the New York Consumers' League, a position she held until 1931.

Through her reform activity in New York City in the 1920s, Molly Dewson met Eleanor Roosevelt. Their association profoundly shaped the rest of her career. In 1928, at Eleanor's request, Dewson joined Al Smith's national Democratic campaign. By 1930 she had transferred her loyalties to Franklin D. Roosevelt's presidential bid, organizing all women's activities in the 1932 campaign. Dewson enjoyed a close working relationship with both Franklin and Eleanor Roosevelt, and she became one of the New Deal's most loyal supporters. Dewson was responsible for many of the appointments of women to high-level positions in the New Deal administration; she played a large role in Frances Perkins's selection as Secretary of Labor in 1933. Dewson also built the Women's Division of the Democratic National Committee into a central component of the newly revitalized Democratic party. She worked for equal representation on all party committees and initiated the Reporter Plan for Democratic women to study the impact of the New Deal on their localities. In the 1936 campaign the Women's Division counted eighty thousand active supporters and supplied 90 percent of the literature for the general campaign in the form of brightly colored fact sheets called Rainbow Fliers.

At the height of her political power in 1937, Molly Dewson returned to her old field of social welfare to become one of the three members of the recently created Social Security Board. She served for less than a year, however, and in 1938 left government service permanently. Dewson spent the rest of her retirement with Polly Porter in New York and Maine and, after 1952, lived exclusively in Castine, where she died in 1962. Polly Porter died in 1972.

Partner and I is not at first glance the most likely title for a book about women's politics, feminism, and the New Deal. It came from a letter written by Molly Dewson that I discovered fairly late in my research. Dewson had recently returned from serving overseas in France during World War I and was now working under Florence Kelley at the National Consumers' League. She used the phrase to open a 1920 letter to Maud Wood Park written in the wake of the final suffrage victory: "Partner and I have been bursting with pride and satisfaction ever since you were elected chairman of the League of Women Voters." It was its very offhand quality—no mention of who the partner was, with the corresponding assumption that Park would know that Molly Dewson was part of a couple—that immediately caught my attention, and my fancy. It offered a clue as to how Molly Dewson presented herself to the world. The choice of that delightful, odd phrase as the book's title was my attempt to direct attention to what I considered the central key to understanding Molly Dewson's life: her fifty-two-year partnership with Polly Porter, a relationship broken only by Dewson's death in 1962.

The Porter-Dewson partnership had enormous consequences for Molly Dewson's career. As she successfully made her way in the man's world of politics and public life, she never left the woman's world that nurtured her, both personally and professionally. Dewson was not alone in this orientation: her lifestyle typified the choices of many late nineteenth- and early twentieth-century educated women who built their emotional lives around other women rather than men. Furthermore, the participation of many women in public life in the early twentieth century was characterized by a similar congruence between informal friendships and public activism. The key instruments were networks that brought together reformers, political activists, and traditional women's organizations on issues of common concern. These networks maximized women's influence and offered a powerful tool with which to influence public policy. Molly Dewson's entire life is testimony to the power of women's networks.

I cannot claim that I had this integrated vision of Molly Dewson's life from the very start of my project, however. Although Molly Dewson had played a large role in the narrative of my first book about women in the New Deal, I thought of her more as part of a network than as an individual. At that point, it had not dawned on me that there was anything unusual or noteworthy in the fact that Molly Dewson had never married. Then one day I remember looking up at a picture of Dewson that I kept on my wall (the photograph at Democratic headquarters, which opens this essay, of a mature professional woman in her fifties, seated at a desk surrounded by toy Democratic donkeys) and suddenly saying to myself, "Molly Dewson, you old fox, you're a lesbian." Why I suddenly came to that realization at that point I cannot, alas, recall, but it represented a new stage of awareness about her personal life that I had been oblivious to when I first wrote about her.

When I embarked on a full-scale biography in 1980, I did not initially plan to focus very heavily on Dewson's personal life. My working title was "From Wellesley to the White House," which summed up the predominantly political orientation of the first draft. Of course, Polly was in the narrative as Molly's partner, but the main emphasis was on Molly Dewson as a political figure and Progressive and New Deal reformer.

I must have taken my role as a biographer seriously at this early stage, because I somewhat self-consciously kept a record of my feelings and thoughts while I worked on the book. This writer's diary turned out to have more historical than literary value. Rereading the diary after the book had been published, I found conclusive evidence of how far I was from an integrated interpretation of the personal and public worlds of Molly Dewson at first. The writer's diary discussed my frustrations at making Molly Dewson come alive given sparse sources at various points in her life, grappled with the problem of balance in how to treat the three decades of her career that preceded the New Deal, and obsessed about how long the manuscript had become (with the subtext, Who would read a long book about a little-known woman?). Only incidentally did the diary dwell on the role of Polly Porter in Molly Dewson's life.

Gradually, as I revised the manuscript and received comments and suggestions from friends, I realized how central Polly Porter was to the story. Although I had all the pieces, I had failed to emphasize (because I didn't realize it yet myself) the fundamental fact that Molly Dewson made practically every career decision in her professional life after 1912 based on how it would affect her relationship with Polly Porter. At first, the two partners were just as likely to be working together—supervising delinquent girls, running a farm, participating in the suffrage campaign, or volunteering with the Red Cross overseas during World War I. By the 1920s, however, Molly moved more directly into political activity, while Polly increasingly devoted her time to raising dogs. When Dewson joined the Roosevelt administration as the head of the Women's Division of the Democratic National Committee in the 1930s, she at first commuted three days a week to Washington, but soon she made New York the primary base for her political activities for women's politics in the New Deal. Once again, I had all this information when I wrote *Beyond Suffrage: Women in the New Deal,* but I did not realize the implications of Dewson's running the Women's Division out of the Biltmore Hotel in New York.

That Molly Dewson refused to put work unilaterally ahead of personal commitments helps to explain the twists and turns of her career. The one time she broke that rule—to take a job in Washington with the Social Security Board in 1937–38 while Polly remained in New York—the separation was such a strain that Dewson resigned after only nine months on the job. After the short stint on the Social Security Board, Dewson retired from professional work (she was sixty-three), and the partners divided their time between New York and Castine, Maine, where Porter had a summer home called Moss Acre. Behind Molly Dewson's freedom to be so selective about her professional pursuits lay Polly Porter's quite substantial family inheritance, which freed them both from the necessity of paid employment.

My conception of the book consequently underwent a profound shift. Instead of my initial plan of writing a "straight" political biography of a major New Deal politician (the word certainly has a double meaning in this case!), I restructured the narrative to integrate Dewson's political and professional choices with the personal priorities of the partnership. And yet I never contemplated making it a joint biography. Molly Dewson's public achievements in the minimum wage fight, her decidedly pragmatic style of feminism in advancing opportunities for women in politics, and her role in the founding of the modern welfare state were the accomplishments that had originally drawn me to her as a subject. These continued to take priority in the narrative over Polly Porter's own choices—her social work training, her involvement with radical politics in the 1920s, and her running a kennel for her beloved Shelties. This concentration on the public achievements of a single subject placed my biography well within the traditional mode, although I suspect that the importance placed on Dewson's personal life sets it off from the vast majority of biographies of men and from many biographies of women.

Having said all this about the centrality of the Porter-Dewson partnership to the biography as I wrote it, I have a small confession to make: there are only two extant letters to support my entire interpretation of these women's deep and abiding love. Actually, there is not a single "love letter" from Dewson to Porter, although two letters exist from Porter to Dewson, written when they were apart during their wartime service in France. Unlike other well-documented female couples (the letters from Janet Flanner to her friend Natalia Danesi Murray come to mind, or the extensive material on Gertrude Stein and Alice B. Toklas), Molly and Polly were rarely separated and thus never wrote to one other. And even if there had been a few letters, my guess is that Polly Porter would have destroyed them out of her intense sense of privacy, at least when Molly died, if not sooner.

All historians are detectives in some way or another, and I became a detective looking for clues about the Porter-Dewson partnership, especially in its early years. I carefully collected small bits of evidence, such as a program book from a museum visit in 1911, annotated "w. Polly," addresses in the Cambridge city directory where Polly lived just before she met Molly, and references to Polly and Molly sharing a flat during the 1912 minimum wage campaign in Massachusetts. After the 1910s, the evidence was often uncovered within more traditional sources, such as the "Partner and I" reference found in the League of Women Voters papers at the Library of Congress.

Luckily I did not have to reconstruct the partnership entirely through circumstantial evidence. At a fairly early point in my research, I had the good fortune to become acquainted with the extended Porter-Dewson clan that is still centered in the Penobscot Bay town of Castine, Maine. The central figure in this group was Virginia Bourne, Molly's and Polly's favorite great-niece who inherited Moss Acre and continues to live in this hulking house with her husband, Standish. The circle also included two of Polly's godchildren, Peter Dobkin Hall and Marion Hall Hunt, both historians themselves and supportive of my efforts to write about the women they remembered as Aunt Moll and Aunt Poll. These family members made available to me a collection of scrapbooks that had been lovingly assembled by Porter and Dewson over the years, their conscious attempt to leave a photographic legacy of their shared lives. In these scrapbooks was all the proof I needed to document the love that bound these women's lives together for over five decades.

Perusing the scrapbooks, I was plunged into the world of the two women known to friends and family alike as the Porter-Dewsons. Here were photographs of Polly's early life that filled in many gaps about her upbringing; scrapbooks on the Dewson side that constructed her genealogy back to a Revolutionary-era great-great-grandfather; photographs of a young, rather masculine-looking Dewson at Wellesley

Molly Dewson and Polly Porter in Maine in the early
1920s. Courtesy of Virginia Bourne and David Hall,
Castine, Maine.

Dewson and Porter in Maine in the late 1950s. Courtesy of Virginia Bourne
and David Hall, Castine, Maine.

College and in her early professional jobs; an entire scrapbook devoted to the farm that they ran in central Massachusetts when they first lived together; a volume on World War I that read like the new social history, with its focus on the impact of war on ordinary French citizens. There were volumes on their European trips and pictures of the extended network of friends and family who came to Castine each summer. And there were innumerable pictures of the dogs, cats, horses, and even farm animals that were so much a part of their life together.[1]

Photographs from these scrapbooks occupy a central place in the final version of the biography. Since I did not have traditional sources like letters to document the love between these two women, I constructed a photo essay designed to convey the dimensions of their relationship. Instead of just including pictures with captions, I crafted an essay that could stand entirely on its own as a pictorial representation of Molly Dewson and Polly Porter's life together. (When writing part of a college-level U.S. history survey text, I had realized the important contribution that photographic sources could make to a written text and had learned how to draw readers' attention to specific details and aspects of the photographs themselves.) I believe the photo essay makes a major contribution to the book as a whole and shows (again, if there was any doubt) the love that bound these women together.

Using phrases such as "two women in love" raises the question of to what extent the label "lesbianism" is appropriate for understanding the Porter-Dewson partnership. All feminist biographers whose subjects were involved in relationships with other women grapple with this issue. Historians must always be wary of transposing present-day definitions back into the past, and nowhere is this more true than regarding sexuality and sexual preference. The caution is reinforced by the fact that Molly and Polly never used the term "lesbian" to describe themselves, nor did their friends and family interpret the relationship in that way at the time.

One option would have been to find linguistic and stylistic ways of conveying their love without using the specific term "lesbian." In some ways, that is what I did, relying more on descriptions of shared lives and the evidence of the photographs rather than repeated references to their sexual preference. In the end, I used the word "lesbian" in only two places—in the introduction and in the chapter defining their partnership.

This labeling was a very deliberate political statement, however, a conscious attempt to overcome what Blanche Wiesen Cook has called "the historical denial of lesbianism." Molly Dewson and Polly Porter loved each other, and I did not want to mask the nature of the relationship nor to sanitize or homogenize it to make it easier for readers to accept. I do not know if they even slept together, nor do I think such intimate knowledge is necessarily central to our understanding of their relationship. We do not demand proof of sexual activity as a badge of heterosexuality. I do know that I have never in my wildest imagination been able to imagine Molly Dewson in love with a man.

The Porter-Dewson partnership, which spanned a critical period in the history of sexuality, sheds light on the changing nature of women's relationships in the late nineteenth and early twentieth centuries. Molly and Polly initiated their partnership in the 1910s, when long-standing and intense female friendships were still a socially acceptable vehicle to a full personal and professional life without the constraints of marriage, especially for privileged educated daughters of the middle class. Families and friends welcomed such couples as an ideal alternative to what was seen as a life of lonely spinsterhood.

By the 1920s and 1930s, however, perhaps earlier, changing notions of psychology, the popularization of Freud, and a general decline in the kind of gender-specific world that had fostered such female friendships had all served to undermine societal support for women who chose to spend their lives with other women. Now love between women was increasingly seen as suspect. Molly and Polly remained unaware or unaffected by such currents, never feeling the need to hide or conceal their lifestyle. In fact, according to their old friend Clara Beyer, there were so many of these relationships among women of their generation that they were hardly even cause for comment.

One of my goals in *Partner and I* was to reacquaint modern readers with this earlier, quite accepted model of female friendship and companionship. In retrospect, I believe that what Adrienne Rich identified as heterosexual privilege allowed me a certain freedom in writing about love between women so forthrightly. My husband is prominently thanked in the acknowledgments (not, I should add, to establish my heterosexual credentials but for his concrete support and help while I was writing the book). But the fact that I am married did, I am quite certain, release me from suspicion that I was writing the book from some kind of hidden personal or political agenda. Of course, it is a sad commentary that the work of gay and lesbian historians is labeled "political," while work coming from others just as affected by class, race, and gender is somehow seen as more objective.

At the same time that I was determined to write sympathetically about love between women, I understood the need not to romanticize women's friendships. Just because the participants in a relationship were women did not make them immune from the problems, tensions, and squabbles that affect heterosexual couples. The goal was to paint these pairings in all their complexity, not to expect that relationships between women would necessarily be any more successful or less tension-ridden than their heterosexual counterparts.

Throughout the project, however, the lack of written sources hampered my ability to assess the ebb and flow of the Porter-Dewson partnership. Even my interpretation that it was stress over their separation that led Dewson to resign from the Social Security Board was deduced from sketchy bits of evidence. Oral history helped to fill in the gaps, but it tends to be more useful in constructing the later stages of a subject's life, when other sources are generally also more prevalent. Only one Castine friend was still alive, Dorothy Blake, who remembered Molly and Polly from the early days out on the farm in central Massachusetts. Over tea hardly seemed the time to ask the very proper eighty-year-old Miss Blake about her friends' early passions, and yet Blake spontaneously contributed a vital bit of information by describing Molly and Polly as "fast friends" from the very start.

My other frustration was that Polly Porter remained such an elusive figure, both in the book and in my own understanding of her. Part of this gap came from working mainly with sources that focused on Molly Dewson, especially her professional and political work. Colleagues of Dewson's often did not know Polly at all because she kept to the background and was not the least bit interested in Democratic politics. In their stories, Polly is something of a cipher. The deep connections that bound the two together, and Polly's quite independent and free-spirited personality, often were not immediately obvious.

Yet there was another side to Polly, one far more intriguing and complex than that of her partner, whom I came to refer to as "Mainstream Molly." Molly Dewson was a totally nonintrospective person who cheerfully accepted what came her way and rarely got discouraged or overwrought. Politically, she accepted the dominant American capitalist system and was almost naively optimistic about the potential for social change through piecemeal reform. She wholeheartedly supported

Franklin Roosevelt, and only once (over packing the Supreme Court in 1937) did she even let herself consider disagreeing with her beloved leader. For her unpublished autobiography, she chose the title "An Aid to the End" and considered that one of her most important contributions to the New Deal was her loyalty to FDR.

Whereas I always knew that Molly Dewson would be squarely in the middle of the American reform tradition (although simultaneously an outsider, with her insistence on raising women's issues), Polly Porter was more complicated, less predictable. There is the question of her radicalism, her possible links to the Communist party in the 1920s. There is her pacifism and her willingness to be critical of dominant institutions, including capitalism and organized religion. One senses a lurking passion, a real feeling for events and ideas that could explode in sometimes contradictory ways: though Polly might philosophically declare herself a communist, she still loved the trappings of her bourgeois lifestyle of fancy cars, foreign travel, servants, and large houses. One suspects that while Molly's conversation would be genial and witty, Polly's would have an edge to it, a bite, an intensity missing from her less introspective partner. I consider my inability to fully capture Polly Porter's spirited soul a missed opportunity, even if somewhat inevitable in the context of writing a scholarly biography of her better-known political partner.

The story of how I came to write about the Porter-Dewson partnership holds various implications for writing biography. Besides rescuing the lives of scores of "lost women," one of the most important contributions of women's history to the craft of biography may be its emphasis on personal lives and their impact on public accomplishments. This is not necessarily a call for more psychological interpretations or psychobiographies, however. Rather, it asks for attention to the ordinary daily lives of our subjects. Whom you share your bed with and how you pay the bills do have an impact on events beyond the household. This insight applies both to men and women but is more salient for women achievers. Women who lived the kind of public life deemed worthy of historical treatment almost inevitably had to make decisions and sacrifices that had potentially profound effects on their personal lives. In charting a woman's public achievements, we need to pay special attention to both the benefits and the costs of such personal choices.

Exploring women in politics and public life through the lens of biography has also convinced me of the ongoing utility of a generational approach for understanding broader patterns of women's history. I employed such a methodological tool in *Beyond Suffrage* and found it even more useful in the Dewson biography. Molly Dewson's Progressive-era reform participation provided her with an optimistic faith that social change could be accomplished through education and legislative reform; the feminism and gender consciousness she imbibed from her education and early professional employment meant that whatever she did, she always raised women's issues as part of her political agenda. These attitudes, forged in the early twentieth century, shaped her ideology and tactics for the rest of her life, as they did for many of her peers.

But were Molly Dewson's priorities passed on to other women? Did her style and political agenda replicate itself? In *Partner and I*, I hypothesized that later generations of women did not approach public or private life with anywhere near the level of gender consciousness exhibited by many members of Molly Dewson's generation. But lurking in the back of my mind was the possibility that if historians dug deeper into the public realm from the 1930s to the 1960s, especially at the state and local level, where women have found greater opportunities, they might nonetheless find continuities and links.

I now feel more confident in categorizing the following generation of political and professional women as quite different from Molly Dewson and her cohort. The main difference is a noticeable tendency to move beyond a separate female political culture to demand competition on an equal basis with men.[2] Women coming of age in the 1910s and 1920s had many more opportunities to move directly into the (male) public realm than Dewson, who graduated into the gender-specific public sphere that still reigned at the turn of the century. Furthermore, these rising generations of women did not necessarily want to work in women's organizations or solely on women's issues. Instead they often preferred to battle shoulder to shoulder alongside men on issues such as pacifism or birth control. Increased cultural and social imperatives toward heterosexual behavior by the 1920s, with a corresponding suspicion of the female world that had nurtured Molly Dewson and her colleagues, also played a profound role in this shift.

The lingering question of what happened to feminism in the generations after Molly Dewson seems to me the most intriguing legacy of *Partner and I*, and it has led me to a new project that addresses similar kinds of issues and employs a biographical approach, but is not about political women. What interests me now are the younger women of the 1920s and 1930s who came of age in a period without the supportive feminist and reform tradition that so nurtured Molly Dewson and her colleagues. And yet such women did have new kinds of role models—the autonomous, independent heroines put forward by popular culture and the media in the 1920s and 1930s. These celebrities captured the popular imagination at the time, rather than political figures like Molly Dewson or Frances Perkins.

Many of these popular heroines are well known—actresses Katharine Hepburn and Bette Davis, athletes Gertrude Ederle and Babe Didrikson, photographer Margaret Bourke-White, artist Georgia O'Keeffe, and social scientist Margaret Mead. The one who seems best to encapsulate the new possibilities for women is aviator Amelia Earhart. Earhart offers clues to unlocking both the fortunes of feminism in the postsuffrage era (she considered herself a feminist and publicly promoted opportunities for women) and the more murky areas of role models, women's aspirations, and the ways in which the popular culture sends out messages that can be liberating and traditional at the same time. Coverage of Earhart's exploits in aviation, and widely distributed images of her short, tousled hair, pants, and silk aviator's scarf, worked as a challenge to traditional status-quo definitions of femininity and women's roles. In turn, this model of female independence drawn from popular culture may have served as a substitute for a more overtly political feminist vision.

After swearing I would not write another biography (at least for quite a while), it is odd to find myself drawn so strongly to the figure of Amelia Earhart. What I have in mind, however, is not a conventional biography but a book that applies a biographical approach to a certain period of women's history. After looking at coverage of Amelia Earhart's flights, her portrayal in the media, and her writings and public speeches, I plan to place her story amid the cluster of women who rose to public prominence in the 1920s and 1930s. By their widely publicized accomplishments and nontraditional lifestyles, such popular heroines suggested that women could be autonomous human beings, could live life on their own terms, and could overcome conventional barriers. Such messages, while not specifically labeled feminism, provided a highly individualistic route for exceptional women to excel. This message of autonomy and independence appeared especially attractive to young women coming of age in the period between the two waves of twentieth-century feminism.

From Molly Dewson to Amelia Earhart—is the transition so abrupt as it seems? Not to me. The questions that animated my interest in Dewson and women in the New Deal—women's achievements, the exercise of power and influence, the fate of feminism in the postsuffrage era—are still in the forefront, but the field of focus has changed from politics to popular culture. I anticipate that it will be a fascinating journey.

NOTES

The photograph that begins this essay, of Molly Dewson at her desk at the Women's Division of the Democratic National Committee, appears courtesy of Virginia Bourne and David Hall, Castine, Maine.

1. These scrapbooks have been microfilmed for the Dewson papers at the Schlesinger Library, Radcliffe College.

2. See, for example, the interviews collected in the Women in Federal Government Oral History Project at the Schlesinger Library, Radcliffe College.

DEE GARRISON

Two Roads Taken: Writing the Biography of Mary Heaton Vorse

MARY HEATON VORSE (1874–1966), born into a wealthy New England family, followed the path of the "new woman" of her time. She studied art in Paris and New York during the 1890s. In 1898 she married Albert Vorse, a newspaperman and aspiring author. After giving birth to two children, in 1902 and 1907, Vorse established a successful writing career, primarily as an author of popular fiction for women. In 1910 her philandering first husband and disapproving mother died on the same day. Cut out of her mother's will, Vorse became the sole support of her family and, in 1912, started her career as a labor activist.

Vorse came late to the support of labor's cause. She was a thirty-eight-year-old mother of two when her observation of the 1912 Lawrence, Massachusetts, textile strike caused her to reorient her life. Henceforth she wrote fiction only to support her children and to finance her work as a foremost American labor journalist. In 1912 she married the socialist reporter Joe O'Brien. Their son was born in 1914, one year before Joe died of cancer.

As an editor of *The Masses,* a member of the Liberal Club, and a founder of the feminist Heterodoxy Club, Vorse was a central participant in the social revolution that took place in prewar Greenwich Village. Her summer home in Provincetown, Massachusetts, became a kind of suburb for the New York intelligentsia; the famed group the Provincetown Players was born there.

Between 1915 and 1922 Vorse lived apart from her children, who were sent away to school or to live with relatives. She reported strikes at home and events in Europe. While in Paris in 1919, she fell in love with Robert Minor, a famous political cartoonist who later became a leading American Communist. For several months she was one of the few American correspondents in Moscow, and she toured Russia to report the famine of 1921. In 1922 Minor left her for another woman soon after Vorse miscarried his child. As a result of the medical treatment for the miscarriage, she became addicted to morphine. For four agonizing years Vorse returned home to recover and to be a mother, in guilty compensation for the years she had spent apart from her children.

Overcoming her addiction, she returned to public life as publicity director of the Passaic, New Jersey, textile strike of 1926. She later reported miners' and farmers' strikes and the early New Deal in Washington, D.C., where she worked at the Indian Bureau from 1935 to 1937. Vorse went on to report the organizing efforts of the Congress of Industrial Organizations (CIO) across the nation. At age sixty-three, she was injured when she dived to escape ricocheting bullets from the guns of company guards during the Little Steel War in Youngstown, Ohio. During the 1930s, she also recorded the rise of Hitler and scenes from Stalin's Soviet Union.

As World War II progressed, Vorse reported on the lives of American women factory workers. After the war she served in Italy with the United Nations Relief and Rehabilitation Administration. Later, in the 1950s, she lived in semiretirement in Provincetown. Her last big story, an exposé of crime in the waterfront unions, was published in *Harper's* when she was seventy-eight. During her eighties and nineties, the scope of her battleground shrunk to Cape Cod, where she helped to organize a protest against off-shore dumping of nuclear waste and voiced her opposition to the Vietnam war. Mary Vorse died in 1966 at her home in Provincetown at the age of ninety-two.

———————

Over the years I worked on Mary Heaton Vorse's story, I read dozens of books and articles about writing biography. Most were written by literary scholars. Few historians have discussed the matter, and most only recently. Outside the comments by feminist scholars, which I will discuss separately, the literature addressing the subject of biography is remarkably repetitive.

One prime theme reminded me of the old question that most historians encounter in the first year of graduate training: Is history (in this case, biography) art or science? For both the budding historian and the prospective biographer, the answer is the same: it is both. Biography demands the skills of both the literary artist and the scientific researcher. The biographer must operate in accordance with strict rules of evidence—measuring the validity of documents, weighing contradictory findings, adding scrupulous footnoting. Yet the techniques of the novelist are also essential. One must shape and order the evidence, deal with flashbacks, develop believable characters, dramatize crucial moments, and analyze human relations—all this without conscious distortion of fact. Of course, all good writing, fiction or not, relies upon central themes and dramatic development. Still, the historical monograph is vastly different from biography's attempt to recreate one human personality in all its mystery and complexity. Every life storyteller knows the difference. As one writer put it, the biographer is "an artist under oath."

Another common conclusion about the biographical process is that no single system of Freudian or neo-Freudian analysis, once so trendy, will suffice, especially since so little is usually known about a subject's childhood. Drawing from an eclectic collection of psychiatric insights, the best modern biographers ponder the psyche without being self-conscious about it, somewhat as we all tend to analyze our friends and families. Feminist scholars, especially, favor social and historical explanations over psychological ones. If one psychological theme emerges from feminist biographers' work, it is a focus on the natural growth of personality, shaped by the changing passages of life as much as by dominant traits and motivations.

The most innovative thought on the writing of biography is relatively new. Only in recent decades—as postmodernist thought and its most radical component, feminist theory, dissolved the old certainties of the Enlightenment and orthodox Marxism—have scholars been willing to see biography anew. I refer to the understanding that part of the biographers' work is detached scientific research, and part an autobiographical process. Leon Edel cast the question: If the poem is the poet, the novel the novelist, and the picture the painter, is the biographer the biography? To a large degree, emphatically—yes. Inevitably so. It is a maxim that even the only moderately self-aware biographer cannot help but sense, despite its jarring impact upon what David Novick has termed "that noble dream" of objectivity.

Biographical interpretation reveals a peculiarly reciprocal relationship between author and subject. The biographer is visible in the selection of documents and testimony, in the intuitive choice of a quote or incident to move along the story, and, above all, in the choice to write this particular life and not another. Surely all scholars to some degree choose their topics in order to enact the main themes of their own lives. The unique nature of the biographer's task simply magnifies that affinity. The elusive link between biographer and subject is a source of analytical and literary power. "Personal involvement is central," the historian and biographer, Blanche Wiesen Cook tells us. "If it fails to emerge in the course of research, I change subjects."[1] The only trouble lies in a self-identification with one's subject that is unexamined and, hence, uncritical of itself. The solution to the dilemma of subjectivity is to be acutely aware of it. The biographer must contend with the impulse to tell one's own life story in the process of writing someone else's.

Initially, I thought that I chose to write a biography of Mary Heaton Vorse because I wanted to teach myself the history of American radicalism and of the American labor wars. As a nontraditional student returning to school in the sixties after years as a housewife and mother, I had, along with thousands of other dissatisfied women, found my way out of domesticity, gained a divorce, and begun a second life. In the late 1970s, when I began the Vorse biography, I was an assistant professor in my first waged position, deeply curious about the socialist protest that I never encountered in my south Texas high school, Southern Baptist household, or conventional marriage. As an eager feminist freed by the second wave of feminism, I was bound to focus on the history of radical women. After I discovered that the papers of Elizabeth Gurley Flynn were not available for research, I traveled to the Walter Reuther Library at Wayne State University in Detroit to check out the archival collection of one of Flynn's closest friends, Mary Heaton Vorse, of whom I knew practically nothing at the time. (Neither did anyone else so far as I could determine. Later, when folks asked me who I was writing about, and I replied, their return query—"Mary Heaton who?"—was so frequent that the phrase became a joke in itself; this led a group of sympathetic friends to present me with a gift T-shirt, inscribed: MARY HEATON WHO? VORSE, OF COURSE!) The extensive size of the Vorse archives intrigued me with its potential revelations. After a few days of reading her diaries and mail, I was possessed by that private significance familiar to every biographer.

Here was the woman whose story was mine to tell. But why Vorse? She was not an obscure woman, like Jean Strouse's Alice James, whose experience could shed light on other notable people, show us just the ordinary details of life, or even illustrate a feature of her time like neurasthenia.[2] Instead, Vorse was a powerfully achieving woman whose work influenced the lives of many others. Erased from historical memory chiefly because she was a political radical of the female gender, she was deeply committed to realization of a world without war, privation, and hate. But she was also a woman who changed her life in mid-passage, became radicalized, endured terror and pain to realize her ambition, and worried about the effect of her choices upon her children: those who knew me best had no difficulty whatsoever in understanding why I chose Vorse.

This haunted relationship, lasting for years, can cause the eyes of my partner, John Leggett, to glaze when he hears the word "Mary" cross my lips: this Mary with whom he spent so many hours, reading draft after draft of her life, endlessly discussing the meaning of her triumphs and defeats. On several occasions, he or some of my friends traveled with me to her home in Provincetown, Massachusetts, to meet her sons, make the pilgrimage to the cemetery hill, or visit her house on the main street facing the bay. So well do those closest to me know Mary Vorse that we sometimes speak of her as though she were a dead relative whom we loved. We comment on her view of this or that or speculate on how she might respond to a political development or note her courage or ironic sense of humor as inspiration during our own moments of small travail.

The biography complete, I can now detach from Vorse. In many ways, she shaped my life as thoroughly as I shaped hers, before we released our clutch on one another. She gave me an expanded context that helped me to trust my ideas, despite their seeming oddity, and to persist through adversity without hope of immediate justice. I have navigated the three stages of biographical entanglement—understanding, writing, and finishing—that have been perceptively described by Elinor Langer, the biographer of Josephine Herbst.[3] Only now can I analyze with some distance the major problems I encountered along the way and enjoy in retrospect the high points of my journey as a feminist biographer.

One major research problem was the enormous pile of available evidence. Perhaps because she lived in one house for fifty-nine years, Vorse seemed to have saved almost every piece of paper she ever touched. She was confident her experience contained lessons to teach another generation; she fully expected to be studied and understood. When Vorse was in her eighties, several efficient archivists, anticipating her death, wrote to ask about the possibility of acquiring her papers for their university libraries. This pleased her immensely. With an archive, she was assured a special kind of immortality as an important person with a unique perspective. Periodically during the ten years before her death, Vorse spent many months sorting through her collection of letters, diaries, and manuscripts, culling from the mass only what she could not bear to reveal but leaving most of it intact. Reading through the accumulated data encouraged a pensive self-analysis for which she had never made time before. She added corrective notes, cautionary reminders, and illuminating references to other materials, carefully dating the new remarks. The bits of paper stashed about her house in nooks and closets took on new meaning—they became the basis for her place in history.

The amount of archival and secondary material was overwhelming. From her "Daily Notes" and "Yearly and Monthly Summaries," I knew Vorse's location and activities (and with whom she had lunch and dinner) on every single day for over fifty years. Then there were her hundreds of short stories and newspaper articles and sixteen books.

The gaps I saw in her autobiography showed me what she left out of her story—concerns about the children, her slow passage to radicalism—and how she wanted her life to be written. Because Vorse was a reporter, she moved quickly from one important event to another, here and abroad. She appeared at major strikes and international conflicts, at sophisticated literary salons, and on dangerous picket lines, at luncheons with senators or meetings with impoverished sharecroppers, at suffrage rallies and CIO strategy sessions. The great variety of her work meant I must explore an unusually large pile of other people's papers and writings and read mounds of secondary literature. Ordering and selecting evidence became an immense task that slowed me down.

In the process, I could follow up on names and interview many who knew Vorse. I could follow closely the development of her writing and sense how it sustained her through daily battles. The volume of material led me occasionally to knowledge I could never have otherwise achieved. As I looked through a book on the Whittaker Chambers and Alger Hiss involvement, the cast of characters lit my memory and sent me back in excitement to Vorse's pattern of engagements in her "Daily Notes." The list of names recorded during her residence in Washington, D.C., during 1933 and 1934 brought the thunderstruck "Aha" of sudden understanding. Mary Vorse regularly attended meetings of the famous Ware Group, a group of leftists named by Chambers as subversive types to whom Hiss was supposedly connected! I would never have guessed this link and its implications, or reached other points of small discovery, without those detailed records she kept of her daily doings.

Another research problem sprang from my growing fondness for her sons, who were still living on her Provincetown property. With the fearless, loving spirit of their mother, they opened their hearts, homes, and memories to me, without restrictions, knowing that their judgment of events might not agree with mine. In some ways, they told me, I knew her better than they did. I had read her diaries and correspondence, much of it about their scrapes and failings and the disappointments they caused her. How could I be true to the central concern of her life—distress over her children and her mothering—and not hurt these lovely old men? Biographers draw boundaries and thus make choices about the privacy of family and friends. What is honorable to leave out—in truth, to hide? How to judge, as a feminist, the questions of confidentiality, of humane sensitivity to others' needs? These were tough decisions, and I think I finally made them well, but only after long thought.

Much of what I knew about Vorse was written by men. It was more difficult to see Vorse through the eyes of women, for few of them left papers or published memoirs. Yet the views of women, their judgment of meaning and importance, are usually so different from that of men, as each of us knows from our own experience. The scarcity of recorded female vision distorts almost all historical findings. A few letters and interviews with women friends and neighbors helped me to widen the span of evidence. The papers of Josephine Herbst and Neith Boyce were invaluable additions. Still, I will never know how much the sparsity of extensive female input may have misshaped my story of Vorse's life.

A final research problem I encountered is common to the work of all historians, not biographers alone: the retrieval of facts one does not wish to find. Jean Strouse eloquently described her spells of angry frustration when she desperately wanted Alice James to just pull up her socks, get out of bed, and get on with life, instead of wasting it on headaches and breakdowns. At some level, we biographers want the lives of our subjects to be a perfect whole, so as to match our own need to overcome personal difficulties. I hated Vorse's reluctance to deal directly with her feelings about her offspring. I read too many affectionate letters to her children that began "Dearest Ellen," or "Dearest Heaton," written on the same day Vorse entered violent diatribes against them in her diary. How could Vorse go on, I stormed, decade after decade, continually moaning about what a lousy mother she was, drowning in seas of guilty fury, refusing to *act*? The type of distress biographers feel is a clear indication of their own bias and preoccupations. It is also the best kind of evidence to humble historians before the infinite complexity of human experience.

If the intricate interrelationship of biographer and subject is often painfully unsettling, the moments of pleasure are equally memorable. I had to know Provincetown, where Vorse lived for over half a century. Mary Vorse first saw Provincetown in 1906, when she came down from Boston by boat, skirting remote shores inhabited only by colonies of seagulls. That summer marked the beginning of her love affair with the fishing village on the tip of the Cape. "I was invaded by the town and surrounded by it," she said, "as though the town had literally got into my blood." In Provincetown she felt "The sense of completion that a hitherto homeless person has on discovering home." Her one-hundred-year-old house on the sandy main street fronting the harbor became her lifelong passion. Vorse wrote of it, spoke of it, loved it, and fumed against it as though it lived. She knew scores of Provincetown residents in both the literary west end and the Portuguese east end of the small town.

Over a period of years I lived in Provincetown for three to four weeks at a time in the late spring. In May, before the summer crowds arrive, the merchants and citizens move outside to repair boats, paint gates, refurbish their stores, and chat in the streets. I spent five months there in all, talking to bankers and fishermen, artists and housekeepers, librarians and bartenders, listening to the gossip, hunting up the old folks, hiking Vorse's favorite path over the dunes to the sea, locating the churches and homes that she loved. I learned how vitally important it is to soak up the feel and atmosphere of the place about which one writes. In Provincetown I heard many stories that were not true, adding immeasurably to my understanding of what was fact. Local legends survive for a purpose and reveal what the people most want to believe.

A few special interviews are engraved in memory. One was with a carefully groomed old man in his nineties who lived on Vorse's block and died the year after we talked. He left town for a long absence in 1907. That is why he could precisely date the time when he drove a highly agitated Mary Vorse in his wagon out Snail Road to search for her errant first husband; he even remembered what Bert Vorse had said when Mary caught him with her secretary in the dunes. There was the ex-minister who told me how he had horrified many of the townspeople when he became one of the first to march against the Vietnam war. Twenty years later, remembering that period, his voice softened. "I knew that Mary Vorse was the intellectual and spiritual giant of the town," he said. "The emotional support she offered me was very, very important to me at the time." An ex–auto worker answered my author's query published in the Provincetown newspaper. He suggested that we meet at the local Veterans of Foreign Wars (VFW) bar at 8 A.M., where we sipped Bloody Marys. During the pivotal Flint, Michigan, sit-down strike of 1937, Vorse's newspaper reports had strengthened his courage to join the revolt. When he retired to Provincetown, he called upon her; the two old-timers had enjoyed several boozy hours of shared memory about their part in a stirring human effort. Even though a trifle tipsy myself, all in the service of historical research, I can never forget the probing sidelong stares of the silent old men seated next to us at the bar as my weeping informant struggled to express all that Vorse's writing had meant to workers.

Another time I visited the Provincetown home of a Portuguese woman who described how during the summers of 1915 and 1916, when she was very young and poor, she had crept under Vorse's wharf at night to eavesdrop on the conversations of Vorse and her friends as they playfully rehearsed what would become the productions of the famed Provincetown Players. The woman had never realized that such a world of sparkling minds existed. She claimed that overhearing Susan Glaspell, John Reed, Louise Bryant, Eugene O'Neill, and other members of the Greenwich Village crowd changed her life. The experience stirred her imagination and sent her off to college when she came of age; but, sadly, the money ran out in the 1930s. She was forced to drop out of school, and eventually she settled for a more conventional female role in life. "Look under the bureau," she told me so purposely that I sensed an impending matter of great import. I pulled out a dusty, typewritten draft of a chapter in Vorse's autobiography. The woman had retrieved it forty years before from a garbage heap. Now, in her old age, she wanted to be rid of this discarded dream of all that might have been.

Research heights like these remind us of why we become historians of women. But I also learned that some of the Provincetown residents who had known Vorse disliked her. They judged Vorse a fraudulent radical—this famous labor reporter with elitist airs who drank far too much, treated her servants badly, and mourned her lost relationship with a domineering male, Robert Minor, for an unseemly length of time. (Other items I did not wish to learn.) Finally, it all helped me to know her better.

Related to this issue of unwelcome findings is another research experience that I am not sure whether to define as a problem or a high point. At the end of years of research, I traveled to the Boston Public Library to see a 1961 film about Provincetown that featured Vorse on camera for about ten minutes. I was incredibly startled to meet her in that dark, empty viewing room, larger than life on the big screen. This woman I fancied I knew better than anyone else in the world, better than her friends, better even than her children, was completely different from the person I thought she would be! I felt a shock so strong it was like a physical blow to the chest. I saw a genteel New England lady ... such a beautiful upper-class accent, her hair combed into a stylish bun, her clothes so carefully chosen and gracefully worn. She was eighty-seven then, but I knew she could not be all that different simply because of age. Mary Heaton Vorse—my wonderful bohemian, sexual radical, and political deviant—looked and spoke like a respectable, wealthy matron. At last I understood why the Provincetown fishermen thought she was too highfalutin to be a rebel. But there was also the Mary I knew, and, several viewings later, I found her, too: energetic, bouncy, telling stories with a sparkle in her eye, exuding childlike enthusiasm. "Oh yes, of course there are ghosts here; we often hear them moving about at night," she said to the camera, nodding toward her home built by a sea captain from the timbers of ships. The face of this proper old lady clipping roses from the hedge glowed with a risk-taking, scandalous impropriety that I recognized.

Researchers will also understand the thrill—and numbing challenge—of finding the notes Vorse insistently addressed to her future biographer. "Life, as it happens," she wrote to me in 1914, "fails often to have a recognizable pattern—for you may bleed your heart out and die of the wound, and yet the pain of which you die, the drama which caused your heart to bleed, will have had neither logical beginning nor logical end, and in the whole course of it, though it has been life and death to you, there will have been none of those first aids to the reader—suspense, dramatic contrast, or plot. You have suffered and died but it may not make a story."

At the age of eighty-eight, four years before her death, she spoke one last time to the future inquirer—a final attempt to give coherence to her living: "You *must* understand," she warned me, "that when I was very young, Life said to me, 'Here are two ways—a world running to mighty cities, full of the spectacle of bloody adventures, and here is home and children. Which will you take, the adventurous life or a quiet life?' I will take *both*, I said." The choice seemed to be between love, security, and warmth—and ambition, creation, and risk. Both were defined and separated for her by the weight of her entire culture. Her words speak still to the decision peculiarly pressed upon women.

The most joyful of research tasks, however, was meeting the female insurgents who worked with Vorse in the past. Even more than all the books or documents I dutifully read, it was her rebellious women friends who taught me most about the history of the American radical movement I originally set out to study. It was not so much what they told me, as it was their vibrant aliveness that instructed me. Many of them were very ill; all were weak with age; most were very poor. Each hummed with happy engagement in the affairs of the world. I learned what devotion to high purpose outside one's own life can bring to living.

In the 1920s, Vorse's friend, Hazel Hawthorne, liked to roll in pools of rainwater on the Cape dunes in celebration of her soaring sexuality. In her old age Hazel was still so beautiful on her sickbed, twisted and bent, unable to rise, informing me matter-of-factly that she was dying—with a wide smile. Vera Buch, the heroine of the Gastonia, North Carolina, textile strike in 1929, met me in a bleak Chicago project; with so little money and time left to her, she was happily organizing, this time for tenant rights. Adelaide Walker organized the group of writers that reported the labor war in bloody Harlan County, Kentucky, in the early 1930s. She lived in a tiny cottage that looked like a picture from a child's fairytale. I could see the books of her famous writer friends piled behind her on the shelf as she recalled for me the stories of the heartbreak and the wild parties and the fight, always the fight.

Jessie and Harvey O'Connor were already legends when I met them; they were fighting against union-busters and for civil rights before I was born. Joseph McCarthy said that Harvey was "the most contumacious witness ever to appear before the committee." Jessie was eighty-one when I visited her and completely blind. Yet she moved about easily, preparing our meal, feeling her way around the kitchen with quick hands, stirring food, finding tea bags. She and Harvey offered me a bed in a tower room on the third floor of their home. Early the next morning, Jessie suddenly appeared at the door of the tiny tower room, having made her way up three flights of narrow stairs and over the twelve-inch abyss of a broken step. Her hands slid lightly over the walls, the doorknob, the bedframe, as she moved along. She seated herself on the bed, drew her feet up, and leaned back like a young coed chatting in a dorm room. It had occurred to her in the night: perhaps I knew something she had not before considered about a 1931 strike she had covered as a reporter for labor's Federated Press? Eager curiosity brought Jessie up the steep stairs. And I learned more of what it must have been like to have worked and played and argued with these women radicals in their youth. They remain for me the best symbols of that generation of American dissidents who were born in bohemian Greenwich Village, transformed by the world's first great socialist upheavals, and buried by the witch-hunt that followed World War II.

But what, if anything, do feminist biographers bring to their work that others do not? It seems to me there is a real difference, not wholly restricted to feminist biographers, of course, but dominant in their work. Feminist biographers, male or female, are much more likely to illuminate the intersection of public and private. They write of the ordinary and rare moments in a subject's external and internal life that do not concern the traditional version of history preoccupied with power and hierarchy. Feminist biographers have the advantage of understanding, far better than the majority of male scholars, that one cannot recreate a subject's public life or intellectual production without acknowledging that person's private activities and intimate relations. In short, the feminist biographer realizes that the private life is no less real or important than the public one.[4] This may seem obvious to many scholars today, even those entranced with conservative versions of post-structuralism; yet books and articles still pour from the presses, free of any apparent consciousness of the personal as political.

Feminist scholars of women's lives are also different because they tend to rely upon knowledge of gender-specific social constructs to shape the central pattern in their work. As biographers, they assume that the restrictions on women's lives, devised by masculinist societies, are more constant and consistent for all women, across all races, cultures, and classes, than the gender boundaries placed around males. Despite the differences in the personal stories of unique women, feminist biographers of women mold their life histories to address the common external framework that determines any single woman's place in the world.

Today a new paradigm is emerging to shape the writing of women's history. It is no longer enough for us feminist historians to "add" women of color and working-class women to our analysis. A new consciousness that white, middle-class privilege is lodged at the root of much of feminist theory and women's history will empower our work. I welcome the change. None of this should diminish the importance of writing feminist biographies, for women's lives are the very foundation of feminist theory.[5]

I leave the last word to Ruth Benedict. She wrote: "I long to speak out the inspiration that comes to me from the lives of strong women. They make of their lives a Great Adventure." Countless women—rich and poor, actors in the public or private world, from every class, race, and ethnic group—have left us a record of their struggle. That inheritance allows us to persevere with more clarity.

NOTES

The photograph of Mary Heaton Vorse in 1930 is from the Archives of Labor and Urban Affairs, Wayne State University.

1. Blanche Wiesen Cook, "Biographer and Subject: A Critical Connection," in Carol Ascher, Louise DeSalvo, Sara Ruddick, eds., *Between Women: Biographers, Novelists, Critics, Teachers and Artists Write about Their Work on Women* (Boston: Beacon Press, 1984), 400.

2. Jean Strouse, "Semiprivate Lives," in Daniel Aaron, ed., *Studies in Biography* (Cambridge, Mass.: Harvard University Press, 1978), 113–31. Also see Strouse, "Responses," in James F. Veninga, ed., *The Biographer's Gift: Life History and Humanism* (College Station: Texas A & M Press, 1983), 37–41.

3. Elinor Langer, "Coming To Terms: Aspects of the Biography of Josephine Herbst," *Pequod: A Journal of Contemporary Literature and Literary Criticism,* nos. 223, 224 (1987): 209–40.

4. Strouse, "Semiprivate Lives," 129; Mary Margaret Fonow and Judith A. Cook, "Back to the Future: A Look at the Second Wave of Feminist Epistemology and Methodology," in Fonow and Cook, eds., *Beyond Methodology: Feminist Scholarship as Lived Research* (Bloomington: Indiana University Press, 1991), 1–16.

5. Maureen Quilligan, "Rewriting History: The Difference of Feminist Biography," *The Yale Review* (Winter 1988): 259–86.

ELISABETH ISRAELS PERRY

Critical Journey:
From Belle Moskowitz to
Women's History

B ELLE LINDNER MOSKOWITZ (1877–1933) was born in
Harlem, New York, where her parents, who had emigrated from East
Prussia eight years earlier, ran a small jewelry and watch-repair shop.
Educated at city schools, Horace Mann High School for Girls, and,
for a year, at Teachers' College, she began her career as a drama coach
at the Educational Alliance, a Lower East Side settlement. She later
became its director of entertainments and exhibits. In 1903 she left
this job to marry Charles Henry Israels, an architect, with whom she
had three children. He died of heart disease in 1911, leaving only a
small estate. Belle immediately sought work to support her children
and retired parents, who were then living with her in Yonkers.

During her early married years, Belle Israels had worked part-time for the social work journal *The Survey* and had pursued charity work, primarily through the Council of Jewish Women. Her special area of interest, working girls' recreation, had led her to campaign for the reform of New York's dance halls. When she became a widow, she turned this experience into salaried work, becoming a field worker for the Playground and Recreation Association and later grievance clerk and then Labor Department head for the Dress and Waist Manufacturers' Association. Politically active among reform-minded Republicans, she joined the Progressive party in 1912 and supported woman suffrage and the election of reform Republican or "fusion" candidates both in Yonkers and New York City. In 1914 she married Henry Moskowitz, a former settlement worker and reformer then serving as civil service commissioner under New York's mayor, John Purroy Mitchel. The Moskowitzes moved to New York City, where Belle continued in labor mediation until the garment manufacturers, unhappy with her prolabor policies, fired her in 1916.

In 1918, despite Alfred E. Smith's Tammany connections, the Moskowitzes supported him for governor because of his legislative record on labor issues. Belle Moskowitz organized the woman's vote for Smith (New York women voted for the first time that year). After his victory, which occurred a few days before the end of World War I, she proposed that he appoint a "Reconstruction Commission" to plan New York State's future. The reports of this commission, which she ran, formed the core of Smith's subsequent legislative program. When Smith was out of office and promoting the establishment of a bistate "authority" for the Port of New York–New Jersey, Moskowitz devised a public relations program that won popular and legislative support for the idea. After Smith returned to office in 1923, she became director of publicity for the Democratic State Committee, managing not only Smith's subsequent reelection campaigns but also his nomination for the presidency in 1928. During the 1928 race, as the only woman on the executive committee of the Democratic National Committee, she directed campaign publicity. After his defeat, Smith became head of the Empire State Building Corporation and tried to retain his leadership of the Democratic party. Moskowitz stayed on as his press agent and led his futile bid for renomination in 1932. In December she fell down the front steps of her house and, while recovering from broken bones, suffered an embolism. She died on January 2 at the age of fifty-five.

Writing the life of Belle Moskowitz took me on a long journey. Because she was my paternal grandmother, learning about her meant learning about a part of my family I never knew, and thus more about myself. Because she was a woman who, in denying her own historical importance, had failed to save many of her papers, writing about her forced me to explore new research techniques. Because I am a historian who happens to be a woman, writing her life led me to confront both her and my own relationship to the women's movement. That last experience took me into women's history, permanently changing the personal and professional direction of my life.

Belle: Almost a Family Secret

I never knew Belle Moskowitz. She died six years before I was born, before my parents, Carlos Lindner Israels and Irma Commanday, had met. They were divorced when I was a baby, and I spent most of my childhood with my mother. Thus I never learned much about my father's family. Occasionally he took me to Connecticut to see his sister Miriam and an older woman we called Aunt Grace, a retired classics professor whom I later learned was his mother's best friend. I remember meeting only one of my father's cousins, Dorothy Lindner Omansky, but I have no memory of my father's youngest sibling, Josef Israels II, a writer and publicist who had worked closely with his mother and died in the 1950s.

I cannot remember my father ever talking about his mother. My first memory of hearing her name dates from when I was about fifteen, and it was my mother's, not father's, family who brought it up. One day my mother's father, Frank Commanday, said, "When you grow up you have to write a book about your Grandma Belle." "Who was she?" I asked. He told me to ask my father, which I did the next time we were together. My father explained (I can still hear his exact words), "She was Governor Al Smith's campaign manager, but you can't write a book about her. No one can because she wasn't a 'saver.' She threw away her papers."

Al Smith had been a governor and thus clearly "important," but his name meant little to me. I had no idea why being anyone's campaign manager, much less a woman in that role, should merit a book. Nor did I understand what "papers" were. But, instead of asking my father to explain, I let the matter drop, probably because I was too embarrassed to reveal my ignorance. Years later I learned that during the sixties he had talked about his mother to a few historians—Judith Mara Gutman, who wanted to know why Moskowitz had hired photographer Lewis Hine to record the construction of the Empire State Building, and Robert Caro, who was writing about Robert Moses, a Moskowitz protégé. But by then I was on the West Coast working toward a Ph.D. in French history and saw my father even more rarely. When we did visit, the subject of his mother never came up. He died in 1969.

Several years passed, during which I earned the Ph.D. and married a historian, Lewis Perry (in 1970), with whom I had two children. One day late in 1974, Lew was reading the *American Historical Review*'s obituary of J. Salwyn Schapiro, a Renaissance historian who had been a boyhood friend and settlement work colleague of Henry Moskowitz. "You know what would be a fun project?" he called out to me from another room. "Belle and Henry Moskowitz, your grandparents." My grandfather Frank's imperative from almost half my lifetime ago echoed in my brain. I repeated to Lew my father's warning that Belle had not saved her papers. By then I knew, of course, that without "papers" historians could not write books. I doubted if any of Henry's existed either. Recent books about Smith and Franklin D. Roosevelt had referred to the Moskowitzes, but without documentation. The project seemed hopeless.

There the matter rested until I mentioned it to my mother. Despite her having left my father years before, she had a lively interest in the Moskowitzes. She had loved Henry, who, during the last year of his life (he died in 1936), had lived with her and my father, then newlyweds. She told me about Caro's new book on Robert Moses, *The Power Broker*. "Your grandparents are in it," she said. Indeed, the book contained not only stories about Henry, the Madison House Settlement, and his work as civil service commissioner but an entire chapter on Belle and the early years of her relationship to Al Smith. All of the material was new to me. I thought, If Caro could find all this without even focusing on the Moskowitzes, what might I do? My excitement began to mount.

The project would not take long, I predicted. I would need only a year's research to prepare a small book on Belle and Henry Moskowitz as Progressive-era social reformers. In fall 1975, my husband won a fellowship to spend a year at a humanities institute at Yale University. We had been living and working in Buffalo, New York, but being in New Haven would bring me closer to New York City and the oral and written sources I would need. Yale's Department of History granted me visiting fellow status, which gave me access to Yale's libraries. I won small research grants from the New School for Social Research and the Center for Research on Women at Wellesley College. Over the following years I won a research grant from the American Council of Learned Societies and a major fellowship from the National Endowment for the Humanities. But my early optimism about speed proved unfounded. I needed time to absorb the American history I was reading. My search for primary sources proved time-consuming and difficult. In addition, I had family and career obligations to meet. Our children, born in 1971 and 1973, were still small. Moreover, my university teaching career had stalled. In order to resume it, in the late seventies and early eighties I took temporary jobs, two of which required me to commute, others of which were in fields requiring new preparations. The jobs put my career back on track and eventually improved the book by expanding my knowledge of American and women's history. But working away from home and in new fields delayed my writing. In the end, twelve years passed between the decision to write the book and its publication.

Research Methodology

As the project took shape, I found my interests focusing more sharply on Belle Moskowitz alone. Henry represented a whole generation of settlement-social workers involved in Progressive-era reform politics, but Belle, as a woman, was the more unusual, and thus intriguing, figure. Also, recent advances in women's history, such as the appearance of the first three volumes of the biographical encyclopedia *Notable American Women* (1971), had stimulated my interest in women's lives and made my task seem less daunting.

I began my research with Oscar Handlin's sketch of Belle in that encyclopedia, her long obituary in the *New York Times,* and tributes sent in to newspapers by organizations on whose boards she had served. There was also a small collection of Moskowitz memorabilia at Connecticut College for Women in New London. In the late 1940s, the daughter of Paul Abelson, a close Moskowitz friend, attended the college. One of her professors wanted to start a "museum of women" that would collect the papers of prominent women of the era. Hearing that Miriam Abelson knew the Moskowitz heirs, he asked her to introduce him to them and then asked for Moskowitz's papers. They gave him what they had, which was not much. The papers contained virtually nothing that illuminated her political relationship to Smith. There was a scrapbook of newspaper articles and photographs from the 1920s, a few unpublished speeches and articles, children's letters home, scattered financial records from her last years, and over a thousand condolence letters on Belle's death that Henry had alphabetized and meticulously answered. There were also letters from her son Josef to his sister Miriam describing how much of his mother's "ancient junk" he had thrown out after her death. So, she was a saver after all! At least she had saved *some* things, but, since they had been unsystematically labeled, Josef had seen the items only as "junk."

That first year of research I followed dozens of leads, some paying off, others not. I searched for Belle's name in the *New York Times* indexes and in guides to periodicals and manuscript collections. I learned that indexes were not to be trusted. By chance, looking for one of her early essays in the social work journal *The Survey,* I came across pieces she had written and references to her that had not been indexed. I then skimmed all *Survey* volumes published while she was a part-time editor there (1906–9), a time-consuming task that taught me much about influences in Belle Israels's early career.

I also sought mentions of the reform campaigns in which she was interested in the indexes and guides I had already consulted for her name. "Dance halls" in the *New York Times* index yielded a chronology of her reform work, many of her policy statements, and a full-page *Sunday Magazine* piece on her from 1912 that had not been indexed under her name. Specialized newspapers and periodicals helped, too. Those from New York's Jewish community mentioned her activities, published her articles, or commented on events relevant to her. The journal *Playground* provided the context for dance hall and other recreation reforms. Through *Women's Wear Daily* I reconstructed her last year with the Dress and Waist Manufacturers' Association. The papers of that association were gone, but the International Ladies' Garment Workers' Union had saved transcripts of the grievance and arbitration proceedings in which Belle Israels (soon-to-be Moskowitz) took part. These provided not only a verbatim record of her ideas and how she conveyed them but a vivid picture of contemporary industrial disputes.

The annual reports and proceedings of social work and women's organizations provided another rich lode. The reports of the Educational Alliance, the Lower East Side settlement where Belle Lindner had worked, included descriptions of her activities. After learning from *The Survey* that Belle Israels had been an officer of the New York Conference of Charities and Corrections, I found her speeches and reports in its proceedings. The National Conference of Charities and Corrections brought similar results. The reports of the Committee of Fourteen, an antiprostitution group, discussed her dance hall campaign. The New York State Reconstruction Commission reports and Smith's published papers helped me trace her later political work.

From the condolence letters at Connecticut College and letterheads of organizations she represented, I drew up a list of her possible correspondents and sought out their private papers. I composed a résumé for her that listed all her organizational memberships and offices. This résumé, mailed in advance to archivists or presented when I arrived to do my research, helped archivists think of collections where I might find traces of Moskowitz activity. Although archivists often warned me I probably would not find much, I learned not to be discouraged, for I found things less often from tracking names of correspondents in card files than I did by following hunches from subject categories. Even if I failed to find a Moskowitz letter, I usually emerged from a collection with a new perspective on an issue in which she had been involved.

Even though one of Smith's biographers claimed that Belle Moskowitz had enjoyed direct telephone access to the governor, I still hoped she had written to him and that I would find letters from her in Smith's unpublished papers in Albany. Imagine my dismay when the curator at the New York State Library warned me that previous researchers, using a name index prepared by Smith's staff, had come up with only a handful of letters of minor import. By then, however, I had been on the Moskowitz trail for two years and had become skilled at the hunt. After exhausting the name index, I worked through the topic list of Smith's files, examining all those on topics I knew would have interested Moskowitz, even if only peripherally. This approach paid off. I soon accumulated a mound of documents. Because I knew her handwriting and the initials of her secretaries, I often could identify unsigned items. One day I hit a delicious find. I opened a file on water power from Smith's post-1929 private papers and discovered fifteen letters from Moskowitz to Smith from the mid-1920s, none of which had anything to do with water power! Teary-eyed, I called the curator over to share my joy. We speculated together on who had put them there. Belle? The governor's secretary? Whoever it was had not thought to serve posterity through rational organization.

Some research experiences were downright frustrating. I won a grant from the Eleanor Roosevelt Foundation to travel to the Franklin Delano Roosevelt Library in Hyde Park, New York. The papers of George Graves, Governor Smith's private secretary, were there, but the head of the library warned me they were mostly of a routine or ceremonial nature. I spent my entire week looking at other papers, including those of Eleanor and Franklin from the twenties, and came up with only a few tidbits. On my last day I asked to see the Moskowitz file in Graves's papers. There were dozens of Moskowitz-Graves-Smith exchanges, but none very important. After finishing them, I had time left and decided to look at the list of Graves's other files. From the names of the correspondents, which included some of Smith's closest friends, I saw immediately that they contained Smith's *private* correspondence from the period when he was in office. I called for a few of them and was astounded at their richness.

I felt betrayed! It was Friday and I was to leave Hyde Park that night. The librarian's warning had misled me and now it was too late. Why had this collection been so misrepresented? I asked to see its accession file and there found the answer. Graves's papers had lain for years in the basement of the Albany home of Smith's state engineer. When he died, his widow asked the state library in Albany to take them but was refused. She then offered them to Hyde Park and was accepted. The processor of the papers recognized their value but quite rightly designated many of them "routine" and "ceremonial." This designation became the central focus of the shortened description sent to the *National Union Guide to Manuscript Collections*. Archivists at Hyde Park were embarrassed but not contrite. "We're experts on Roosevelt, not Smith," one said. Thus the Smith-Roosevelt rivalry dogged me fifty years down the line. That Friday I left Hyde Park in frustration but did manage to return some years later to spend more time in the Graves papers.

Fortunately, there were serendipitous finds as well. During my first year of research I interviewed my Aunt Miriam several times. Most of her recollections were from childhood. In 1925, at the age of eighteen, she visited England and was married there. Unfortunately, she saved no correspondence from those years between herself and her mother. In 1936, three years after Belle's death and shortly before Henry's, she and her husband, Cyril Franklin, were divorced. She later married the sculptor Naum Gabo, and after the war she came back with him to the United States to live near "Aunt" Grace Goodale, Belle's best friend.

Some of Miriam's childhood memories proved important. She remembered, for example, the moment when her mother realized she would have more influence over Smith if she did not accept a government post from him. She also described Henry Moskowitz's reception into the family and how family life was when she was a teenager. Sometime during my first visits, she found a packet of letters Grace had written her in the 1930s and 1940s. In handing them to me she said, "There's probably not much here that will help you." But buried in those sixty-odd letters were reminiscences about Grace's friendship with the young Belle Lindner and graphic narratives of key events in Belle's early life. Thus I found out about Belle's enthusiasm for the "poster" fad in the 1890s and that she had invented a monologue character called "James, the Tailor-Made Girl," a sobriquet her young women friends continued to apply to her for many years.[1] I also learned the circumstances of her courtship with her first husband, the birth of her first child (my father), and her husband's death. The letters touched me deeply, intimately. They referred to my parents' marriage and subsequent divorce and to my visiting Grace when I was a small child. On one such visit, Grace wrote Miriam that she had taken my face in her hands and said, "Yes, she is my James's granddaughter." Grace's linking me in that way to the grandmother I never knew closed a circle for me.

Since all of my potential oral sources were elderly, I rushed to see them before I knew enough to ask good questions. Many talked mainly about themselves or the Roosevelts, who had died more recently, or gave me only one or two anecdotes or vague impressions. Frances Perkins's transcribed oral history contained rich insights into Belle's character, but some of her memory lapses made me worry about reliability. For example, she confused the identities of Belle's two husbands and then, forgetting that Belle had died in 1933, charged her with having turned Al Smith toward conservatism in 1936. My best living source was the actress Aline MacMahon, with whom Belle traveled to California in late 1932. During MacMahon's annual six months in Hollywood, she wrote almost daily to her husband, Clarence Stein, a New York architect and a friend of the Moskowitzes. MacMahon had kept their letters, parts of which she read into my tape recorder. The written record jogged her memory of poignant details about Belle's last days.

Robert Moses, burned by Caro's book, turned down my first request for an interview. Thanks to MacMahon's intercession, he finally agreed to see me but (his secretary informed me) only on condition that I not discuss "the Caro book." This turned out to be a handicap, for I could have made productive use of parts of the book as a discussion point.

Moses, at ninety still charismatic and domineering, kept the interview under tight control. Banging the flat of his hand on his desk to punctuate his points, he ranted for an hour about Frances Perkins, whose abilities he compared unfavorably to Belle's and whose lack of loyalty to Smith still irked him. Given Moses's feud with FDR, this perspective was hardly surprising but gave me little I could use in my book. Moreover, I was so fascinated, as well as cowed, by Moses's performance that I never dared try to change the subject. When I asked for details of Belle's advice to Smith, Moses replied, "My dear, if I remembered I wouldn't tell you." His most specific remark was to say that she was a "real woman with the brains of a man," a phrase that to him was a compliment. It illustrated gender stereotypes typical of his generation. Men of the 1920s and 1930s used to make the same characterization of Frances Perkins, but I didn't know that then, and even if I had I'm not sure I would have dared mention it.

Interpretive Issues

The research experience most crucial to the book's final shape was my discovery of women's history. I still remember how that process began. I was in my first year of research. I had gone to visit the New York Council of Jewish Women to look for signs of Belle Israels's activities in its old minute books, which the council kept in a locked cabinet at its offices. The minutes convinced me that the organization, by identifying social problems and training its members to solve them, had transformed Israels from a settlement worker into a skilled social reformer. To learn more, I began to read the published proceedings of the council's national meetings, which had started in 1893. Reading the speeches of nineteenth-century Jewish women leaders, I was astounded at the depth and power of their oratory. More important, their oratory advocated reforms I had previously associated exclusively with male politicians.

Who were these women, and why had I never heard of them? No history class or text I knew had covered women's political activism. Indeed, had I then been asked what women had done of historical importance, I probably would have said "not much," with the exception of a handful of royal or aristocratic women and women like Belle Moskowitz. But, as she had apparently conquered the man's world of politics, I had thought of her as an "honorary man," not as part of a larger tradition of female activism. My growing acquaintance with the Council of Jewish Women opened up that tradition to me, as did my later work in the records of the Women's City Club of New York, the group that fostered Moskowitz's nonpartisan politics in the 1920s. In linking the Council of Jewish Women and Women's City Club to the nineteenth-century woman's movement and to women's history in general, I began to place her accomplishments into a broader, female-centered context.

I had yet another step to take. The woman's movement had taught Moskowitz how to bring about social and political change; it had also won women the vote, thereby advancing women on to a new level of political power. But knowing this did not help me interpret some enigmas in her behavior. If she were an "honorary man," why hadn't she consistently behaved like one? Why had a woman with a reputation for practical politics devoted so much energy to visionary social reform? How could unionists in the 1910s think her bossy, arrogant, and domineering, and politicians in the 1920s praise her for being calm, modest, and motherly? How could she be "Al Smith's campaign manager," as my father had described her, and yet never carry that title in any of his campaigns or hold political office? How could she have been a critical figure in Smith's "kitchen cabinet" and yet spend its meetings, as Robert Moses recalled, sitting against the wall knitting? Answers came only when I stopped trying to understand her from a male perspective. My research had showed me Belle Moskowitz's strong connections to women. I needed to move to a female-centered analysis.

The female spheres in which Moskowitz had functioned had not only taught her how to work for change but also had provided her with behavior patterns for influencing men. Models came from several sources—the service ideal of Victorian "true women"; the Jewish woman's commitment to help the less fortunate; the zest for reform of the turn-of-the-century "new woman." Moskowitz knew that men ran the world. She believed they always would. Ever conscious of this limitation, she was strong when she could be and self-effacing when she needed to be. In fact, she was not at all what I originally had thought she was—an "honorary man" who had "conquered" the man's world of politics. She had accepted the boundaries laid down by her times and had sought only to work effectively within them.

Once I came to this realization, much fell into place. I saw that she could be both bossy or modest, depending on her circumstances. Working in an advocacy position in the 1910s she had to impose her personality upon that of the men across the bargaining table; in the 1920s she had to work amicably with the men who controlled the Democratic party. To her, there was no contradiction in being both politically visionary and practical. Combining the two was, in fact, characteristic of the woman's movement that had helped form her. Her refusal to accept a position from Smith also made sense. It was not out of "womanly" modesty, as many (mostly men) thought at the time. Her refusal emerged from the belief that informal advising would give her more power than any government post, which, by its bureaucratic nature, limits an official's sphere of action. When she knit during meetings, she was doing what many women did at their own meetings and what she in particular felt comfortable doing—keeping their hands busy while they did other things. More important, perhaps, the activity enhanced the motherly, unthreatening image she wished to convey.

This is not to say that she "put on" a motherly image for the benefit of men. To her own mind, she was a professional: knowledgeable, experienced, and skilled, with much to offer anyone willing to take her advice. But she accepted motherliness as an integral part of her own sense of what it meant to be a woman. This gender sensibility permeated her activities, including the way she wrote publicity for Smith. Smith's personality and style appealed to her "mother heart," so much so that in 1928 she came to believe that a publicity plan that highlighted his warmth and humanity would win over the American electorate. Her publicity strategy, which stressed his childlike love of practical jokes and animals, tended to evade substantive issues and almost infantilized him. The strategy was also powerless against the strong prejudices that motivated the ideological opposition to Smith's candidacy.

Understanding Moskowitz as a woman also improved my understanding of her entire generation of female social reformers. Like most of her friends, including Eleanor Roosevelt and Frances Perkins, Moskowitz avidly supported women's causes, especially the entry of more women into the professions and political offices. But, even though these were feminist causes, she seldom if ever called herself a "feminist." Like most of her friends in social reform, she also opposed the Equal Rights Amendment. She went further, in 1926 stating publicly that, while women's intuitions were superior to men's, women could never be the intellectual equals of men. In holding such views she was not alone, however. In expressing them in the 1920s, she may even have enhanced her political effectiveness.

In 1976, when I gave my first paper on her at the Berkshire Conference on Women's History, I did not yet have this perspective on Moskowitz. The commentator on the paper took me to task for writing about someone who was not a "feminist" and suggested I would contribute more to the field by writing a collective biography of nonelite women. Later that same day, at a colleague's suggestion, I asked a historian working on the topic of prostitution if she had ever come across any material on Moskowitz, who had been involved in Progressive-era antiprostitution campaigns. The historian made it clear that she had no interest in my work. I left the conference depressed and angry. When I had first "found" women's history, I had thought I was joining a united crusade for the rediscovery of women's past and thus the reinterpretation of the entire human experience. But some feminist scholars were grinding political axes that put others of us on the defensive. In my view, these feminists were doing as much harm to the history of women by leaving certain "politically incorrect" women out as the misogynists had done by leaving women out altogether.

Over the following years, the politics of women's history and women's liberation became clearer to me and I was able to place this experience into perspective. By the mid-1970s, *Notable American Women* had been out for some time. Many historians thought the "compensatory" task of the first stage of women's history had been finished. In addition, the new social history of the sixties was rising in popularity, making the study of the inarticulate seem more challenging. To make matters worse for biographers of some notable women, the Equal Rights Amendment was failing. This made women who had opposed the amendment in the past or who had defended protective legislation for women ipso facto "nonfeminists." Despite their many accomplishments on behalf of and with women, antiegalitarians became "the enemy," at least to some.

Fortunately, the field has changed since then. Many scholars now realize that studying the masses neither invalidates nor makes less necessary a study of "notables." The biographical job will never be done: hundreds of women have never been studied, or, if they have been, not from a feminist perspective.[2] And we cannot pick only those women with whom we agree or who seem most like us. I date the start of this turnaround from Eleanor Roosevelt's centennial in 1984, an event that led to a reevaluation of the social reformers of her generation who, out of a commitment to the principle of protective legislation for women, opposed the ERA. In 1986 several books came out that continued this trend. Sylvia Ann Hewlett's *A Lesser Life* chronicled how she and other professional women had been hurt by "equal" (in the sense of "same") treatment with men, feminists' traditional goal. Histories of the ERA suggested that the quest for an equality defined by men and interpreted by a male-dominated society might, in fact, hurt more than help women. In 1988 Linda Gordon's study of the history of child abuse criticized social control models of the work of child protectors, thus opening up for reevaluation the lives and programs of other Progressive-era social reformers.[3] All of these books, and others, prepared the way for a new perspective on women like Belle Moskowitz who, constrained by their times, gave more credence to notions of "difference" than many of us would today.

Special Challenges

Biographies require hard decisions. What is there to do when a crucial piece of information is missing? A study of a movement or an event can gloss over gaps with examples; in a biography, missing facts leave big holes. My strategy was not to become paralyzed by gaps but to fill them with contextual material. This is risky. One can get so caught up in context that the narrative thread disappears. When this happened, I tried to remember that I was writing the story of Belle Moskowitz and not that of the Council of Jewish Women or another equally fascinating group. I saved unused material for future essays.

Because of the paucity of Moskowitz papers, I had to rely more than I would have liked on context. I also relied on materials found in many other sources and personal papers. In one sense, these seeming disadvantages served me well. Because biographers are writing the story of one person's life, they are often tempted to make their subject the center of the universe, the fount of all policy and action. My own temptation to ascribe everything during the Smith years to Moskowitz was very strong. Not having her papers saved me from this pitfall. I had to confirm and document everything she did from sources drawn from the outside. This meant I had to recognize how many other people were involved in the same endeavors that engaged her. Of course, I would have rejoiced over the discovery of cartons of papers she herself had kept. But I think I learned more about my subject by seeking her from the outside looking in rather than the other way around.

Having so little material also forced me to probe deeply for meaning in the documents I did have. One Moskowitz letter, a lengthy hand-written description of Smith she sent to the settlement worker Lillian Wald in 1923, became the basis for a psychological and cultural analysis of the Moskowitz-Smith relationship. When I had first read that letter I had not thought of it as important. But when I later joined it to other evidence of how the relationship worked, it provided an unexpected linchpin to my argument. Another surprise was the use I was able to make of Belle's formal photographs. I had looked at them dozens of times without seeing anything special in them beyond her handsome beauty. Then, inspired by Martha Banta's work with women's images in turn-of-the-century America, I began to read the photographs as texts, finding in them messages that clarified Belle's changing conception of her gender identity as she moved from adolescence into womanhood.[4] Thus a paucity of sources stretched my abilities as a historian, a process I found exhilarating.

Some historians think biography organizes itself. A life begins, matures, ends. But it's not so simple. In Moskowitz's case, because she engaged in so many different kinds of activities—settlement work, Jewish charity, social reform, industrial reform, public relations, politics—

I had to blend a thematic and chronological approach. This blend evolved from my decision to prepare two articles for scholarly journals before attempting the whole book. Thanks to a note from the historian Nancy Cott I learned that the Schlesinger Library held an unindexed transcript of a Moskowitz speech on why she had become an "industrial reformer" in 1913. Reading the speech I felt I now knew enough about the subject to start there. I then turned to dance hall reform because it made a complete and colorful story in itself. But writing the articles took more time than I expected. In the articles I had to focus on the broader historical significance of Moskowitz's work; when I rewrote the articles as chapters, I had to tie them back into a narrative of one person's life. Whether to follow the article path is a judgment biographers must make for themselves. For my own part, they helped convince colleagues—and reviewers of grant and book proposals—that a Europeanist could write American history.

My kinship with Moskowitz created a personal dimension to my subject that not all biographers will share with theirs. Sometimes the kinship was an advantage. For example, it gave me entrée to places closed to others. When I visited the Women's City Club of New York, its president at first refused me access to board minutes because I wasn't a member. After some thought, she decided that since I was a member's granddaughter I could read them after all. Being a granddaughter also gave me access to people such as MacMahon, Moses, and Dorothy Rosenman, widow of the Roosevelt "brain truster" Sam Rosenman. When others learned I was interested in my grandmother's life, they sent me mementos—the choreographer Agnes DeMille Prude, for example, whose mother Anna George was one of Belle's closest teenage friends, sent me an evocative photograph of a "Poster Party" at her mother's house, the home of Henry George.[5] Through my aunt Miriam I met her friends Lewis and Sophia Mumford. Lewis, who had known Belle during the postwar "Reconstruction" era, gave me a wonderful impression of her and made our visit to his home and garden in Amenia, New York, memorable. In the summer of 1986 I had a longer stay with Miriam. I installed myself in Gabo's former sculpture studio to bang out the final version of the entire manuscript. Sophia Mumford visited for two days and, after reading some of my chapters, gave me superb editorial advice. She had been an editor on *The Dial* when she met her husband and had edited all his books. I will never forget our discussion of what life was like for professional women in earlier years, especially for those married to "famous men" such as Mumford and Gabo.

But being related to Moskowitz was difficult in part. Some discoveries about family members disturbed me. I fretted over which to use, finally deciding to include only those that reflected or directly explained something in her life. Most difficult was reconciling being both granddaughter and critical scholar. I could not hide the relationship or pretend it was not relevant. Because I was a granddaughter, would I be able to maintain scholarly detachment? To colleagues who worried about this I said that, since I had never known her, I did not "love" her in the way one loves a grandmother. I protested further, "I'm a historian, not a hagiographer." But only the final product could sustain that claim. I think now that I may have compensated for my kinship by striving for standards of detachment higher than those an unrelated historian might have sought.

There were other ways in which my family relationship was not always to my advantage. My first grant proposal to the National Endowment for the Humanities elicited the comment that I seemed to be "just writing a book about my grandmother." When my husband moved to a job at Indiana University, the department newsletter announced that his wife was writing "a history of her family." Indeed, some people thought I was a genealogist: why else would I be interested in my grandmother? I can smile about those remarks now, but at the time they hurt.

On the whole, the ledger on my kinship to my subject is more positive than negative. I had never felt close to my father or known or understood him well. Learning about the early death of his own father and the frequent absences of his mother helped me to understand him better. This knowledge has given me a certain peace about our troubled relationship. Writing about my grandmother also brought me closer to my daughter. Watching me discover my family relationship to the history of women and of feminism, she began as a teenager to express a transgenerational "bond of womanhood" with me. We have a strong friendship now, a rare phenomenon today between mothers and daughters. Finally, there is no doubt that my personal link to Belle Moskowitz gave me the drive to see the project through, despite its length and difficulty and despite the discouragement I often felt. Somehow I believed I owed her and her generation its completion. As reformers, advocates for women's rights and protection, and political activists, they deserved to be recognized. But Belle had been my grand-mother, too. No future project I undertake will ever provide such a powerful stimulus.

NOTES

The photograph of the young Belle Moskowitz (1896), posing as her mon-ologue character, "James, the Tailor-Made Girl," is from the author's collec-tion.

1. After the biography was published, Lewis Perry came across a reference to *The Tailor-Made Girl: Her Friends, her Fashions, and her Follies,* a popular collection of humorous dialogues that Philip Henry Welch, a journalist, pub-lished in 1888. Belle most probably based her monologue character on Welch's sketches.

2. See Hilda Smith's comments in this regard in the *Organization of Amer-ican Historians' Newsletter,* February 1987, and Gerda Lerner's plea for "fem-inist biographies" of notable women in *Perspectives,* Newsletter of the Amer-ican Historical Association, April 1988.

3. Joan Hoff-Wilson and Marjorie Lightman, eds., *Without Precedent: The Life and Career of Eleanor Roosevelt* (Bloomington: Indiana University Press, 1984); Sylvia Ann Hewlett, *A Lesser Life: The Myth of Women's Liberation in America* (New York: W. Morrow, 1986); Jane Mansbridge, *Why We Lost the ERA* (Chicago: University of Chicago Press, 1986); Joan Hoff-Wilson, ed., *Rights of Passage: The Past and Future of the ERA* (Bloomington: Indiana University Press, 1986), esp. xix–xx and 5–6: "it is possible to recognize some-thing quite modern about those well-educated and often well-to-do women who emerged from the Progressive movement opposing the ERA." See also Linda Gordon, *Heroes of Their Own Lives: The Politics and History of Family Violence* (New York: Viking, 1988).

4. I first heard Banta speak about photographs at Indiana University in the early 1980s. The book she was then writing later appeared as *Imaging Amer-ican Women: Idea and Ideals in Cultural History* (New York: Columbia University Press, 1987).

5. "Poster parties" derived from the "poster" craze, which began in the early 1890s, when magazine publishers started using lithographed poster art to advertise their weekly or monthly issues. Guests came dressed in costumes, struck poses, and asked others to identify which poster they represented. See Victor Margolin, *American Poster Renaissance* (New York: Watson-Guptill, 1975), Introduction, 17–21.

JOYCE ANTLER

Having It All, Almost: Confronting the Legacy of Lucy Sprague Mitchell

LUCY SPRAGUE MITCHELL (1878–1967) was born in Chicago, where her father and his brother built Sprague Warner and Co., the largest wholesale grocery in the world. As a shy, introverted girl who was tutored at home, she came to know several individuals in the city who helped frame her earliest ideals, among them Jane Addams, the director of Hull-House, and Alice Freeman Palmer, a former president of Wellesley College. Palmer rescued Lucy Sprague from a miserable home life in southern California, where the family had moved in 1893 because of her father's tuberculosis. Living with Alice and her husband, the Harvard professor George Herbert Palmer, in Cambridge, Sprague began Radcliffe College in 1896, studying philosophy with George Palmer, William James, Josiah Royce, and George Santayana.

In 1903 Lucy accepted a position working with women students at the University of California at Berkeley. In 1906 she was appointed its first dean of women and assistant professor of English. At Berkeley she worked to improve housing conditions for women and to strengthen women's organizations and their participation in campus life.

After marrying the economist Wesley Clair Mitchell in 1911, Lucy Sprague Mitchell moved to New York and began working in children's education. She took courses at Teachers' College, Columbia University, with John Dewey, worked as a volunteer visiting teacher in the public schools for the Public Education Association, and taught nursery school, kindergarten, and language classes at Caroline Pratt's Play School (later known as City and Country). With her cousin, the chamber music benefactor Elizabeth Sprague Coolidge providing the financing, in 1916 she established the Bureau of Educational Experiments (BEE) to teach and do research concerning "progressive education and educational experiments."

Mitchell guided the BEE's pioneering work in early childhood education. In 1919, it launched an experimental laboratory nursery school for children under the age of three, linking classroom procedure to scientific research. In 1931 it began a cooperative school for experimental teachers known as "Bank Street," where the school was located. The school's innovative pedagogy included courses in language and the environment, taught by Mitchell, and creative workshops in dance, drama, painting, and writing, which were combined with practice teaching, field trips to city institutions, and internships in social organizations.

In 1938 Mitchell began a writers' workshop at Bank Street to help writers of children's books understand the developmental needs of children and to assist them in using the direct imagery and sounds of children's speech. In 1943 she inaugurated a series of public school workshops to bring experimental teaching methods to a wider public. In 1950, six years prior to Mitchell's retirement, the BEE was chartered as the Bank Street College of Education.

Mitchell was influential as a writer as well as a teacher and administrator. Her *Here and Now Story Book* (1921) was considered "revolutionary" and "epoch-making" in its attack on fairytales and in its argument that stories for young children should derive from the world of their experiences and that their form should correspond to children's play with words and sounds. Other important works include *Young*

Geographers (1934, 1963, 1971), *Our Children and Our Schools* (1950), and *Two Lives: The Story of Wesley Clair Mitchell and Myself* (1953), an unusual account of the couple's independent and joint lives.

I came across the life story of Lucy Sprague Mitchell quite unexpectedly one day during the course of my doctoral research on educated, professional women in the early twentieth century. Mitchell made a brief appearance in my dissertation; on its completion, however, I would turn over the better part of the next ten years of my life to rendering meaning from hers. Mitchell's story compelled my interest because it seemed a perfect reflection of the struggles of educated women of her era to emerge from the dark shadows of Victorianism into the light of modernity. Her attempt to combine an intellectually fulfilling career with marriage and motherhood suggested great contemporary relevance as well. My research into Mitchell's life confirmed these initial judgments and led me also to a new understanding of the importance of the life cycle in forming women's historical choices. Mitchell's story also prompted me to reconsider the historical place of female progressive teachers and their connection to earlier generations of reform-minded women.

My rendezvous with Mitchell was intensely personal as well as historical. Perhaps I learned as much about myself during the process of doing her biography as I did about Mitchell, since every aspect of her story—her struggles about intimacy, independence, child rearing, and creative and professional development—had resonance in my own. For the long years I worked on the project, Mitchell's life story in fact "possessed" me.[1]

At the time of our first encounter, Mitchell's contributions to social history were not well known outside of a relatively small circle of educators. As the founder of New York City's Bank Street College of Education, Mitchell had had a distinguished and pioneering career in teaching and writing for young children. Yet even Lawrence Cremin's redoubtable book on progressive education, *The Transformation of the School* (1964), contained only brief references to Mitchell as a teacher, author, and founder of the Bureau of Educational Experiments, Bank Street's predecessor.[2]

While the significance of Lucy Mitchell's work in education needed to be explored, it was not this aspect of her life that had first attracted my attention. Rather, I was intrigued by her private life; she was one of the first professional women in the twentieth century to write about her struggles in combining marriage, child rearing, and career. Among the small body of letters in the Lucy Sprague Mitchell Papers at Columbia University was a fascinating 1911 courtship correspondence between Lucy Sprague and the economist Wesley Clair Mitchell, which set out Sprague's reasons for hesitating to marry Mitchell with unusual clarity and frankness: in essence, marriage would rob her of her independence and remove her from the "alternative" professional life she desired. Despite her misgivings, Sprague yielded in the end.

She told the story of her marriage in *Two Lives: The Story of Wesley Clair Mitchell and Myself* (1953), a literary tour de force that combined biography and autobiography.[3] After their marriage in 1912, the Mitchells established the close family life each had desperately wanted, adopting two children and having two biological ones. Lucy's career in education, stimulated by her own mothering, flourished. "It was a highly focused life," Lucy recalled, "with everything concentrated on children, each aspect of my work illuminating the others." Given her earlier caution about the effects of marriage on a woman's career, Mitchell's success in combining professional work with an active family life seemed to offer a role model for women of my own generation. In 1976, after the birth of my first child and with the completion of my dissertation imminent, I began to contemplate what I could learn from Lucy Sprague Mitchell.

The project began in earnest when I received a two-year fellowship at the Bunting Institute of Radcliffe College, funded by the Lilly Foundation. I hoped to write a full-scale biography of Mitchell despite the fact that she had not left a diary, and, except for the courtship correspondence, there were few letters relating to her private life. Most of the papers in the Columbia University collection concerned Mitchell's work at Bank Street or her professional publications. Nevertheless, the materials in the collection that did address issues of personal development were exceedingly rich: in addition to the love letters, there were copious reports that Lucy and Wesley Mitchell made of their four children's early development, and nineteen years' worth of poems (really psychological outpourings) that Lucy wrote during the painful years of widowhood. With the oral history and published biography, these materials covered the full range of Mitchell's life cycle: the formative years of her childhood and adolescence; her education at a private secondary school and at Radcliffe College; her courtship with Wesley and the first years of their marriage; her early career in education; the stages of her motherhood; her mature professionalism; and the last decades of her widowhood. Revealing the personal and professional transformation of a shy, young Victorian-born girl into a "modern" twentieth-century woman, they could illuminate many of the issues that I had explored in my thesis and provide added insight into the lives of educated women in the early twentieth century.

While Mitchell was a wealthy woman, and thus not a representative one, I believed that her story held significance beyond the boundaries of class. Throughout her life Mitchell was unusually anxious to understand her own processes of learning; in her professional life she also focused on issues of growth and development. The habit of recording her thoughts—even "half-thoughts"—-about anything that entered into her current experience lasted until her death at the age of eighty-nine. Through this "incurable" habit of writing she expressed her conflicts and explored solutions to personal, intellectual, and professional problems. At the same time, in generalizing her situation to understand her own choices and feelings, she came to illuminate those of educated women more broadly. These characteristics made me hopeful that despite the class privileges Mitchell had inherited, and which had shaped many of her choices, her life history could suggest generational patterns and offer a link between individual experience and larger changes in the social order.

This belief guided and shaped my research, but, as I was to discover almost immediately, very little else went according to plan. Because of the scarcity of diary materials, for example, I contemplated finishing the book within a relatively short period of time. But I soon learned of two other extensive diary sources, each of them requiring considerable research. Lucy's aunt Nan Sprague, her mother's sister and the wife of her father's brother, left a diary of family life in Chicago that illuminated the course of Lucy's childhood, adolescence, and early adulthood. Nan was the center of the Sprague family, especially after the death of Lucy's parents in the 1900s, and she kept much of Lucy's correspondence as a part of her diaries. The Schlesinger Library at Radcliffe College acquired the diaries shortly after I began work on the project, and I immediately became absorbed in them. I recall the day I emerged from the library red-eyed, having finished the account of Lucy's mother's slow death from tuberculosis, the disease that had wasted her husband, after a lifetime of having submerged her own personality and interests to his care and well-being. "What's the matter?" one of the librarians asked. "Lucy's mother is dead," I sobbed, "and she never had a chance to do her music."

Even more important was my discovery of the diaries kept by Wesley Clair Mitchell. The founder and longtime research director of the National Bureau of Economic Research, a founding member and officer of the Social Science Research Council and the New School for Social Research, and, at various times, president of the American Economic Research Association and the American Statistical Association, Mitchell was widely considered to be the "dean" of American economics. After his death in 1948, at the insistence of Arthur Burns, Mitchell's former student and his successor at the National Bureau, Lucy gave the diaries Wesley wrote for most of his adult life to another former student, a professor of economics who wanted to undertake a biography of Mitchell. The diaries became the personal possession of this economist, who refused to allow other scholars to examine them. I first learned about their existence from an economic historian who had been unable to gain access to them.

When, however, I went to interview the scholar who owned the papers about his acquaintance with Lucy Mitchell, he offered to let me see Wesley's diaries. But they would not be very useful to my work, he explained, since they dealt only with the substantive matters of Wesley Mitchell's work in economic research. If I would agree to use them in a library under the supervision of library staff, he would agree to send me the complete microfilm reels of the diaries.

With my expectations low, I began perusing the diaries at the Schlesinger Library. Imagine my astonishment, then, to find that, in his meticulous hand, Wesley Clair Mitchell had recorded not only every contact he had with Lucy Sprague before marriage, as well as family events thereafter, but also fairly complete accounts of Lucy's daily appointments. The diary was in every sense a family diary: it recorded details of the children's births and adoptions, their illnesses and lessons, visits from friends and relatives, and vacation trips, outings, and the like. Wesley also paid a great deal of attention to Lucy's work in education. In the first decade of their marriage, for example, the Bureau of Educational Experiments was a joint venture, with Wesley serving on many of its committees. All of this material, a gold mine of information for historians of families and of women's lives, had been invisible to Wesley's biographer, who, in his pursuit of information about Wesley's professional work, simply ignored it. The biographer eventually opened access to the diaries, and they became part of the Wesley Clair Mitchell Papers at Columbia University Library. Though they added years to my research, the diaries gave me a unique insight into the nature of Lucy's work and of her marriage. The larger lesson I learned is that materials considered irrelevant by biographers of male subjects or other traditional historians may hold enormous value to those writing women's lives or the stories of families. Contextual material about daily family life can be equally valuable to scholars studying male lives if the biographer's task is defined to include telling the story of private life as well as that of public achievement.

Another unexpected discovery was a cache of papers in the basement library of the City and Country School on West Twelfth Street in Greenwich Village that detailed the early years of the Bureau of Educational Experiments. Lucy had owned a group of buildings on West Twelfth and Thirteenth streets that housed the City and Country School, the offices of the BEE, and the Mitchells' apartment. Lucy provided space for the school, founded by Caroline Pratt, and supported its many ventures; she also taught language classes there. All four Mitchell children attended City and Country at various times, and Wesley Mitchell cut short his classes at Columbia University and the New School to teach carpentry there. When the children were young, Lucy was able to nurse or otherwise tend to them at home, then resume her teaching at the school. Locating the school and her administrative work at the BEE in proximity to her home was one of the ways she brought "unity," as she called it, to her roles as mother, teacher, author, executive, and researcher. Like Wesley Mitchell's diary, the school and the bureau were family projects.

The Bureau of Educational Experiments, founded in 1916 by Lucy and Wesley Mitchell and Lucy's friend and associate Harriet Merrill Johnson, came into being to promote experiments in progressive education. But it was not until I came across many of its early papers in musty cartons in City and Country School's basement that I realized the scope of its ventures and its significance within the fields of both progressive education and child development.[4] The dozen members of the bureau—in addition to the Mitchells and Harriet Johnson, they included Caroline Pratt, the labor leader Helen Marot, Evelyn Dewey (whose father, John, was an honorary member of the group), and Elisabeth Irwin, the founder of the Little Red School House—worked as a cooperative, with Lucy as its guiding force, pioneering much innovative work in progressive education: educational testing, vocational education, day nurseries, rural schools, the Gary School idea, and many other projects. In 1919, under the leadership of Lucy and Harriet Johnson, the BEE established the nation's first laboratory nursery school for infants and children up to three years of age, conducting extensive psychological and physical research on its young students for over a decade. Individuals associated with the BEE founded two influential journals, *Progressive Education* and *Child Development,* and helped shape both parent fields (progressive education and child development) in myriad ways. My accidental find of Lucy's BEE papers in the basement of her former home helped to reveal the major significance of her earliest work in education.

My growing understanding of Lucy's institutional significance to the world of experimental education was matched by my recognition of the innovative qualities of her writings, particularly *The Here and Now Story Book,* published in 1921 to critical acclaim and an appreciative popular audience of parents.[5] Later in my research I came to understand that Bank Street was not only a pioneering teaching college, children's school, and research institution but the central focus of an allied group of "experimental" educators (a term Lucy preferred to "progressive") interested in social and political reconstruction.

Just as my conceptions of Mitchell's professional work changed dramatically during the course of my research, so did my views of the private dimensions of her life. While *Two Lives* and various unpublished memoirs revealed a great deal about the Mitchells' domestic relations, the experience of parenthood remained curiously elusive, especially in view of the fact that in *Two Lives* Mitchell chose to portray the successful synthesis of work and family as a central theme of her life. After interviewing Mitchell's three sons (an adopted daughter had died at the age of forty some two decades earlier), the question of parenting and the place it played in Mitchell's life became even more intriguing.[6] To varying degrees, all three children admired and respected their mother, yet they strongly resented her work and her manner of child rearing. The eldest son, who was also adopted, was the most critical, attributing the various disappointments of his own life to his mother. In particular, he blamed the progressive schools she sent him

to for failing to prepare him for the real world. The youngest son—
the one most directly formed in the image of his parents—was less
inclined to blame his mother for the consequences of his schooling,
commenting that his own abilities compensated for what experimental
schools did not provide. Nevertheless, this son expressed other deep-
seated resentments, as did the middle brother.

All three complained that they felt like grist for their mother's mill,
guinea pigs in the laboratory of progressive education, and spoke dis-
paragingly of Lucy's cerebral, nonemotional care giving. Although as
determined progressive parents, the Mitchells strove to promote the
children's independence and self-respect, nevertheless their demand for
appropriate behavior and their high ethical and intellectual standards
diminished their offspring's self-confidence. "Standing in the shadows
of such tall columns," the youngest son told me, made the children
feel inadequate. "Somehow or other," he observed, "it was taken away
from us to create our own world."

Even though this son, a writer and researcher at the Stanford Research Institute, also acknowledged more positive aspects of the Mitchells' parenting, his comments and those of his brothers challenged my
initial interpretation of Lucy Mitchell as a pioneering feminist who
had successfully combined family life and career. I began to reconsider
my views and to probe the issue of mothering from a feminist perspective more carefully.

It seemed significant to me, for example, that the Mitchell children
recalled very little of their mother's actual presence in their lives, focusing on her neglect rather than involvement. Sometimes the dis-
crepancies appeared so major that I wondered if there were two different versions of family life: the parents' and the children's. For
example, the sons felt that the family housekeeper took over most of
the standard mothering functions. They were surprised when I told
them that not only as recalled in *Two Lives,* but also according to
Wesley Mitchell's authoritative diary, Lucy sewed and knitted for them,
stayed home with them when they were ill, took them to doctors and
lessons, met with teachers, and did many of the normal tasks that
mothers perform for growing children. The Mitchell children seem to
have shut out of their memories many of those activities that dem-
onstrated their mother's daily concern with their lives. In this respect,
Mitchell's professional work was an important factor. Not only did
she have a full-time career when most mothers of school-age children

did not, but it was a particularly distinguished and ever-present career at that. Though work problems were rarely discussed at home, job and home were closely connected in a physical sense; moreover, the children attended the school at which their mother taught. While the children in later years resented their mother's work all the more because of this proximity, nevertheless, from Lucy Mitchell's perspective, her merger of career and family life was successful. And Mitchell's solution to the problem of her absences from home—to bring in a permanent, reliable, and sympathetic housekeeper—also succeeded only too well. The children became deeply attached to the housekeeper, comparing their mother unfavorably to her and resenting Lucy all the more.

In considering the discrepancy between Lucy's view of her mothering, as recorded in her autobiography, and her children's evaluation, I came to question both parties' perceptions of the past. The fact that Lucy was writing the book as a tribute to her husband and to her marriage colored her presentation. Helping to assuage her long-standing guilt about her own brashness and egotism in contrast to her husband's gentleness and humility, as she perceived it, *Two Lives* placed a premium on a benevolent interpretation of the Mitchells' domestic life. But oral interviews can be as problematic as the written word. For example, the Mitchells' oldest son, who described himself as a persistent failure, admitted that his childhood was carefree and rewarding. It was only as an adult, when he realized that he was not getting ahead in the world, that he became resentful toward his mother. (The field in which the son, in his own opinion, was so notably unsuccessful was the very field in which his father had been a superstar: economics.) Furthermore, this son was sixty-five years of age when I interviewed him, not only a father of three sons but a grandfather. Might not his attitudes toward his childhood have reflected his less-than-happy interactions with his own children?

The parents' eminence might also have affected the children's evaluations of their child rearing. Each Mitchell parent was a founder of an educational or research institution, served as its director, wrote many books and articles, and became prominent locally, nationally, and internationally. The style of the Mitchell household was a cerebral one in which learning and discussion dominated. With the parents caring so much for intellectual discourse and with their interest wrapped up in the cause of human betterment, how could the children not consider themselves as failures when they chose very different occupations and developed different social and personal interests?

In my quest to understand the parent-child dynamic at the Mitchell household, I also focused on Lucy Mitchell's personality and the nature of her specific interactions with her children. But ultimately I found myself questioning whether it was possible for biographers of women to judge the quality of parenting at all. How much of the Mitchell children's resentment toward their mother, for example, was a product of her career? Were their attitudes colored by the social context of the time, which did not approve of working mothers, as much as by her personal qualities? All the Mitchell children were generally more critical of their mother than their father, for example, despite the fact that they each conceded that he was the more remote and uninvolved. If there were a family crisis, she may not have responded the way the children wanted—in a direct, spontaneous, intimate way—but it was she, not the children's father, who attempted to resolve the problem. That the children nevertheless resented their mother more than their father was a result of the different temperamental qualities of each, but also of the double standard in the way mothers and fathers were judged at the time.

I wondered, also, whether it was appropriate to consider the whole question of feminist lives, particularly the struggle to merge public with private demands, from the point of view of children's attitudes toward parents. How much of these attitudes reflected retrospective remembrances of grown children who recalled the past from the vantage point of the present? How reliable can adult children be, furthermore, as reporters of their own childhoods and critics of their own necessarily ambivalent relationships with parents? Do children ever understand the limitations imposed upon parents by the parents' own socialization and childhood experiences? Is the capacity to parent thus in some way dependent upon the availability and quality of role models inherited from the past?

I asked myself, too, what the question of parenting, and especially mothering, had to do with understanding the contours and contradictions of feminism. Should we even consider the quality of mothering as an aspect of feminist biography? To say of a subject, Yes, her accomplishments in the world were great, but was she a good mother? might not only be an irrelevant question, but one that runs the risk of turning the spotlight right back onto women's traditional sphere of domesticity, from which women like Lucy Sprague Mitchell struggled so hard to escape. As the biographer Justin Kaplan has remarked, it is the work and career, the public manifestations of self, that is one way we distinguish major lives from lesser lives.[7] If feminist biographers attempt to take a multidimensional approach to correct the overly political and masculine bias of traditional history, do they not run the risk of setting unrealistic expectations, of wanting their subjects to achieve too much: to be great writers, businesswomen, artists, or professionals as well as great mothers, wives, or companions? Would we not find all women wanting if we peer too deeply into the crevices of the private life as well as onto the public faces of achievement?

Finally, I wondered how success in parenting could be measured. Must our children like us? Must they turn out to be successful, with happy marriages, achievement in work, and the like? Or could they also be successful in a deeper way, as reflective, caring human beings, understanding of themselves and others? Perhaps a biographer's objectivity is no more reliable than that of the autobiographer, but I found two Mitchell sons to be remarkably thoughtful, with a deep understanding of self and the same kind of integrity and honesty that they considered characteristic of their parents. They were leaders in their communities as well, liked by colleagues and friends. Were their mother and father—individually and together—responsible at least in part for these successes as much as they were for the failures the children cited?

The very complexity of these parenting issues persuaded me of their significance to women's life stories and of the biographer's responsibility to explore their multifaceted aspects. But in my own biography I had not yet resolved the question of how much voice to give to the Mitchell children, or where and how to locate this voice. My book, after all, would be Lucy's story: her children's reflections played an important role in the tale but should not, I felt, preempt the unfolding drama of their mother's life. The solution that I arrived at was to describe and analyze the parenting strategies of the Mitchells in detail in one of the chapters of the book dealing with the Mitchells' home life and to include additional references to parenting in other chapters. However, I delayed presenting the children's full perspectives until the epilogue. This allowed me the opportunity to reflect on some of the conceptual issues involving the evaluation of parenting and to appraise Lucy Mitchell's performance as mother along with her other life work as teacher, writer, executive, and wife. Such a comparative, interpretative discussion was better suited to an epilogue, I felt, than to the narrative of my subject's life. Ultimately, however, the reader has to decide which version of historical truth about Mitchell's parenting—hers or her children's—is more accurate. Hopefully, the cultural perspectives about gender that informed the biography help to explain not only the nature of Lucy Mitchell's mothering but also its place within her life development.

Almost from the beginning of the project, it had been clear to me that a gender-based analytical perspective could best shape my telling of the story. In part, this was because at various times in her life Mitchell consciously addressed questions regarding gender. "Every stage of life has its song," she acknowledged in a poem at the very end of her life; "my song has been a woman's song." The concluding pages of *Two Lives,* in particular, speculated on the changes in sex-role relationships that had taken place over Lucy's lifetime, changes dramatically revealed in the accounts she presented of her parents' marriage and her own. Indeed, in 1953 the reviewer for the *New York Herald Tribune* commented that *Two Lives* offered a "better look at changing human and sex relationships than Simone de Beauvoir gives," no small compliment.[8]

Yet Mitchell placed her hopes in the radical possibilities of education, not feminism. She was generally unconcerned with the political struggles of women as a group; not until the teens did she enthusiastically support suffrage, for example. When, several years into my research, I learned from a 1911 *New York Times* article that she feared that the passage of the suffrage amendment in California might set back opportunities for women's higher education, I reacted with visceral disappointment. To separate my own feminist convictions from my subject's historical place and point of view was difficult but essential. That Mitchell was influenced by concerns of gender was clear to me, but I needed to sharpen my understanding of how, exactly, her life choices reflected these concerns when she seemed emphatically not a feminist.

Mitchell was not a political feminist who actively supported equal rights for women, at any rate. Yet consciousness of women's plight influenced the unique character of the institution she founded. Bank Street's cooperative management and its nonsexist curriculum suggested one dimension of the feminist point of view implicit in her educational philosophy and practice. In her own life, moreover, Mitchell challenged and eventually overcame many of the restrictions that limited women's options in the early twentieth century. She sought to work out the major issues confronting women on an individual basis, a pattern that became more common in the next generation. Although she explicitly turned away from collective political action in the cause of women's emancipation, she was a pioneer of what I call "feminism as life process," a personal rather than a collective attempt by women to mold their destinies in the world and achieve autonomy.[9] The unfolding of this process in Mitchell's life highlighted the successive stages of growth for women and suggested a clear developmental framework for the book.

In youth, for example, Mitchell's drive for autonomy focused on breaking away from the filial obligations that limited her opportunities; in early adulthood, on developing an independent professional identity as a woman and establishing intimacy within her personal relationships; in later adulthood, on balancing her professional ambitions with family cares. The creative feminism of her old age reversed earlier patterns, for in her last decades she sought a new sense of self by breaking the bonds of dependency created both by her marriage and by her attachment to her work identity. As she explained it, she had "become more so," or more herself. I suspected that these gendered life stages reflected patterns common to many professional women not only of her own era but of others as well.

I was struck, for example, with the generational continuities between Mitchell's work in experimental education and the reform goals of an older group of women professionals—pioneering settlement women like Jane Addams and Florence Kelley—whom Lucy knew personally. These continuities suggested to me that the activism common to Progressive-era reformers was sustained in the women-centered ideals and programs of Mitchell and her colleagues during the mid-decades of the twentieth century. Reinterpreting Mitchell's career within the context of life-cycle choices thus led me to reevaluate teaching as a profession for women and to reaffirm the radical possibilities for social change within education.

A gendered analysis of Mitchell's work led me also to appreciate the similarities and differences between her intellectual approach and those of men with whom she studied, like William James and, especially, Wesley Clair Mitchell, whose scientific approach to social problems influenced her deeply. The philosophy papers Lucy Sprague wrote for her Harvard professors and the many reports she later prepared as director of the BEE led me to recognize, first, her dissent from a curriculum she declared too "abstract" and "academic" since it neglected women and children and, second, her rejection, albeit tardy, of a scientism based on quantification rather than more organic, qualitative conceptions. Influenced by James's philosophy of pragmatism and her husband's institutional economics, Lucy Mitchell enshrined experience as the guide to behavior, but it was a different, nonscientific, female-centered experience—the experience of a daughter, wife, mother, and teacher—that mattered most to her.

While in these varied respects, thinking and writing about a woman's life raise important new issues for feminist biography, the most critical task of the biographer—to fathom the subject's "real self," hidden behind the individual's public mask—is a universal, not a gender-specific, one. For me this task was difficult and ongoing. Who was the "real" Lucy Sprague Mitchell? The shy young girl who became a self-effacing professional mentor and then an insecure, deeply emotional widow, one whose poems of loss, attachment, and guilt could not fail to bring tears to my eyes, no matter how many times I read them? Or the woman who began life as a child of privilege, self-absorbed and haughty, who grew into a commanding, domineering mother and executive, alienating colleagues, relatives, neighbors, and others not integrally connected with her work? The mixed responses I received from acquaintances of Lucy whom I interviewed—adoring and resentful—testified to the complexity of her personality and to the fact that the "real me," as she liked to call herself, could be several different personages. Artist and entrepreneur, romantic and rationalist, she was the daughter of her aggressive, demanding, authoritative merchant father and of her delicate, caring mother, a talented musician whose abilities were repressed under her husband's stern rule. These qualities shaped Lucy Sprague Mitchell's outlook and her talents; ultimately, however, she was as open to experience as she was guided by her heritage. Her deep concern with learning and growth—and, in my view, the gendered nature of these processes in her life—revealed the key to the continuities of her personality. I concluded that from childhood to her oldest age, the "true self" who was Lucy Mitchell—her "real me"—was, in fact, a constant, a self focused on learning, despite its varied surfaces.

My journey through Mitchell's life taught me much about the dynamics of personality as they ripen and evolve throughout the life cycle;

it taught me not only about Mitchell but also about a generation of women like and unlike my own. While my view of the extent of her accomplishment and the nature of her feminism changed during the years I worked on the book, I continually uncovered a great deal of material that was deeply meaningful to my own life. Most important was the lesson I learned about balancing what I now knew was a trilemma—marriage, child rearing, and career. Initially, Mitchell had stood as a model for the kind of integration I hoped to make between my private and professional lives; in the end, her life served, too, as a warning.

Despite her best intentions, her parenting (according to her children) turned out differently than she had hoped. With the enlarged insights I gained through doing her biography of the precarious relationship of parents to children, work to family, I determined not to make similar mistakes. Yet as I look back, the pattern of my life turned out to be not very different from Lucy Mitchell's. She described her routine as a "four-ring circus—family, teaching, writing, research and executive work." I had two children rather than four (a second daughter was born in 1984), but otherwise, as a wife and mother, writer, faculty member at Brandeis, and director of the Brandeis Women's Studies program, my life definitely had its circus aspect, and a four-ring one at that. And just as Lucy's life was "highly focused" despite her varied roles, since "everything concentrated on children," so women's studies has played a similar role in my own life. My teaching, writing, research, and executive work each concerned women's historical lives; even the Mitchell biography became a family project.

Every summer since shortly before my older daughter's second birthday we went to Greensboro, Vermont, where Lucy Mitchell had established a family compound that she considered the "gyroscope" that kept the Mitchells together. Originally, I had traveled to this lovely village on Caspian Lake in Vermont's Northeast Kingdom to interview one of Lucy's sons who had retired there. Encountering grandchildren, other relatives, and neighbors who had known Lucy well, I extended our stay, learning the pleasures of Greensboro at first hand. As Lucy and Wesley had discovered, it provided an idyllic setting in which to combine writing with family vacation pleasures. We rented a house near the Mitchell compound, where I researched and wrote various chapters of the book. And thus the biography took on a very personal meaning to my older daughter, Lauren, who became good friends with several of Lucy's great-granddaughters, as well as to my husband, who also became acquainted with Lucy Mitchell's family, former neighbors, and her environment.

These connections enhanced my family's interest in the biography and led me to assume that my children would not experience the competitive feelings that the Mitchell offspring had toward Bank Street. Essentially, this was the case. Yet an incident that occurred at the very end of the project drove home to me that even with the wisdom I gleaned from the new scholarship about women, the supports provided by the contemporary feminist movement, and what I hoped was a more warm and open personality than Mitchell's, I could not escape the inherent conflicts between the work I loved and my family's desires.

At the end of 1984 the writing of the biography was nearly complete, and with ambivalence I contemplated my separation from Lucy Sprague Mitchell. One day at dinner I announced that I had finished one of the last chapters of the book, a section that chronicled Wesley Mitchell's sad death, and about which I had been apprehensive because of the poignancy of the event as recalled in *Two Lives*. I was relieved that writing the chapter had not been as painful as I had imagined. "Are you finished with the book?" Lauren, then eight, asked. "Not yet," I responded. "I still have to write Lucy dead." Since Lucy lived on for almost twenty years following her husband's demise, it was several weeks before I emerged to announce to my family that yes, Lucy was gone, and it hadn't been as bad as I had imagined. Lauren could not contain herself. "The book is finished!" she squealed in delight. But again I had to tell her not yet. There would be an epilogue, I said, although I had already written some of the material for it and imagined I would complete the section fairly swiftly.

The following Monday night, again at dinner time, I was able to announce to my family that the book was finished at last. Although Rachel, my nine-month-old, couldn't appreciate the significance of that moment, the rest of us enjoyed a gala celebration. Two days later, at dinner, I was enthusiastically chattering to my husband about the new book I was already thinking of, paying little attention to Lauren's shocked countenance. Suddenly she pushed her chair back from the table, shouting, "*Another* book? *You can't do this to me!*"

It was I who turned out to be the most startled, since my daughter's outburst made me recognize the inevitable feelings of anger and jealousy she had about my work, despite her interest in it. Her comments became a beacon to me that my passion for work needed at times to be restrained; henceforth, I told myself, I would implement the rhythm method of writing, alternating deep involvement in a subject with lesser degrees of absorption in lesser projects. But I knew that I need not temper my scholarship for the sake of my children. Alongside of my older daughter's resentment of my work was her deep pride in it: a few months after this episode took place, Lauren's third-grade class began a biography project. With no prompting from me, Lauren chose to read a collective biography of the Lowell mill girls. Upon finishing it, the students were asked to write their own biography, answering the question, "What will your biographer write about you, fifty years hence?" "She owns a hospital, school, and other things," Lauren responded. "She has her own job, house, and pet." And, finally, "She wrote a 1,500-page book" (a volume that would have been, by the way, twice the length of my original manuscript). I rest my case!

When *Lucy Sprague Mitchell* was finally published, it was of great interest to me that most of the reviews focused more on Mitchell's attempt to balance career and family life than on any other aspect of the book. "She Wanted It All, and She Got It," ran the headline in the *New York Times Book Review.* "Having it All in the 20s," the *Washington Book World* put it. "Story of a Woman Who Had It All in the 20s," agreed the *Christian Science Monitor.* "Superwoman and Child," announced the *Times Literary Supplement.* Although reviewers neglected other issues that her life brought into focus, Mitchell did have it all—almost—as I hoped the book would explain. As I was learning in my own life, having it "all" is as unlikely today as it undoubtedly was for the most energetic and privileged women of Lucy Mitchell's generation. Yet how much we want to believe that everything is possible!

NOTES

The photograph of Lucy Sprague Mitchell, ca. 1906 appears courtesy of the Bancroft Library, University of California, Berkeley.

1. The idea of a biographer's being "possessed" by his or her subject was discussed by Richard Holmes in the preface to his biography of Shelley. Cited by James Atlas in "Choosing a Life," *New York Times Book Review,* January 13, 1991, p. 23.

2. Lawrence Cremin, *The Transformation of the School: Progressivism in American Education, 1876-1957* (New York: Alfred A. Knopf, 1961).

3. Lucy Sprague Mitchell, *Two Lives: The Story of Wesley Clair Mitchell and Myself* (New York: Simon & Schuster, 1953).

4. I discussed the significance of the BEE in "Progressive Education and the Scientific Study of the Child: An Analysis of the Bureau of Educational Experiments, 1916-1940," *Teachers College Record 83* (Summer 1982): 559-91.

5. Lucy Sprague Mitchell, *The Here and Now Story Book* (New York: E. P. Dutton & Co., 1921).

6. The material that follows was first presented in " 'Was She a Good Mother?' Some Thoughts on a New Issue for Feminist Biography," in Barbara Harris and Jo Ann McNamara, eds., *Women and the Social Structure* (Durham, N.Car.: Duke University Press, 1982), 53-66. Some of the issues are also discussed in Joyce Antler, *Lucy Sprague Mitchell: The Making of a Modern Woman* (New Haven, Conn.: Yale University Press, 1987), 360-62.

7. Justin Kaplan, "The Naked Self and Other Problems," in Marc Pachter, ed., *Telling Lives: The Biographer's Art* (Philadelphia: University of Pennsylvania Press, 1981).

8. Ernestine Evans, "A Happy Family Album," *New York Herald Tribune Book Review,* June 14, 1953.

9. Also see my article, "Feminism as Life Process: The Life and Career of Lucy Sprague Mitchell," *Feminist Studies 7* (Spring 1981): 134-55.

LOIS RUDNICK

The Male-Identified Woman and Other Anxieties: The Life of Mabel Dodge Luhan

MABEL DODGE LUHAN (1879–1962), writer, patron, and salon hostess, was born in Buffalo, New York, the only child of upper-class parents, Sara and Charles Ganson. In 1900 she married Karl Evans, a young man from her social set. The birth of her only child, John, in 1901 was soon followed by the accidental hunting death of her husband and by the death of her father. These deaths, accompanied by the termination of an affair she had been carrying on with her family doctor, led to a nervous breakdown and to her being sent to Europe to recuperate.

On board ship she met Edwin Dodge, an architect from Boston, whom she married in Paris in 1905. Her second marriage was succeeded by the first of a series of severe neurasthenic depressions that accompanied her intimate relationships with men. When the Dodges moved to Florence and purchased a magnificent Medician villa, Mabel's depression lifted, as was often true when she found herself in the presence of a place or cause that aroused her creative energies. In Florence from 1905 to 1912, she adopted Renaissance modes of dress and decor, attempting to find her identity by appropriating a ready-made European past. She entertained emigré royalty and expatriate artists, including Leo and Gertrude Stein, whom she met in 1911. The Steins emancipated her from what she called "the dead forms of the past" by showing her the possibility of creating her identity through the psycho-aesthetic principles of modern art.

In the fall of 1912, Mabel moved to New York City, separated from Edwin, and launched a salon at 23 Fifth Avenue. Seeing herself in the vanguard of a revolutionary age, she cultivated friendships with Emma Goldman, Lincoln Steffens, Alfred Stieglitz, and scores of other modernists, whose debates over anarchism, psychoanalysis, postimpressionist art, and sexuality brought her gatherings national fame. She supported prominent artists, writers, and numerous political and social causes that she hoped would help bring about a world in which she could be "at home." A leading advocate of the avant-garde and an exemplar of the "new woman," Mabel was described in the press as a "national institution." In 1915 Mabel retreated from the urban world of the avant-garde to Croton-on-Hudson. Here she met the postimpressionist painter, Maurice Sterne, whom she married in 1916.

In January 1918, the Sternes settled in Taos, New Mexico. In 1923, after separating from her third husband, Mabel married Tony Luhan, a full-blooded Pueblo Indian. As a result of her relationship with him and her contact with the Taos Indians, Luhan underwent a conversion experience so compelling that she spent much of the rest of her life trying to convert others to an understanding and appreciation of the Pueblo way of life. With she and her husband leading the way, Luhan envisioned Taos, "the beating heart of the universe," as the center of spiritual and cultural redemption for Western civilization.

Luhan called others to Taos to help celebrate and preserve the Eden she believed she had discovered: Georgia O'Keeffe, Marsden Hartley, and John Marin, to immortalize its beauty; John Collier, to protect the Indians' land, rights, and culture; and Mary Austin, Willa Cather, and D. H. Lawrence, to write the gospel of her new world vision. In the Indian Southwest Luhan finally found her own creative voice. She published seven books in the 1930s and 1940s: *Lorenzo In Taos* (1932), *Winter In Taos* (1935), *Taos and Its Artists* (1947), and her four-volume autobiography, *Intimate Memories*, each volume of which deals with one phase of her search to make herself "real" (*Background*, 1933; *European Experiences*, 1935; *Movers and Shakers*, 1936; *Edge of Taos Desert*, 1937). Mabel died in Taos in 1962 of a heart attack. She never fulfilled her messianic dream, but she captured the spirit of place powerfully in her works and drew to her large estate many men and women of achievement and vision who did the same.

―――――――――――――

I am continually struck by the naïveté with which reviewers write about biographies. With rare exception, they evaluate the biography as a more or less accurate and interesting portrait of the life. They compliment or criticize the biographer for bringing, or not bringing, the person and his or her times to life. And they devote their review primarily to retelling the highlights of the subject's life. What they fail to notice is that biographers are active agents. Like fiction writers and historians they create their subjects from a particular angle of vision and with a particular set of strategies that help determine the outcome.

A few biographers—and it seems to me that they are often women—have begun talking publicly about the relation of their writing to their own lives, times, and interests. They have revealed the subjective, partial, and context-bound nature of biography, thereby demonstrating the importance of our paying close attention to the writer, the writer's narrative voice, and the dialogue that is established between biographer and subject.[1]

Biography is one of the last literary genres to hold out the promise of objective "truth." It is also one of the most Western and male-dominated genres. This is true not just in terms of the subjects traditionally chosen but also in terms of how the subjects' lives typically adumbrate the myth of the individuated heroic—or antiheroic—self. Integral to that myth is the distanced, authorial voice that provides the illusion that the life actually was as it is presented.

Women's lives have rarely fit the model of the normative biographical hero-type. As feminist biographers have carved out a major domain within the genre, we have not only uncovered and restored "lost" women, many of whom were not heroic in the traditional sense, but we have also called into question the masculinist grounds on which biography has conventionally been defined and accepted.

Perhaps we have helped to unmask the once-presumed objectivity of biography because of our sensitivity to the many ways in which women have been socially constructed. We do not assume that how a woman is defined determines who she "really" is. Our unmasking of our strategies and processes as writers of biography should lead to the creation of more authentic texts and to more probing and artful criticism of our work. But this can only happen if we are self-critical as well. As feminist scholars we sometimes impose subtle and not-so-subtle limitations on our subjects and our treatment of them. The new gender, class, and ethnic orthodoxies constrain us in some of the same old ways.

These issues are central to this essay. As I explore my intellectual and political autobiography, the influences of old and new historical and literary orthodoxies, and my choice and use of sources, I hope to further our understanding of the complex notion of biographical "truth."

Mable Who?

The question, complete with misspelling, was emblazoned in large white letters on a green T-shirt, presented to me by my cousins at the family book party celebrating the publication of my biography of Mabel Dodge Luhan. The question was a standing joke, and not only among my family members, who had no reason to know who she was. Whenever I brought up the subject of my biography among friends and colleagues, the few who had heard of her knew only that she had some connection to Greenwich Village before World War I or that she was associated with D. H. Lawrence's years in America. I assume that the "Mabel Who?" question is one that is asked of many biographers, even those who choose more celebrated subjects, although I believe that it is far more likely to be asked of biographers who are writing about women.

The question of who Mabel Dodge Luhan was seems to me particularly provocative, for she was hardly an obscure figure in her own lifetime. She organized what was perhaps the most interesting and infamous salon in American history. She participated in most of the avant-garde and radical movements of the 1910s; she had made her estate in Taos, New Mexico, a creative center to which numerous writers, artists, and reformers flocked in the 1920s and 1930s. From 1911 through 1940, her life story and character had figured in at least a dozen published novels, short stories, poems, and plays. Harcourt, Brace had published four volumes of her memoirs during the 1930s. She was lionized, patronized, and excoriated in scores of elite, radical, mainstream, and pulp newspapers and magazines at the local, regional, and national levels from her arrival in New York in 1912 through her declining years in Taos, in the 1950s. Yet by 1974, when I began my research, she was all but forgotten by scholars and public alike.

Mabel Dodge Luhan was lost to history for a number of reasons, not all of which I understood when I first began my research. I discovered her at a crucial moment in my own career—I needed to find a dissertation topic. I wanted one that no one had treated before, or at least one that was relatively unexamined. I knew that I wanted to write about a writer, but someone who did not fit easily into already established categories. As an American studies Ph.D. candidate, encouraged to cross disciplinary boundaries in the pursuit of an understanding of American culture, I had a kind of freedom of choice that would not have been allowed me at that time in a traditional English or history department. Although I had not determined to write about a woman, I can see in retrospect why such a choice was logical for me. I was starting my dissertation at a time when scholarship on women's history and literature was beginning to come into its own.

I first encountered Luhan in Christopher Lasch's *The New Radicalism in America,* a book that reexamined twentieth-century reform movements through biographical profiles of Progressive-era social and cultural leaders. In his chapter "Mabel Dodge Luhan: Sex as Politics," Lasch reinscribed her in the annals of American historical scholarship only to dismiss her as having only peripheral relevance to that scholarship. To be fair to Lasch, it is unlikely that my attention would have been attracted to Mabel Luhan if he had not offered more than a dismissive evaluation of her. Lasch was intrigued by her for one of the major reasons that held my attention over several years—the ways in which she served as a symbol for an age in transition, from the rigid and hollow but seemingly self-satisfied certainties of Victorian America to the exhilarating but chaotic new freedoms of the modern world.

As a scholar at the entry level of her career, however, I had to ask myself why I would want to undertake the study of a woman whom a reputable historian described as "a pioneer in the cult of the orgasm," one of those women purportedly responsible for the neurotic culture of narcissism that has undermined the moral fabric of society.[2] Only later, when I had read extensively in the Luhan archives and in women's history, did I begin to realize the profound misogyny of Lasch's stance toward Luhan, who epitomized for him his dislike of the "new woman" that first came of age in the early twentieth century.

Emily Hahn's subsequent biography, *Mabel* (1977), did little to restore Luhan's place in American cultural history. Hahn clearly disliked her subject, whose life she recreated primarily through gossip and anecdote with no documentation of her sources. In 1972, when I was just beginning my research, I called Hahn in order to learn whether her intended biography would preempt further work. I feared that such a forgotten and recently maligned figure as Mabel Luhan would not merit two biographies. She was kind enough to tell me that she had no scholarly intentions that would compete with mine.

Lasch's and Hahn's estimations of Luhan provide important clues to her historical demise. In their view, she did not contribute anything of "significance" to American history. She was a culture-carrier rather than an originator. She did not do "her own work" but depended for her identity on the work of creative artists, mostly men. She did not, in other words, achieve in the masculine realms of public activity. She was "merely" a muse, a catalyst, appearing fleetingly in the autobiographies and biographies of famous men, and thus relegated to near oblivion in scholarly works. In opposition to their point of view, I came to regard Mabel as an artist of life, whose realm of work had been undervalued, like that of many other women whose time and energy have been invested in the creative use of space and place to nurture the genius of others and who have provided arenas for the rich and contrapuntal discourse of the avant-garde; for example, Madame de Staël and Margaret Fuller.

Part of the transition to modernism, which Lasch did not discuss, was that of women who were reared, as Virginia Woolf puts it, to be "looking glasses" for men, but whose adulthood coincided with the second wave of feminism. These "new women" were among the first feminists to openly address issues of gender and sexuality along with the more traditional political and legal issues of women's rights. Mabel Luhan's life and writings exemplify some of the most complex issues faced by her generation of women, and they also help to clarify similar issues faced by our generation of feminists.

Like Mabel Luhan, I am a product of a transitional generation. I grew up in the seemingly safe, apolitical, and "feminine" 1950s. My father's involvement in the Communist party in the 1930s and in the Progressive party in the 1940s was a family secret kept from the children until we were adults. In college I was drawn to the study of American society and culture by Jesper Rosenmeier, a student of Perry Miller's. His thematic approach to teaching the survey course in American literature was to follow the millennialist strain in American thought and letters that defined the American mission from the earliest days of its "discovery" onward. This was my first encounter with an idea that made sense of the dominant culture within which I lived. It also moved me powerfully because of the distance I perceived between the realities of the American dream and its promise.

While discussing my biography with Rosenmeier at lunch one day, I realized that I was continuing to pursue the theme he had first introduced me to. The way that I make sense out of the broad outlines of Mabel Luhan's saga is to see her as part of the long history of American utopianists, for whom the promise of a brave new world lies just beyond the next frontier. They have always lived in a terrible contradiction between the desire to make the world over in their own image and their desire to find an Eden where the self can be subordinated to something larger than an all-consuming ego. In Luhan's case, the contradictions were exacerbated by her gender. She had been brought up in the late Victorian era to believe that as a woman she needed to depend on men to achieve power and to realize her identity; she came of age during the Progressive era, in a time and place when many women of her class were seeking to define themselves and to achieve their own dreams.

I came of age politically in graduate school. As a college undergraduate I was vaguely aware of the civil rights movement and the expanding war in Vietnam and considered myself politically liberal. But I had never tested my beliefs in any active way. Nor had I thought much about my personal responsibilities in relation to the social, economic, and political injustices of which I was intellectually aware and critical. While studying for my master's degree at Tufts University, I worked part-time in an Upward Bound program—where I discovered that I could be disliked on sight for being white and Jewish. In my first years of doctoral study, I joined the antiwar movement at the same time that I had my first academic exposure to the radical activists of the pre–World War I era.

When I discovered Mabel Dodge Luhan in 1974 and began to explore her life and times in greater depth, I recognized the striking connection between her generation and my own intellectual and political autobiography. The men and women in the Luhan circle were among the earliest to respond to the human costs of our emergence as a major urban industrial power and world empire. They were the first generation of American radicals to argue with equal passion for cultural and social revolution. For them, poetry, drama, painting, and the latest theories of psychoanalysis were as important to transforming the consciousness and social reality of the United States as labor union organizing and the building of an anarchist or socialist Left.

Those of us who have been engaged in the challenging process of recovering women's literature and history have often been driven by a desire to understand how the decisions we have made as scholars and teachers, lovers and friends, have been shaped by a past that we are both discovering and reinventing. Along with most of my colleagues in this volume, I am a product of the third wave of feminism that grew up and out of the civil rights movement, the war in Vietnam, and the counterculture of the 1960s and 1970s. In its various manifestations—hippies, yippies, new leftists, earth watchers, communalists—this rebel generation was seeking to transform America from a predatory military-industrial complex into a society that recognized equality, individuality, and the interdependence of all forms of life.

Luhan's generation of early twentieth-century activists asked and tried to answer many of the most salient questions that faced my generation of professionals and social activists: how to balance the personal and the political, how to cross the class and educational boundaries that separated us from "the masses," how much to work within, as opposed to against, "the system," and, most important for those of us who were feminists, how to construct our own gender identity. Researching and writing Luhan's biography provided me with my first sense of the historic legitimacy of my own (and my father's) political radicalization and created a link between my academic life and my life outside the academy.

It was fascinating work to trace Luhan's evolution—from an emotionally and intellectually deprived upper-class Victorian adolescent who had a passionate hunger to find and create a world of beauty; through her expatriate years in Florence, where she took on the well-established role of salon hostess and muse in her Renaissance villa; to her entrée into the revolutionary world of the avant-garde, where she broke out of the more debilitating constraints of her class and gender. Among other activities, she devoted her time and energy to supporting labor union organizers, bailing socialists out of jail, providing a meeting place for the birth control advocates, introducing Gertrude Stein to her American audience, helping to organize the Armory Show (the first exhibit of postimpressionist art in the United States), and writing for what was arguably the best radical journal of the pre–World War I era, *The Masses.*

The Male-Identified Woman

As I became further enmeshed in my research and in my career, I discovered that "Mabel Who?" was not the most difficult question to answer. When I talked about Luhan to my feminist peers, in what I thought was an engaged and engaging manner, the response I often got was a polite nod on the part of my listener, who soon changed the subject. My first clue to this response came during a conference when I was introduced to a colleague who asked me about my work. When I mentioned that I was writing about Mabel Dodge Luhan, Professor X replied, "She was male-identified, wasn't she?" Since this phrase was new to me at the time, it only dawned on me slowly that she intended the question, rhetorically, to cut off further discussion—and perhaps to put me in my place.

In terms of certain feminist and leftist notions of "correct" scholarship, I had chosen the wrong woman to write about, and she was wrong for numerous reasons. She was white, rich, and spoiled, with the financial wherewithal to do as she pleased with her life. She was a popular purveyor of her generation's versions of "new age" nostrums. She was a headhunter of creative geniuses and seemed to give legitimacy to Freud's ideas about penis envy. She was manipulative, domineering, and often suspicious of other women. She was a New Yorker who went to the "primitive" West of New Mexico, married a Pueblo Indian, and exploited the third-world culture of Native Americans, which she marketed to the nation through her writings and the works of her invited guests.

As I began to see how Luhan looked from the perspective of those I was ideologically aligned with, I became very uncomfortable. My discomfort increased when a colleague mentioned that she found biography a problematic genre because it privileged the individual in a way that was false to the complexities of the social fabric and thus reinforced political and social values we did not admire. In other words, why was I spending—or wasting—several years of my life writing about a single person, even if I placed her within a complex historical fabric?

At times these challenges made me feel defensive about my work. I was particularly concerned with the kind of reception my biography would have among feminists. In hindsight, it seems that I was overly concerned, for the reviews of my book have generally been very positive across the spectrum of political, critical, and scholarly opinion. Perhaps I made my case for Luhan well enough to preempt the kinds of criticisms I expected. However, I feel that some of the fears I had then about the reception of my work still need to be addressed, since I have no doubt that they affect the work of others as well.

If we are really committed to examining openly and honestly the lives of all of the varieties of women who have gone before, there can be no party line—spoken or unspoken—in terms of biographical subject choice. Certainly most women in the past have not transcended their gender boundaries. Many have been, and many still are, "male-identified," if what we mean by that is that they define a primary part of their identity in terms of their intimate relationships with men. In *The Female Imagination*, Patricia Spacks criticizes Luhan for needing men "to make herself real." She had, Spacks tells us, the wealth and personal freedom to do as she pleased, and yet her life and work convey "the essential confusion of the woman whose sense of reality was always vicarious—unable fully to accept herself" as a model or guide who points the way for other women, "unable fully to exist as a separate self."[3]

It is precisely this "essential confusion" that interested me in Mabel and that makes her representative of her times in ways that her more traditionally accomplished women friends, like Margaret Sanger and Georgia O'Keeffe, are not. In the introduction to my biography, I note that in spite of all Luhan's accomplishments, "the outstanding fact of Mabel's life is that she never found a clear and coherent direction for herself" primarily because "she believed that women were dependent on men to realize their destinies" (p.xii). The fact that Mabel had both the desire and the income to determine her own life made it all the more interesting to explore the reasons for her inability to discover her own route to self-fulfillment.

Luhan was certainly not oppressed in the more obvious ways that women of color and the working class have been. Nor did the men she married put any obvious impediments before her that made it impossible for her to do her own work. As a child, however, she suffered from a syndrome that I call, for want of a better phrase, upper-class child abuse. She was never physically punished, as far as I can tell, but she was intellectually deprived and psychologically damaged by parents who were emotionally frigid. Sara and Charles Ganson's lack of love for one another and for their only daughter exacerbated the problems inherent in the child-rearing practices common to their class. As is often true of physical forms of child abuse, Mabel continued the pattern with her only child, John Evans.

While doing my research on this period in Luhan's life, I could find little of substance that had been written about upper-class family life, parenting, and schooling in Victorian-age America. In fact, the first volume of Luhan's memoirs, *Background,* was my most important source of insight into this world. She understood better than many of her contemporaries how the upper classes of America transmitted their ruling-class hegemony to their children. The substitution of power for love began in the nursery, when they were turned over to nannies. Mabel remembers her five-year-old self seeking to escape loneliness by licking the Mother Goose figures on her bedroom walls. As she fights to establish her presence in the household, we see her discover how domination over others fills the emotional vacuum left by her parents. We also observe how her upbringing and education teach her the ways in which women of the upper classes must use their power—not in their own right, but to get what they want through men.

This is a subject with rich and complex dimensions that needs to be further explored by social and cultural historians as well as by biographers. It makes particular sense for those of us who define ourselves as leftists to devote some of our scholarly efforts to exploring the social fabric of the "power elite." Luhan was class-privileged in ways that were damaging to the development of her intellectual, emotional, and moral capacities and that limited her capacity for and interest in political discourse. But at her best in her memoirs she is an analyst of how and why this happened and of the ways in which she represented both a widespread social and cultural malaise and the attempts of one of America's most creative rebel generations to "cure" it.

The publication of Luhan's memoirs during the 1930s was greeted with the kind of political orthodoxy that one can also find today on the scholarly left. While some mainstream critics praised her volumes, most of the radical press greeted them with hostility. There is a fascinating irony in this because Luhan's indictment of pre–Depression America had much in common with theirs. She, however, went further than many of her critics, who accused her of being the personification of the bourgeois degeneracy that had brought on the Depression. Her memoirs demonstrate that in certain respects her life epitomized the psychological and social destructiveness of Anglo-American culture. It had produced individuals who lived by their will to power and domination over nature and people: the men seeking to master the earth, the women seeking to master the men.

One of Luhan's overriding purposes in publishing her memoirs was to offer herself as "a twentieth-century type" (her words), a paradigm for the decline and fall of Western civilization. It is not surprising that her memoirs were misunderstood and underrated in the 1930s, given the self-confessional nature of her writing and the seemingly self-indulgent life that she led. It is unfortunate that they are all but neglected now. Aside from my brief discussion of the writing of *Intimate Memories* in my biography, there exists only one other published essay on the subject, to my knowledge.[4]

While Luhan's writing is sometimes rhetorically excessive and tedious—the volumes certainly could have been better edited—this is not untrue of much of the literature of "ordinary" and sometimes extraordinary women who have been recovered from the past. She creates a vibrant, if at times infuriating, representative self—and she reveals that self within a richly elaborated social and aesthetic context that makes an important contribution to twentieth-century American social and cultural history.[5]

Intimate Memories is rooted in the tradition of the conversion narrative, a genre that imagines history as a journey from imperfection to perfection, where the search is for a paradise to be regained and where new beginnings are associated with new frontiers. One aspect of the originality of Luhan's work resides in her subversion of this primarily male-defined tradition, through which she radically alters the mainstream American journey myth.[6] *Intimate Memories* culminates with an Indian captivity narrative. Only here the white woman is not brought back to civilization from the "savage" world of the Indian. Luhan depicts the Anglo world as the anti-Christ or, in her more secularized imagination, as the exploiter of the earth and the destroyer of human community. The light of true faith and community lies in the world of the Pueblos and is brought to the Anglo world by one of its own, who has been captured and redeemed within the Indian world.

The Pueblos, Luhan believed, offered Americans what no so-called advanced twentieth-century society was able to: the model of a fully integrated society that was achieved through an intimate connection between the individual and community, work and living space, play and art. Their seeming lack of interest in material wealth, their devotion to spiritual values, their healthy respect for human limitation, and their adaption to, rather than exploitation of, the natural environment are presented throughout her writings as sane alternatives to a chaotic and self-annihilating white civilization. Because of the equal respect their worldview paid to the importance of male and female powers, Luhan associated the Pueblos with an essentially androgynous psychology in spite of their clearly differentiated gender roles.

The Indian-Identified Woman

When I first approached Luhan's work with and for the Indians, I saw it as unproblematic. Viewed from the perspective of the highly racist and nativist 1920s, the small but important achievements of her and her friends in trying to promote and preserve, rather than to denigrate and decimate, Native American cultures was highly admirable. The first national Native American protest movement of any consequence occurred in the 1920s. The primary seat of political activism on behalf of Indian land rights and cultural integrity was northern New Mexico, where numerous Anglo writers and artists worked in consort with the Pueblos. Mabel's husband Tony was an important go-between among them.

When I was at work on my biography, I never would have used the concept of cultural imperialism to describe Luhan's writing and activism on behalf of the Pueblos. But the rudest shock I received as her biographer occurred as a result of my not knowing why and how her work could be viewed in this way, and—by extension—my own work.

Following the publication of my biography I was invited to be part of a book project that focused on the creative work of Anglo, Hispanic, and Native American women in the Southwest. At one point, all the contributors appeared as part of a public forum at the University of New Mexico. I spoke on the work of Luhan and two other Anglo women writers, Mary Austin and Alice Henderson, who also wrote about and were influenced by the indigenous cultures and landscape of the Southwest.

At the close of my talk a woman in the audience got up and lambasted Mabel for coming to New Mexico and "ripping off" the Indians. Another woman stood up, turned to her, and, in a shaking voice, proclaimed that if it had not been for Mabel Luhan's writings she never would have discovered New Mexico, which was now her home. Later on that day one of the sponsors of the event informed me that there had been a complaint that I had been invited to speak. A member of the audience asked why a person from Massachusetts was working on "our" regional writers, the implication being that, like Mabel Luhan, I was an appropriator of other peoples' cultures.

After my initial astonishment—"Don't writers in New Mexico write about Emerson?" was my first thought—I simmered down and, over time, began to understand that I needed to confront the issues raised by the angry audience responses. Anglo women have, after all, been important patrons of minority writers and artists, and, in the case of Native Americans, many of the first major interpreters, translators, and promoters of their work and culture. This has been, I have come to realize, a mixed blessing.

The influence of Anglo reformers on the arts of indigenous cultures and their influence on Anglo artists are important and fascinating subjects of study. But I now understand why the work of Anglos as cultural interpreters and negotiators is problematic. A number of cultural historians and ethnographers have written about "the arts of the fourth world," the products of third-world indigenous peoples who have been influenced by first-world market demands. Those who have written specifically about Anglo patronage in the Southwest have brought to the fore the less attractive elements of their good intentions: their tendency to view Native Americans in static, romantic, and essentialist terms, their encouragement of individual artists among peoples for whom art was communally oriented, and the undermining of cultural integrity by the use of religious objects as decorative art.[7] My essay on Austin, Henderson, and Luhan, written after the conference, was influenced by these criticisms.[8]

One of my advantages as a biographer of Mabel Luhan is that I approached her life from a historical perspective that many of those in her more immediate neighborhood did not have. Yet my perspective suffered because of my too uncritical acceptance of Luhan's identification with and respect for an oppressed minority that I romanticized for some of the same reasons that she did. I also began to learn why my regional affiliation might make me suspect, as I have become more aware of the sensitivities of westerners, who have too often had their cultural productions relegated to second-class status by the Northeast's critical establishment. In fact, Luhan's most condescending reviewers were eastern critics who often patronized her affiliation with the "Wild West."

The Subject-Identified Biographer

My identification with Luhan's interest in and support of the Pueblo Indians, among other causes, did not mean that I identified with her—or so I once thought. I was initially surprised by how many readers of my book told me they assumed a close identification between Mabel Luhan and myself. I do not know if this assumption is made of most biographers, but I would not be surprised if it is more often made of female biographers writing about women than of male biographers writing about men.

The first time I came up against the suggestion that I identified with Mabel Luhan, I remember laughing in disbelief. Who, me? Independent, professional me, who had always worked hard in school and been clear about my direction in life? Yes, I had married when I was twenty-one and a junior in college, but there was a clear understanding between my spouse and myself that I was going on to graduate school. I had always assumed that I could be a wife, a mother, and a professional. I had followed the straight and narrow path to tenure. How could I identify with a woman who never held a job, who was a terrible mother, and who, although capable of enormous generosity of purse and spirit, was also capable of cruelty and mean-spiritedness?

Luhan's negative characteristics irritated me, but they were not an inhibition to my writing (although my voice sometimes took on a sarcastic tone that my editor made sure I amended). I have never believed that the only women feminists should resurrect from obscurity are the "nice" ones. Certainly no one has ever expected the subjects of male biographies to be "nice." Although I certainly understand the impulse for historically oppressed groups to look for admirable role models, our scholarship must include the full range of female personalities, just as it must include the full range of gender and class identities, if we are to understand our past and present.

In any case, I did not identify with Mabel in the sense of finding her wholly or even mostly admirable. I was fascinated by her, and I recognized her importance as a cultural indicator and as a cultural historian, but I was fairly dispassionate about her. I still feel that my perspective benefited from the fact that I had no axe to grind. When I began to think more about the issue of identification, however, I realized that I could not let myself off the hook quite so easily.

One night, not long after the publication of my biography, I was having dinner with a friend, who asked me about my relationship to Mabel. In answering her, I realized that Luhan appealed to the side of my imagination that likes to fantasize about being the queen of my own universe, with the money, creative power, and imperious will to do good and interesting things, to know adventurous people, to influence my times, and to live on the edge—psychologically and politically. While researching and writing my biography, I discovered that one of its most paradoxical delights was entering worlds that helped to explain my own but that were at the same time the antithesis of my own. Luhan's generation of cultural radicals was—for good and ill—kin to my own, yet they experimented with life and took risks that my personal and professional choices have not allowed. Writing about Mabel Luhan, her friends, and her associates allowed me to step through the looking glass that separates the academy from "real life." It has enriched my personal life by nourishing my imagination. In terms of my subsequent scholarship and teaching interests, it has also benefited my professional life in ways that I could never have imagined when I first encountered Luhan in Christopher Lasch's essay.

The Tar Baby of Biographical "Truth"

Perhaps because I was not always consciously aware of the personal and political forces that influenced my presentation of Mabel Luhan, I found dealing with the "objective" sources the most challenging and anxiety-producing element of writing. In his essay, "Hidden Name and Complex Fate," Ralph Ellison uses the African-American folk character Tar Baby as a symbol for the "sticky" world of reality that creative writers must labor with in trying to name their truth.[9] Perhaps Tar Baby is a particularly good symbol for biographers, who have to negotiate the dual realms of literature and history.

Sharon O'Brien has pointed out that biographers have to deal with contradictory expectations from their readers, for whom the goal of a good biography is to provide a true and convincing portrayal of a life while reading like fiction. Readers of biography expect something like a nineteenth-century Victorian novel, which may be one reason biography has become so popular a genre at a time when poststructuralist conventions affect literature as well as literary criticism.[10]

In recreating Luhan's life, it seemed as though I had the makings of a Victorian novel. I drew on some fifteen hundred pages of her published writings and on most of her available private papers, including hundreds of letters and seventeen scrapbooks of newspaper clippings of her and her friends' public activities. I also drew on the works and lives of the numerous male and female writers and artists who have given her their own imprint in autobiography, poetry, fiction, drama, painting, and photography.

In spite of what seems like an overabundance of sources, however, there were some large gaps in my information. The published memoirs of her years growing up in Buffalo and one schoolgirl copybook were the only materials I had available to me for the first twenty years of her life. The same was true for the last twenty years of her life, when she was rarely involved in public life and often ailing. In the Luhan archives at the Beinecke Library, there were several manuscripts belonging to her unpublished and "unexpurgated" memoirs that were restricted and thus not available to me.

In order to write about Luhan's childhood and adolescence, I had to rely on recreating the world that she lived in. I traveled to Buffalo, where I discovered that much of the neighborhood in which she grew up had been preserved or restored, including the building that housed her first school and the church she attended. A neighborhood preservation group that published an architectural guide to Victorian Buffalo and the archives of the Buffalo Historical Society brought the high-society life of the Gilded Age very much to life, providing me with a lode of resources for developing a historical context.

For her early and later years, I mined Luhan's published memoirs, which was perhaps one of my most difficult challenges, since I needed to keep in mind that I was using a highly mediated source. At the same time I did not want to sound like I was writing about her memoirs rather than about her life. It is a tribute to her rarely acknowledged abilities as a writer that her vivid perceptions and intelligent commentary provided me with some of my best insights. But her autobiography is sometimes a treacherous source. Luhan's letters make clear that she was conscious of creating a symbolic persona and of manipulating her self-presentation.

One-third of my biography is devoted to the fictional portraits of Luhan created by the writers and reformers in her circle. For writers as different as Gertrude Stein, Carl Van Vechten, John Reed, Max Eastman, D. H. Lawrence, Jacques Blanche, Witter Bynner, and Myron Brinig she figured as the "new woman" who introduced the modern era. Stein, Van Vechten, Eastman, and Reed celebrated her as the muse of a more enlightened and freer culture; Lawrence, Blanche, Bynner, and Brinig condemned her (although not altogether) as a virago who symbolized the United States' coming-of-age as a world power.

My decision to treat the fictional portraits of Luhan with as much seriousness as my other sources led to my experimenting with autobiographical form in a way that I felt did justice to my subject's breaking of conventions. Ironically, it also led to my manuscript being rejected the first time it was sent out to a reader. Because I interrupt my chronological narrative with sections on Luhan's relationships with the above-mentioned writers, the reader insisted that I had failed the simplest requirement of biography—to write chronologically.

For the last two decades of Luhan's life, I had very little factual information. Thus, I collapsed them into an epilogue and relied for my ending on a wonderful fifty-page letter that Mabel's granddaughter wrote to me. Bonnie Evans's portrait of her grandmother, whom she came to know best in Mabel's last years, was ideal for my purposes, not only because Bonnie saw her vividly but also because she was so clear-sighted about Mabel's strengths and failings. She helped me to understand how, in spite of her primary identification with men and her often decidedly unfeminist behavior, Luhan was a strong and independent woman who could serve as a role model for younger women. As Bonnie put it to me, "When it comes down to it, she did just about as she pleased her entire life and the sky did not fall in on her. . . . She is not seen, at this time, as a feminist heroine. When I knew her she was more than equal to anyone I ever saw her in relation to.[11] Bonnie also acknowledged an unintended benefit of this letter, as she finally came to terms with her relationship with her grandmother, which she had been trying to put into writing for years.

In my biography, I attempt the task of creating a coherent portrait at the same time that I try to remain true to the ambiguities and complexities of a woman who was viewed by herself and others from myriad and contradictory angles of vision. The difficulty of this task can perhaps best be seen in the final story I have to tell. It certifies for me the tenuous nature of our search for the authentic life in the writing of biography.

Many biographers have archive horror stories to tell, but those of us who write about twentieth-century subjects probably have more of them relating to restrictions that deny us access to documents important to our work. Many of our subjects have living relatives who are not always happy to have family stories retold for public consumption. In Luhan's case, her son John Evans was not only unwilling to talk with biographers about her but also insistent that certain of her papers not be opened until the year 2000. One of the reasons for his concern had to do with papers that reveal the ambiguity of his paternity, for Mabel's affair with the family doctor began before her son was conceived. (I learned about this from other sources before finishing my biography.)

For the past decade I have tried to get the restrictions lifted on the Luhan papers at the Beinecke Library, motivated in part by the fact that at least two other researchers have been given access to the restricted papers. One of these researchers, whom I met two years ago, discovered information that had I known of it at the time I was working on my book, would have undoubtedly affected my interpretation of Mabel Luhan.

I was calling her about another matter when she mentioned her interrupted dissertation on Luhan to me and casually asked whether or not I knew that Mabel had contracted gonorrhea from her family doctor and that her second and third husbands both had syphilis. I was dumbfounded to hear this, since the only information I had, based on interviews with native Taoseños and on Emily Hahn's statement in her biography *Mabel*, was that she had contracted syphilis from Tony Luhan at some point in her early forties. On my last research trip to Yale, I discovered that one of the restricted manuscripts had been released. When I read it, it corroborated much of what my informant told me.

While I must reserve judgment on the manuscript that Luhan wrote in her seventies about her early experiences with venereal disease until I can see the earlier manuscripts, I have no reason to disbelieve the essence of what she reports here about her first lover and three of her husbands. Luhan's essay is written in a somewhat bemused tone, perhaps because she was past the point in her life where the real tragedy of what she had experienced affected her any longer (she had taken the penicillin cure as soon as it was available). But the facts are horrific in spite of that. There was no cure for syphilis until the 1940s. If she started treatment in the 1900s, it was with a mercury compound, taken orally, that was often highly toxic. By the early 1920s, she was being treated with an arsenic compound that was less toxic. But she had to have weekly injections that caused a great deal of pain.

Dr. Parmenter was a married and prominent Buffalo physician who, if she is accurate in this essay, was simultaneously making love to her mother as well. When he told Mabel he had the "clap," she says she offered to "take it" from him, apparently unaware of the likely results. Mabel's second husband, Edwin Dodge, a more upright individual, informed her that he had been infected with syphilis but that because he was not in an infectious stage, he was safe (a common belief at the time). Her psychoanalyst, A. A. Brill, apparently discovered during therapy that her third husband, Maurice Sterne, was syphilitic. Mabel suggests that Tony's syphilis was contracted from a woman at the pueblo. At the end of her essay, she asks if it is possible that there is so much venereal disease in the world.[12]

I could not help but ask the same question myself. My curiosity led me to Allan Brandt's social history of venereal disease, *No Magic Bullet.*[13] Because I had some questions his book did not quite answer, I telephoned him. Although statistical data on the rate of infection are very fragmentary, estimates range from 10 to 50 percent of the male population in the early part of this century. Brandt feels that the higher percentage may be more accurate because no satisfactory treatment existed before penicillin.

Given the extraordinary social stigma associated with venereal disease, as well as the difficulty of finding primary source evidence by and about its sufferers, the Luhan papers dealing with this subject may be important sources for a field that still needs a great deal of investigation. Brandt spoke to me of the anger of some of the feminists involved in the social hygiene movement during the Progressive era, who attacked men for infecting women and destroying the lives of children. Even if the rate of infection was closer to 20 percent, the public health experts who spoke of an epidemic do not seem to have been exaggerating.

This new information has led me to have more compassion for Luhan and to wonder how much of her psychological and physical suffering—as well as the pain she sometimes inflicted on others—was due to her continual exposure to, and perhaps reinfection with, venereal disease. It also casts a more tragic light on the deep-seated hostility that underlay her dependency on men. In the 1930s, Luhan described herself to her friend Una Jeffers as always having been "frigid," a remark that I talk about in my biography as related to a number of factors, including her early socialization in the belief that a woman's sexuality was her major route to power.

My initial reaction to this new—and still incomplete—information was a mixture of anger and embarrassment. I was angry that I had been deprived of knowledge that would have allowed me to create a more accurate portrait of my subject; I was embarrassed that I was conveying misinformation to my readers. Although I am still angered by Yale University's most recent ruling that the remaining restrictions on the Luhan papers cannot be removed, I have also recognized another way to learn from this experience. No matter what evidence we have access to as biographers, the stories that we tell will always change over time because of our own changing personal histories and historical moments. Although we may re-create the lives of our subjects more clearly and fairly than they or their peers were able to, our portraits will always be unfinished.

As Doris Kearns has suggested in an essay on writing biography, this is a truth that should keep us modest: "We rummage through letters, memos, pictures, memories, diaries, and conversations in an attempt to develop our subject's character from youth to manhood to death.

Yet, in the end, if we are honest with ourselves, the best we can offer is a partial rendering, a subjective portrait of the subject from a particular angle of vision shaped as much by our own biography—our attitudes, perceptions, and feelings toward the subject—as by the raw material themselves."[14]

But, as the members of my women biographers group have suggested, this is also a truth that should exhilarate, not humble us. For we bring to our chosen genre the feminist challenge of creative indeterminacy—the continuous possibility of enriching and transforming our own—as well as our subjects'—lives.

NOTES

The photograph of Mabel Dodge (Sterne?) in Taos, New Mexico, ca. 1918, appears courtesy of the Yale Collection of American Literature, Beinecke Rare Book and Manuscript Library, Yale University. I want to thank my biographers group, Susan Quinn, Megan Marshall, Judith Tick, and Joyce Antler, for their help with the final insight in this essay.

1. See Bell Gale Chevigny, *The Woman and the Myth: Margaret Fuller's Life and Writings* (Old Westbury, N.Y.: Feminist Press, 1976), and her essay "Daughters Writing: Toward a Theory of Women's Biography," *Feminist Studies* 9/1 (Spring 1983): 79–102; see also Elinor Langer's dialogic narration in *Josephine Herbst: The Story She Could Never Tell* (Boston: Little, Brown, 1983).

2. Christopher Lasch, *The New Radicalism in America: The Intellectual as a Social Type* (New York: Vintage, 1965), 118.

3. Patricia Spacks, *The Female Imagination* (New York: Alfred A. Knopf, 1975), 225–26.

4. Jane Nelson, "Journey to the End of Time," *Biography* 3/3 (Summer 1980): 240–51.

5. The University of New Mexico Press has republished the last two volumes of Luhan's memoirs, *Movers and Shakers* and *Edge of Taos Desert*, in paperback (1985 and 1987, respectively). I am hoping to get the first two volumes republished as well.

6. See William Spengemann and L. R. Lundquist, "Autobiography and the American Myth," *American Quarterly* 17/3 (Fall 1965): 501–19.

7. See Nelson Grabhorn, ed., *Ethnic and Tourist Arts* (Berkeley: University of California Press, 1976).

8. Lois Rudnick, "Re-naming the Land: Anglo Expatriate Writers in the Southwest," in Vera Norwood and Janice Monk, eds., *The Desert Is No Lady:*

Southwestern Landscapes in Women's Writing and Art (New Haven, Conn.: Yale University Press, 1987).

9. Ralph Ellison, *Shadow and Act* (New York: Signet, 1953), 150.

10. Sharon O'Brien, "Feminist Theory and Literary Biography" (Paper presented at the December 1988 meeting of the Modern Language Association).

11. Quoted in Lois Rudnick, *Mabel Dodge Luhan: New Woman, New Worlds* (Albuquerque: University of New Mexico Press, 1984), 327.

12. "Doctors—Fifty Years of Experience," TS, Luhan Collection, Beinecke Library, Yale University.

13. Allan Brandt, *No Magic Bullet: A Social History of Venereal Disease in the United States since 1880* (New York: Oxford University Press, 1985).

14. Doris Kearns, "Angles of Vision," in Marc Pachter, ed., *Telling Lives: The Biographer's Art* (Philadelphia: University of Pennsylvania Press, 1985), 91.

JACQUELYN DOWD HALL

Lives through Time:
Second Thoughts on Jessie Daniel Ames

> They're prima donnas ... they're troublemakers ... and they
> all write their autobiographies in their latter years.
> —Lulu Daniel Ames, speaking of the
> women in her family (1972)

J ESSIE DANIEL AMES (1883–1972), a suffragist and civil rights
activist, is best known for her contributions to the fight against lynching. Ames was born in Palestine, Texas. Her father was a train dis-
patcher; her mother was a devout Methodist church worker. In 1893
the Daniels moved to Georgetown, Texas, where both Jessie and her
older sister Lulu attended Southwestern, a coeducational Methodist
college. At twenty-one, Jessie married a friend of her father named

Roger Post Ames. During most of their nine-year marriage, Roger was an army doctor in Central America. When he died in 1914, she was thirty-one and pregnant with her third child.

Ames launched her reform career in 1916, when she and her mother formed a county suffrage organization. Moving from local to statewide activism, Ames was in the thick of the battle that won for women the right to vote in primary elections and made Texas the first southern state to ratify the Nineteenth Amendment. She became the first president of the Texas League of Women Voters. As an officer of the Texas branch of the American Association of University Women, the Joint Legislative Council, the Committee on Prisons and Prison Labor, and the Federation of Women's Clubs, she pursued progressive social welfare goals throughout the 1920s. In 1924 she took a paid position as field worker for the Commission on Interracial Cooperation (CIC), the South's major interracial reform organization. In 1929 she moved to the commission's headquarters in Atlanta as director of its women's division. She continued the division's efforts to bring black and white middle-class women together in a campaign against racist stereotypes and for the improvement of segregated facilities. She channeled most of her energy, however, into a new organization, the Association of Southern Women for the Prevention of Lynching, which she directed from 1930 until 1942. During World War II, Ames initiated a series of meetings that culminated in the founding of the CIC's successor, the Southern Regional Council. Envisioning herself at the helm of a postwar campaign for voting rights and integration, she found herself forced into retirement and onto the sidelines instead.

In 1968 Ames lost a lifelong battle for autonomy to the ravages of age. She was in her eighties and too sick to live alone. Yet she refused to be institutionalized. In the end, her relatives took her—by force, sedated—from the little house in the North Carolina mountains she called "the wren's nest" to a nursing home in her native Texas. She died in Austin four years later, so thoroughly forgotten that her death went unnoted even by the Southern Regional Council, the organization she had helped to found.

When my study of Jessie Daniel Ames and the women's campaign against lynching appeared in 1979, I put it away, out of sight. I was moving on to new research in working-class history and leaving behind the years to which that book belonged. As it happened, though, I was not through with Jessie Daniel Ames, or rather she was not through with me. Asked to contribute to *Powers of Desire,* an anthology on the politics of sexuality published in 1983, I took the opportunity to refine my analysis of repressive violence and explore the connections between lynching and rape.[1] Two other events—a conference at the University of North Carolina on "introspection in biography" and an invitation to speak at a Smith College workshop on new approaches to women's biography and autobiography—brought Ames herself to mind.[2]

How, I wondered, had context and consciousness shaped my rendition of Ames's story? What new stories might I tell in different times and under different circumstances? Obviously, the answers called for self-reflection. But they also called for an understanding of the collaborative nature of the biographical enterprise, for *Revolt against Chivalry* was not fashioned by me alone. It was also produced by a circle of women who refused to let Ames and her antilynching campaign disappear into "the twilight zone that lies between written history and living memory."[3] Those women ranged from Ames herself, who saved the documents that made my project possible, to her daughters and coworkers, to the feminist historians who helped to create the discursive context in which my book made sense. Closing the circle, but also setting it in motion, was a postpublication encounter with Ames's niece, whose writings, inspired in part by my book, encouraged me to take a second look at some of the key documents on which *Revolt* depends.[4] Whatever its value to scholarship, I am sure that thinking back has been salutary for me. Intellectual tasks, like emotional ones, take their own time and carve their own spiraling paths. If the publication of *Revolt against Chivalry* seemed somehow premature, the essay that follows has the feel of a timely reckoning, a necessary settling of accounts.

The Association of Southern Women for the Prevention of Lynching, to which Ames devoted herself single-mindedly from 1930 until its dissolution in 1942, won nominal support from most major women's groups in the region. But the association's ability to effect grass-roots change depended on a network of Methodist women's missionary associations. Blending the evangelical impulse with the secular leverage of the vote, Ames asked local women to sign antilynching pledges, committing themselves to three kinds of female influence. As wives and mothers, association members tried to constrain the violence-prone men in their own families. As voters and members of small-town elites, they pressed county sheriffs to uphold the law. As members of a far-flung communications network headquartered in Atlanta, they beamed a withering light of publicity on local affairs.

Ames prided herself on careful organization and pragmatic action. But she also saw herself as a secular revivalist engaged, in the most serious sense, in a war of words. She sought to demystify and defuse the language through which white southerners expressed their racial fears and asserted their racial power. The black rapist, the chaste but vulnerable white lady, and her alter ego, the wanton black woman—these representations explained and justified racial practices ranging from segregation to extralegal violence. These were not just irrational fantasies. These were words invested with power, capable of shaping social reality. The Antilynching Association set out to turn this language on its head. In place of the black rapist as symbol of disorder, the association placed a white man—a lyncher of innocent black men, a fornicator, an exploiter of powerless black women.

Above all, the association rejected what Ames called "the crown of chivalry that has been pressed like a crown of thorns on our heads."[5] In this powerful counterimage, the same emotional logic that burned black men at the stake crucified white women. The "false chivalry" of lynching cast women as Christ-like symbols of racial purity and regional identity and translated every sign of black self-assertion into a metaphor for rape—black over white, a world turned upside down. Dependent on white men for protection and circumscribed by an image of the self as a symbol, women could not assert, sometimes could not even discern, their own individuality, their human needs. In place of the white lady as potential sexual victim, the Antilynching Association offered the autonomous woman citizen, requiring not the "crown of chivalry" but the equal protection of the law.

This is not to say that association members rejected the ideal of ladyhood outright. On the contrary, their chief strategy was to play on the image. Asserting their claim to gentility, they used their moral capital, as well as their class position, to persuade men to abide by the law. They spoke as insiders, and their effectiveness lay as much in what they were as in what they did.

By the time I began reconstructing this story, Ames and the Anti-lynching Association had found their way into the history books mainly as footnotes to the saga of southern liberalism. I first encountered them in a biography of Will Alexander, head of the Commission on Interracial Cooperation, a circumstance that would not have pleased Ames at all.[6] She blamed Alexander for forcing her to resign from the Southern Regional Council, and she had been highly annoyed by what she regarded as his biographers' offhanded and sentimental treatment of her role in the commission. Anne Firor Scott's *The Southern Lady,* by contrast, placed the Antilynching Association firmly in a female reform tradition.[7] As I pursued my research, a generation of feminist scholars was developing an increasingly dialectical understanding of that tradition, an understanding that turned on the relation between middle-class women's culture—the values, rituals, and networks formed under a system of sex segregation—and women's efforts at reform. From this angle of vision, the historical significance of the Antilynching Association emerged.

Unfortunately, there was a wild card in this interpretation: Jessie Daniel Ames, the founder, leader, and chief ideologue of the movement. The Antilynching Association, for all its racial daring, appeared to be a late-blooming variation on what were essentially nineteenth-century themes. Updating the "cult of true womanhood"—the belief in women's passionlessness and moral superiority—antilynching reformers saw their influence as radiating outward from the home. But Ames seemed to be cut from a different cloth. She sometimes used the rhetoric and methods of earlier reformers, but she had much in common with the breakaway generation of single women who sought not indirect influence but professional opportunities and political power. Her career depended on a constituency of small-town churchwomen whose courage she admired but whose piety she did not fully share. She wore ladyhood as a mask, employed evangelical language for reformist ends, and remained an outsider even in the organizations she ran.

At the time, this marginality sometimes made me feel victimized by my subject. Why was I writing about such an anomalous figure? Why not a Jane Addams or an Eleanor Roosevelt, who seemed to epitomize their times?

Looking back, I can see that Ames's marginality was part of what drew me to her. Feminist biographers are often engaged in acts of rescue, trying to restore to their rightful place foremothers who have been ignored, misunderstood, or forgotten. Ames suffered triple invisibility: as a woman in a region whose history has been measured by men; as a southerner in a women's movement that has been understood from the perspective of the urban Northeast; and as an individual whose talents and sensibilities were in some ways out of step with her circumstances and her times. I too was a product of the small-town Southwest, the first in my family to go to college, and for me, as for Ames, race and gender issues were always intertwined. I was not conscious of this at the time, but writing Ames into history was surely a way of asserting a view of feminism and of women's experience, indeed of the American experience, that was capacious enough for me and the women I knew.

In any case, my interpretation of the Antilynching Association evolved relatively smoothly out of the counterpoint between my own research and the cumulative efforts of other scholars. But when it came to *Revolt against Chivalry*'s biographical theme, I stumbled over problems of evidence and timing. Ames's correspondence was rigorously impersonal; it told little about the private experiences that shaped her public choices. And I gained access to the sources that revealed her personal story only after I had drafted the history of the movement she led.

The collaboration that made biography possible began when I arrived at the Austin home of Ames's youngest daughter, Lulu Daniel Ames. Tape recorder in hand, I was intent on asking personal questions about a woman who had already become a rather formidable figure in my mind. I knew from her mother's records that Lulu had suffered from infantile paralysis, but I was unprepared for the apparent frailty of the wheelchair-bound woman who met me at the door. Luckily, there was no time for diffidence. Lulu Ames summoned me indoors in a throaty voice uncannily like her mother's, brought out a bottle of Jack Daniels, and started to talk. The story she told me was compounded of family tradition, her own observations, and her reading of the letters, diaries, and autobiographical fragments that her mother left behind. From her I first heard about the "tragedies" in Jessie Daniel Ames's life: her father's open preference for her older sister, Lulu Daniel Hardy; Jessie's short, unhappy marriage; the agonizing search for her daughter's cure.[8] In the months that followed, Lulu Ames continued to go over her mother's papers, sending them to me with her own commentary, box by box, and calling at all hours to compare insights and interpretations. Those papers enabled me to add to my portrait of a reformer whatever psychological depth it may contain.

Several years later, after the book came out, one of Ames's co-workers gave me a letter Lulu Ames had written at a critical juncture, a letter that reminded me of the contingencies that shape historical research. Written just before Lulu decided to turn her mother's papers over to me (except, heartbreakingly, those she had destroyed the summer before), the letter sought to explain her motivations: "I do not mean that I didn't love Mother, that she didn't do a tremendous job, that she wasn't magnetic and creative and brilliant, that all her public life and work weren't remarkable.... But ... the whole ... person isn't known and the whole person was human and real and good and bad. And if Jackie writes a thing on Mother, I want it to be on all of Mother."[9]

Lulu Ames's desire to honor her mother without simplifying her complex life made biography possible. Yet the very factors that made the daughter's testimony so valuable also made it problematic. Lulu's father died before she was born. She spent her early life in and out of hospitals; in later years her mother was always on the road. Like her brother and sister, she sometimes felt neglected. Yet there was no denying the intimacy of the mother-daughter bond. All their lives, Lulu and Jessie kept up a steady correspondence. Until she was well into her twenties, Lulu filled her letters with a private language of endearment, mixing professions of love and dependency with news of progress or backsliding in her efforts to please. Ames reserved a special tenderness for her "sweetest ... gentlest ... most sensitive child." But mainly she dispatched instructions about what Lulu should eat, do, and wear. "I have no lectures for you," she might begin—and then proceed with detailed instructions about diet, exercise, money, and school.[10] When Lulu began writing her autobiography, Ames responded with a literary critique. End the story with your graduation from college, she advised. "I am the antagonist from this point on and overcoming that hatred for me which is akin to love and becoming close friends with me marks the end in fact of your psychological struggle."[11] As an adult, Lulu shared her mother's sense of irony, her taste for introspection, and her commitment to politics and reform. And she never ceased to view her mother with compassion and respect. But she also blamed Ames for holding her to impossible standards of "normality," for pushing her too hard.

Ames, for her part, may have seen her own psychic injuries embodied in her child. "I must destroy my wall of self-protection and take chances . . . even though I may be shot at, wounded, crippled," she once wrote.[12] At other moments she gallantly (if unrealistically) likened her daughter's accomplishments to her own. "I'll tell you right now," she admonished an interviewer when she was eighty-two and already suffering from the arthritis and osteoporosis that would soon make it impossible for her to manage on her own, "being on crutches is not a handicap—either for her or for me."[13]

When I met Lulu Ames, her mother had died only nine months before. Lulu had had a heart attack; a few years later, she too would die. Her willingness to help me was entangled with a process of "life review"; she was sorting out for the last time where her personality ended and her mother's began.[14] No wonder Lulu seemed to have been waiting for my arrival, preparing herself for exactly the project I had in mind.

It is difficult to describe the emotions this relationship with Ames's daughter evoked in me. I felt gratitude and excitement, to be sure, but also trepidation. How could I do justice to such intensely lived lives? How could I maintain my intellectual independence against the force of Lulu's interpretations? Mindful of the dangers, I circled around her testimony, supplementing it with other interviews and comparing it to written sources. All in all, I concluded that Lulu Ames was a remarkably reliable witness. And I would, for the most part, stand by the interpretations that grew out of our encounter.

Yet even as the story fell together, gaps remained. Chief among them was the private dimension of Jessie Daniel Ames's middle years. By and large, the documents that shed light on Ames's inner life had been written either before her antilynching career began or after she had retired. Other diaries had been destroyed, and I had only the public record of her forties, fifties, and early sixties, when she was at the height of her career.

But evidence was not the only problem. In retrospect, I would say that the intellectual context in which I worked was less helpful here than elsewhere. I would also say that although my own life experience made me sensitive to certain aspects of Ames's personal history, it may have hindered my understanding of other dimensions. Indeed, these two factors were closely related—the state of feminist scholarship at the time and the state of my own consciousness.

The problems with the literature are fairly obvious. The nineteenth-century preoccupations of women's history told us little about the modern era. The periodization that grew out of studies of the urban, industrial Northeast obscured the timing of generational change in other regions. Perhaps most important was the inadequacy of available models of psychological development. Even biographers like myself, who rely primarily on what might be termed disciplined empathy, need psychological tools. And those tools, as applied to women, were exceptionally crude. To be sure, feminist critiques of psychoanalysis had gone a long way toward modifying Freudian biases. Yet those critiques remained focused on the Oedipal romance and had little to say about sibling bonds or about the possibilities of growth and change over time. Developmental psychology, to which a biographer might naturally turn, was premised almost entirely on studies of men.

Among my own limitations was an unrealistic belief in the promise of sisterhood, nurtured by an idealistic view of the women in my own family, by the early women's liberation movement, and by the scholarship on the nineteenth-century female world. Once I discovered Ames's conflicted relationships with men, I looked for evidence that she relied for support and intimacy on women instead. But I found that even as she devoted herself entirely to a female public world, her private relationships with women were often marked either by distance and reserve or by stormy competition. The question then was what to do with these unwelcome signs of ambivalence where I had hoped to find female bonds. Nineteenth-century biographers often went to great lengths to prove the femininity of their heroines by suppressing traces of ambition, anger, or passion. With the popularization of Freudianism after World War I, scholars turned to portraying successful women as aberrations from a healthy feminine norm. In either case, where a man might be assessed wholly on the basis of his public accomplishments, a woman also had to prove herself in gender-specific ways in the private sphere.[15] Given this double standard, it occurred to me that writing about Ames's difficulties with men would reinforce sexist stereotypes. But that fear was allayed by confidence that the women's movement had created an audience that would not reduce public accomplishment to a compensatory flight from private failure. Ames's attitudes toward other women, along with her political rigidity and her devotion to intellect at the expense of the emotions and the body, were something else again. Here I had to struggle not just with concern about discrediting an admirable woman, but with my own feelings of disappointment—even, perhaps, dislike.

In the end, I argued that Ames's relationships with her father and her husband taught her the risks of intimacy and denied her a secure sense of feminine identity. At the same time, those experiences were a source of her insight and power. They mobilized her resistance, her distrust of paternalism, and her struggle for autonomy. Had all this occurred under other circumstances, Ames might have found her place within a separate, nurturing female world. As it was, she could neither wholeheartedly adopt the values of her mother's generation nor reject those values in exchange for such new ideals as sexual liberation or assimilation. Nor could she choose a single, professional life. She was trapped between Victorianism and modernism, finding neither fulfillment in women's networks nor success in male-dominated institutions. She transcended her dilemma through practical activity that linked her with other women in pursuit of political goals. But because she equated womanhood with weakness, dependency, and competition over men, she kept her distance from her coworkers, viewing them as followers to be influenced or dominated and not, for the most part, as equals and friends.

In response to this interpretation, a few reviewers gently suggested that I treated Ames's relationships with other women too negatively or that I placed too much emphasis on her personal limitations.[16] My own feeling is that the problem lay rather in my tendency to posit too sharp a distinction between the realm of intimacy and affection, from which she fled, and the realm of competence and instrumentality, in which she found satisfaction. Having assumed this dichotomy, I tended to underestimate both the emotional significance of Ames's relationships with women and the continuities in her inner life.

If I were writing *Revolt against Chivalry* today I would look harder at Ames's middle years. I would focus more sharply on her involvement with her sister, Lulu Daniel Hardy. Above all, I would amend my view of Ames's rejection of conventional femininity, stressing instead her attempt to heal the split between the masculine and feminine voices within.

Such a reframing would reflect my own passage through time. Since I wrote *Revolt against Chivalry,* the women in my family have grown up or grown old; we didn't turn out to be a latter-day version of *Little Women* (plus one loved brother) struggling through life in perfect unity. Instead we have had to come to grips with difference and distance and, over the years, to discover a new basis for solidarity that takes all that into account. I have also found myself on my own in the world in a way I never expected to be. The end of a marriage; a career that took; a right-wing offensive whittling away at gains my political generation hoped were secure. All this has given me a sense, which I could not have had when I started out, of what it means to survive—from one role to another, from one era to the next—and to combine, over time and in daily life, ways of feeling and behaving that I was raised to believe must be split apart.

More immediately, this revision would draw on the insights I gained from an encounter with a final member of the remarkable Daniel-Ames clan. I never met Ames or her sister Lulu. My sources reflected primarily Jessie's side of their story. But after *Revolt* came out, Lulu's daughter, Laura Hardy Crites, came to see me in Chapel Hill, bringing with her an essay she had written in response to my book. Entitled "The Sisters," it confirmed my basic conclusions, but it also encouraged a second reading of my critical texts. In the light of "The Sisters," I saw sub-

Jessie Daniel Ames and her sister, Lulu Daniel Hardy, in 1955. Courtesy of the Lulu Daniel Ames Papers, Southern Historical Collection, University of North Carolina at Chapel Hill.

themes in Ames's autobiographical writings I had not noticed before. Or rather, I took seriously comments that I had seen and not seen, read but in effect dismissed.

Looking back, Jessie Daniel Ames portrayed her marriage as a series of reconciliations and painful partings in which she was always being sent away to live, a Cinderella in exile, in her beautiful, well-to-do sister's home. By contrast, in her sister's account, Ames experienced her husband's sexual demands as an assault and sought asylum in her sister's home at every opportunity. Ames's first two children were born there, rather than with her husband in Central America or her parents in Texas, and she gave her last-born daughter Lulu's name. This is how "The Sisters" described those days: "Lulu surrounded her sister with constant care and attention, understanding and love. Her home was Jess's home. The two young women sewed together, read aloud, cared for their children, played cribbage, went for long afternoon buggy rides, planned the extensive entertaining that was called for by Lulu's [p]osition as wife of the commandant of [a military academy] and mistress of a large staff."[17]

Ames's father died in 1911; her husband's death occurred three years after that. Only then did she establish her own household, settling in Georgetown within walking distance of her mother, then moving into her mother's larger home. She and her children continued to spend summers with her sister's family. When Lulu's husband died, Jessie took care of her sister's children while she returned to school; Jessie's daughter, in turn, lived with Lulu during the Ames's move from Texas to Georgia in 1929. Clearly, Jessie was enmeshed in an intergenerational extended family in which she, her mother, and her sister relied upon one another's support and raised two sets of children as if they were one.

By the time Ames began writing the surviving versions of her autobiography, her memories hinged on resentment against a sister whom her father had outrageously adored. This is true of a relatively light-hearted memoir written when she was thirty-nine, as well as of the psychological self-scrutinies of later years. Starting out to examine her marriage in an essay called "Daniel-Ames Family Life," she wove back and forth between her husband and her sister, ending with an effort to absolve herself of guilt for "this antagonism, this dislike." Her goal was not reconciliation, but getting "this poison . . . out—and for good and for the last time."

Yet however much she might emphasize her present "antagonism" and "dislike," Ames also acknowledged other, earlier themes, themes more consonant with Lulu's recollections. When Jessie's honeymoon was cut short, "there was one comfort in being sent home that helped me. Lulu . . . wanted me to go back with her. I was delighted, made happy." After a long catalog of her sister's faults, particularly her helplessness and need for constant sympathy and attention, Ames ended with the claim that only by severing the relationship altogether could she avoid being reabsorbed by the "adulation and worship I used to have for her."[18]

I tended to discount such affirmations of sisterly love in part because of the force of Ames's more negative recollections. I also assumed that youthful feelings of "adulation" could even then have been manufactured from converted rage. There was, in any case, little doubt about Ames's later rejection of her sister or of the reverberations of that rejection in her public and private life.

The very rhetoric of the antilynching campaign mirrored Ames's rebellion against a model of femininity she explicitly identified with her sister. Where her sister was protected by men, she would reject protection in the name of autonomy. Where, in her view, her sister got her way through manipulation, she (and the Antilynching Association) would use the franchise to punish and reward. If her sister epitomized the southern lady as beloved wife, lavish hostess, and apolitical club woman, Ames would use the image of the lady for political ends.

Ames played herself off against her sister in her personal style as well. Photographs show Jessie to have been an attractive, soft-featured young woman with striking, luminous eyes. Yet her sister had occupied the place of beautiful daughter. Jessie had been the "tomboy," learning her first lessons in survival on the back lots of what she remembered as a desolate East Texas town. One game lodged in her memory with particular force. As a girl playing with "less respectable" children in an abandoned brick kiln, she was always the tail in "crack the whip," whirled outward to slam against the brick ovens until she fought her way close to the head of the line. Throughout her life, she prized physical vigor, hid weakness, despised sentimentality, and unnerved her male coworkers with her "direct way of walking and talking" and her strength of will. By contrast, she portrayed her sister, in later years, as a seductive hypochondriac and a "clinging vine."[19]

The importance of this motif is underlined by the frequency with which it crops up in writings on subjects with which it seems to have little to do. In a journal kept while her son Frederick was dying of cancer in 1958, Ames returned from the hospital to title that day's entry "Memories," devoting it to her sister and their childhood games. Sixteen years earlier, in a letter written to Frederick during World War II, she followed a familiar logic that linked her feminism, her self-image, and her sister's contrasting personality and views.

> Women in war work are demonstrating without a doubt that this ancient idea that women are delicate, fragile . . . creatures is being so fast exploded that soon a woman who can't do things will be as obsolete as the women who used to faint around and have the vapours. Your auntie thinks it is a shame and that women will be degraded by working in steel mills and boiler factories and other heavy industry. . . . If I were younger I would certainly be doing physical war work of some [kind] but the old gal at nelly bout sixty is not what she used to be. Though I still think I can do anything I really have to do at whatever the price.[20]

To a certain extent, Ames's relationship with her mother echoed the ambivalence of this sibling bond. In contrast to her comments about her sister, her writings acknowledged only minor conflicts with her mother. Laura Daniel fully supported her daughter's reform career, and Ames attributed to her mother the qualities she most valued in herself: devotion to principle and to keeping one's "chin up, fighting thro."[21] As a child, she had sided with her evangelical mother against her agnostic father, and she went on to build the Antilynching Association primarily on a base provided by Methodist missionary societies. Yet Ames wrote of her own conversion experience with a sense of distance and irony that was echoed in her stance toward the evangelical women she led. And she remembered her mother as remote and preoccupied, too busy to notice the loneliness of a little girl.

One might assume—and to a certain extent I did assume—that Ames's rejection of her sister's and mother's models would lead her to abandon the conventional feminine domestic role. But nothing could be further from the truth. She had three children to raise; she could hardly avoid domesticity. Moreover, it was through her ability to take care of her children, to support them without a husband's help (thus combining masculine and feminine roles), that she achieved the adulthood upon which she built her public success. In another sense, too, her public and private lives were inseparable. The respect and allegiance accorded her by coworkers in the Antilynching Association was based in part on their perception of her as an effective and heavily burdened mother.

Two incidents that occurred during Ames's middle age underline the depth of her investment in this nurturing role. In 1937 her mother died of cancer; in 1951 her niece Verona (Lulu Daniel Hardy's oldest daughter) succumbed to the same disease. Both women chose Ames, rather than her sister, to nurse them through their final days. Verona had already, from childhood, shifted her allegiance from her mother to her aunt, whom she took as a model of worldliness and political commitment. It is significant, I think, that Ames viewed nursing the sick and caring for the old not as burdens to be avoided but as privileges to be fought for, as opportunities to prove that she could blend the competence and control on which she staked her career with the ability to nurture, to take care. Emotional need thus blended with altruism; Ames saw these moments as victories over her sister, a vindication of her brand of womanhood, proof that she loved and was loved.

Ames wrestled all her life with these two sides of the self. Each, of course, is socially constructed—the instrumental, masculine mode; the affective feminine mode. In Ames's case those two voices spoke more loudly, warred against one another more painfully than they do in most of our lives. As a child, she played with boys but saved her affection for other girls. As a wife, she felt herself to be an impostor, a substitute for the womanly woman her husband might have had. As a mother, she played a double role. She was shadowed to the end by the ghosts of her father and her husband, but her existence turned on relationships with women. And the difficulty of those relationships did not detract from their emotional power. Beneath coolness, there was passion; difficulty was not the antithesis of love but rather its occasion. Alongside Ames's more visible self-assertion in the public realm ran an abiding desire to reclaim and express an affective life that she associated with weakness and rejection. Thus her lifelong obsession with her sister reflected more than sibling rivalry. She saw her sister not just as a negative prototype of femininity but also as an alter ego, an embodiment of a side of herself she could neither fully express nor abandon.

Nowhere is this struggle more evident than in her autobiographical writings of the 1950s. For Jessie Daniel Ames, this was a time of deep depression, and the reasons are not hard to find. Political fashions had shifted, leaving her stranded, a relic of a silenced feminist past. Her mother was dead; she had "broken" with her sister and left the church. She was dependent on her children for financial support, and she could be vicious in demanding her due. She concealed much and, of course, was misunderstood. In the past, she would have saved herself through work. Alone in retirement in the North Carolina mountains, she set out to conquer depression through self-knowledge. "My task now," she wrote, "is to break the habit [of a lifetime, to discover] what, if anything, I can do ... to attain peace within for the years that may remain to me."[22] Of all the distances she had traveled, perhaps none took more courage than this journey within.

That said, I would reaffirm, and even emphasize more strongly, my original perception of the satisfaction Jessie Daniel Ames won from her public role. If the spiritual quest of her late sixties reveals her private pain, an oral autobiography constructed fourteen years later attests to her resilience. Conducted by a journalist in Atlanta about

Jessie Daniel Ames, in Austin, Texas, May 24, 1965. Courtesy of the Lulu Daniel Ames Papers, Southern Historical Collection, University of North Carolina at Chapel Hill.

1966, this interview was initiated by a friend named Josephine Wilkins, who had shared and admired Ames's work. If Lulu Ames was responsible for salvaging the evidence of her mother's private life, it is to Josephine Wilkins that we owe our most vivid glimpse of Jessie Daniel Ames's public persona.[23] In this interview, grievance and self-doubt give way to serene self-possession. Ames minced no words about the shortcomings of her old colleagues or the importance of her own contributions. She voiced no regrets. Had the board members of the Interracial Commission disliked her? "They would have liked me if I had been submissive." Had their successors in the Southern Regional Council sent her packing? "They were blotting me out of existence—but I kept on breathing just the same." What, in the end, had motivated her? "It was my sense of justice and fair play, and it was the only thing that ever moved me and it always has."[24] The autobiographies of nineteenth-century women often stressed self-denial and played down achievement.[25] By contrast, when asked to order her life's meaning for posterity, Ames did so in structure, language, and detail that conveyed a triumphant conviction of competence and worth. Yet public performance and introspection must be read side by side. Together they constitute more than evidence of a life, grist for the historian's mill. They are, in themselves, a major achievement, a bid for transcendence and for immortality.

The construction of subjectivity has been central to women's history since the field's emergence in the 1970s. Indeed, the enduring appeal of biography—and its essential role in feminist scholarship—lies largely in its privileged access to that process. Biography also attracts us as writers and readers because of qualities it shares with literature. Puzzling out the narrative of another woman's life, we recognize dimensions of her character to which she herself is blind and consequently discover new dimensions and possibilities in ourselves. That project of self-discovery is open-ended, for just as we "remain a mystery to ourselves," so the biographies we write remain incomplete.[26] We have challenged the illusion of objectivity and given up the arrogance of believing that we can, once and for all, get our foremothers right. Second readings thus come with the territory of feminist biography. For only by telling new stories and telling our stories anew can we glimpse the truths that emerge not once and for all but all in their own good time.

NOTES

The opening photograph of Jessie Daniel Ames in 1937 in Atlanta, Georgia, appears courtesy of the Lulu Daniel Ames Papers, Southern Historical Collection, Wilson Library, University of North Carolina at Chapel Hill.

1. Jacquelyn Dowd Hall, *Revolt against Chivalry: Jessie Daniel Ames and the Women's Campaign against Lynching* (New York: Columbia University Press, 1979), and " 'The Mind That Burns in Each Body': Women, Rape, and Racial Violence," in *Powers of Desire: The Politics of Sexuality,* ed. Ann Snitow, Christine Stansell, and Sharon Thompson (New York: Monthly Review Press, 1983), 328–49. The following essay is a revised version of "Second Thoughts: On Writing a Feminist Biography,"*Feminist Studies* 13 (Spring 1987): 19–37.

2. Carl Pletsch and Samuel H. Baron organized the Chapel Hill conference and edited a volume of papers entitled *Introspection in Biography: The Biographer's Quest for Self-Awareness* (Hillsdale, N.J.: Analytic Press, 1985). This essay owes a good deal to them and to Susan C. Bourque and the participants in the Smith College Project on Women and Social Change 1983 summer workshop. I am also grateful to Joyce Antler, Mari Jo Buhle, Jeanne Clark, Peter Filene, Mary Hill, Robert Korstad, Elizabeth Minnich, Carol Stack, and Kathleen Much for their comments and encouragement. Grants from the National Endowment for the Humanities and the Andrew W. Mellon Foundation enabled me to complete the revision of this essay during a wonderful year at the Center for Advanced Study in the Behavioral Sciences.

3. C. Vann Woodward, *The Strange Career of Jim Crow,* 2d rev. ed. (New York: Oxford University Press, 1966), xii.

4. Laura Hardy Crites, "The Sisters" [1981], 12, in Laura Crites's possession. I am indebted to Della Pollock for the metaphor of a "circle in motion."

5. The quotation is from Wilma Dykeman and James Stokely, *Seeds of Southern Change: The Life of Will Alexander* (Chicago: University of Chicago Press, 1962), 143.

6. Ibid., 142–52. Kenneth T. Jackson, my advisor at Columbia University, introduced me to this book and encouraged my turn to southern history.

7. Anne Firor Scott, *The Southern Lady: From Pedestal to Politics, 1830–1930* (Chicago: University of Chicago Press, 1970), 194–99.

8. Lulu Ames, interview by Jacquelyn Hall, Austin, Texas, Nov. 11, 1972, Southern Oral History Program Collection, and Lulu Daniel Ames Papers, both in the Southern Historical Collection, Wilson Library, University of North Carolina at Chapel Hill.

9. Lulu Ames to Benjamin Mays, Jan. 22, 1973, Lulu Daniel Ames Papers.

10. Jessie Daniel Ames to Lulu Ames, Apr. 16, 1929, Lulu Daniel Ames Papers.

11. Jessie Daniel Ames to Violet Kimberly of Canada, Jan. 25, 1943, Lulu Daniel Ames Papers. Lulu apparently used "Violet Kimberly" as a pseudonym.

12. This reference to a "wall of self-protection" is contained in an autobiographical essay, "Post-Ames-Family," that Ames wrote about 1951 (in Lulu Daniel Ames Papers). It signifies the Berlin Wall and, more generally, the arms race, in an extended metaphor of "cold war." Jessie Daniel Ames drew on her private experience to understand social life. At the same time, she drew on her politics—in this case, an avid interest in international relations—in introspection. Thanks to Susan Bourque for drawing this aspect of Ames's thought to my attention.

13. Jessie Daniel Ames, interview by Pat Watters, Atlanta, Georgia, [1966], Southern Oral History Program Collection.

14. For the concept of life review, see Paul Thompson, *The Voice of the Past: Oral History* (New York: Oxford University Press, 1978), 100–113.

15. Jill Conway, "Women Reformers and American Culture, 1870-1930," *Journal of Social History* 5 (Winter 1971–72): 164–77; Joyce Antler, "Was She a Good Mother? Some Thoughts on a New Issue for Feminist Biography," in *Women and the Structure of Society: Selected Research from the Fifth Berkshire Conference of the History of Women,* ed. Barbara J. Harris and JoAnn K. McNamara (Durham, N.C.: Duke University Press, 1984), 53–66.

16. See, for example, *Oral History in the Mid-Atlantic Region Newsletter* 5 (Summer 1981): 1; and *Science and Society* 45 (Summer 1981): 236–39.

17. Crites, "The Sisters," 12.

18. Jessie Daniel Ames, "Daniel-Ames Family Life" [1951], 24, 18, 19, Lulu Daniel Ames Papers.

19. Jessie Daniel Ames, "The Story of My Life" [Feb. 27, 1922], 4–5, Lulu Daniel Ames Papers; Dykeman and Stokely, *Seeds of Southern Change,* 116; Ames, "Daniel-Ames Family Life," 23

20. Jessie Daniel Ames to Frederick Daniel Ames, Aug. 30, 1943, Lulu Daniel Ames Papers.

21. Jessie Daniel Ames to Mrs. W. A. Newell, Aug. 25, 1938, Jessie Daniel Ames Papers.

22. "Daniel-Ames Family Life," 22, 18. See also "Post-Ames-Family." For an eloquent description of a similar experience, see Elinor Langer, *Josephine Herbst: The Story She Could Never Tell* (Boston: Little, Brown, 1983), 299–331.

23. Josephine Wilkins, interview by Jacquelyn Hall, March 21, 1972, Southern Oral History Program Collection.

24. Jessie Daniel Ames interview.

25. Patricia Meyer Spacks, "Selves in Hiding," in *Women's Autobiography:*

Essays in Criticism, ed. Estelle C. Jelinek (Bloomington: Indiana University Press, 1980), 112–32.

26. Robin West, "Economic Man and Literary Woman: One Contrast," *Mercer Law Review* 39 (Spring 1988): 870. Thanks to Charles Lawrence for drawing my attention to this article.

SARA ALPERN

In Search of Freda Kirchwey:
From Identification to Separation

F REDA KIRCHWEY (1893–1976), born into a highly educated progressive household, is best known for her work on *The Nation,* one of this country's oldest political journals. She grew up in New York City, attended the Horace Mann School and Barnard College, and joined *The Nation* in 1918, clipping articles for its International Relations Section. She advanced to editor of that section the next year, became managing editor in 1923, then literary editor in 1928, and finally owner and publisher as well in 1937. She molded the journal until her retirement in 1955.

Kirchwey was a "new woman" of the 1920s who got some of her political education by working for woman suffrage and advocating the legalization of the dissemination of birth control information. Since she came of age in an era of changing morality, her story tells us much about the personal conflicts young people faced during that period. She and many of her contemporaries tried to balance a career with marriage and family, but, in addition, Kirchwey had to cope with the death of two of her three children. Her first son, born one year after her marriage to Evans Clark, died in 1917 at eight months of age; a second son died in 1930 at the age of six. Grief over this second loss prevented her from working for some time.

When she came back to work at *The Nation* in 1932, she merged her life with that of the journal. As the executive editor of a board of four, she used *The Nation* to examine the grievous problems of a world beset by the Great Depression and growing fascism. In the 1930s and beyond she conducted open forums increasingly focused on world events. Aroused by the firsthand reports of atrocities from Nazi Germany, she issued a sustained cry of outrage against fascism. A consummate journalist and a strategist proclaiming herself a "militant liberal," she transformed the formerly pacifist *Nation* into one that advocated collective security and eventually war. She publicized the horrors fascism wreaked on Germany, Italy, and Spain and pressed for homes for the refugees from the dreaded system and specifically a national homeland for the Jews. Once the United States declared war, Kirchwey declared a "Political War," to be fought in the pages of her journal, that gave a voice to political leaders ousted from their countries by fascists. When the atomic bomb ended the war but left the residue of death and destruction in Hiroshima and Nagasaki, Kirchwey spoke out for the public control and peaceful use of atomic power and for peaceful coexistence through the United Nations. After retiring from *The Nation,* she traveled, wrote for the *Gazette and Daily* of York, Pennsylvania, and served as United Nations delegate from the Women's International League for Peace and Freedom. In the 1960s, despite ill health, she worked for the Committee for a Democratic Spain. In 1971, after the death of her husband, she traveled to Switzerland to visit her son Michael and his family, residing with them for a year. She died in Florida on January 3, 1976.

In 1973, recently separated from my husband, I moved with my two-year-old son to Cambridge, Massachusetts, to do something I considered important. I would conduct research at the Schlesinger Library and contribute a dissertation to the then relatively new field of women's history. The next year I found Freda Kirchwey, or rather, the historian Kathryn Kish Sklar introduced her to me—not the living Kirchwey (at the age of eighty-one, she was already too ill to be interviewed), but boxes of her recently donated papers. I had come to Kitty Sklar's office to discuss problems I was having with the research topic "Women in the Twenties: What Happened after Women Got the Vote?" Sklar gave me some suggestions for that topic but also said a study of Kirchwey would lead to an excellent piece of original research.

I identified with Freda Kirchwey almost immediately after I read her description of a woman facing the changing morals of the 1920s: "Out in the world, in contact and competition with men, she is forced to discriminate; questions are thrust upon her. The old rules fail to work; bewildering inconsistencies confront her. Things that were sure become unsure. And slowly, clumsily, she is trying to construct a way out to a new sort of certainty in life; she is seeking something to take the place of the burden of solemn ideals and reverential attitudes that rolled off her shoulders when she emerged."[1]

These words from the introduction to the book *Our Changing Morality,* a collection of essays originally published in *The Nation,* piqued my interest in Kirchwey. I delved into her papers to get a feel for what was in those nine uncataloged boxes. Then I rushed off to Stamford, Connecticut, on a hot, humid July 4th on a standing-room-only Amtrak train to ask my advisor for approval to change my dissertation topic. He found Kirchwey a plausible subject because of *The Nation*'s stature as an important political journal but wondered about the influence of her husband or her father on her career as editor, owner, and publisher. In time I would be able to refute assumptions such as these—that women in nontraditional fields of power for women must be there because of a father or husband. Then, I was happy that he agreed to the change of topic and supported my decision to investigate the life of Freda Kirchwey.

When I returned to Cambridge I began my search. Kirchwey's pithy, forceful, witty editorials, her speeches, her diaries, and her correspondence continued to sustain my interest. One package of personal letters in her collection "hooked" me. These made me care about who she was and made me determined to know more.

"Letters During Jeff's Illness" read the words on the torn white sheet of paper tucked under the frayed ribbon. I carefully unknotted that ribbon and read and reread the letters it had protected since 1930. Freda had written these revealing letters to her husband, Evans Clark, while she cared for their terminally ill child, Jeffrey. She wrote of her fears, her joys, and of her and Evans's sexual life together and apart. No longer was she simply the polished writer I had come to admire. With her insecurities and dreams intact she came to life for me. This connection with the human being was a turning point in my search.

I had been drawn to Freda Kirchwey as a prospective role model. My seven-year marriage had broken up primarily over the conflicts of a two-career family. Influenced by the times, the nascent years of the women's liberation movement, I came to believe that my marriage could be saved only by sacrificing my career. Instead I chose my career. I still longed to combine a nuclear family with a profession. There must be a way to have it all. Freda must have found it, for she was successful in her work and had a lifelong marriage and three children. I set out to find out how she had done it.

I wanted answers to all the questions I faced as a woman, historian, and mother. How did Kirchwey work so successfully in a "man's profession"? How did she manage to fulfill society's "feminine" role when she did such unusual work for a female? Did she have time to be a productive editor and publisher and a good mother? How did she and her husband work out the problems of their dual-career family?

Although I wanted answers, I found more questions as the research I did revealed information that challenged my preconceptions. Why did the senior who graduated "Best Looking" from Barnard worry about being feminine? Why did she feel guilty about her children? Why did she take some three years out of her career to have "a little breathing spell"? Why did she bite her fingernails, have trouble sleeping, and suffer from persistent migraine headaches? Why would a successful career woman with a supportive family, money, and friends worry about being a "normal" woman? If the spunky, self-confident Freda Kirchwey, with all her advantages and accomplishments, suffered from the pressures of being true to herself yet wanting to be judged normal by her society, social strictures for women were more entrenched than I had thought. After all, I had begun by believing that in the 1920s, the years of Kirchwey's early career, women did do it all, successfully combining career, marriage, and family. Kirchwey's story of painful struggles convinced me that in her own time, solutions for successful integration had yet to be found. I also came to see that some of us modern women, misinformed about our heritage, had accepted impossible standards against which to measure our current efforts to combine private and public lives. I wanted to share this knowledge as a contribution to women's history.

Freda would have been uncomfortable with my armchair psychologizing. Although she believed in analysis and underwent psychotherapy during at least two stages of her life, she was a public figure who craved and protected her private life. But she might have been interested in my thesis that her personal story illustrated shared themes of women in history.

Kirchwey was a feminist and had no qualms about saying so. Although she had vigorously supported the suffrage movement and had advocated a number of reforms for women in the 1920s, by the 1930s other issues became more important to her than those of gender. To tell Kirchwey's story I had to move beyond the women's history questions that had originally interested me. But that research would come later.

Research Process

I began my search in Kirchwey's manuscript collection and resumed it there at various times over many years with fellowships from the University of Maryland, the Woodrow Wilson Foundation, the American Association of University Women, the Radcliffe Research Support Program, and Texas A&M University. Initially I found the Kirchwey collection in extreme disorder, but library policy prevented my disturbing or reorganizing it. Therefore I had to devise a unique note-taking system to accommodate the nine uncataloged cartons of manuscripts. When the collection was cataloged many years later, my return research trips yielded more efficiently gathered material.

Another challenge was to find out exactly which editorials Freda Kirchwey had written for *The Nation* so that I could read all of them. *The Nation* published some signed articles, but many editorials were left unsigned. To determine which of the unsigned editorials Kirchwey had written I followed the suggestion of Michael Wreszin, who had written a biography of Oswald Garrison Villard, Kirchwey's predecessor at *The Nation*. Wreszin told me that an annotated set of the journal existed and was accessible for use in the New York Public Library. (When I inquired in 1986, a librarian told me that this set had become too fragile for public use.) In this set, the handwritten initials of the writer appeared at the end of each piece. I checked through all the back issues of the annotated set during Freda Kirchwey's tenure, looking for the familiar "FK" signature.

Kirchwey's family gave me permission to conduct research with the stipulation that I not attempt to interview her. Her sister, Dorothy Kirchwey Brown, and her son, Michael Clark, did not want her bothered. At the time, she was only periodically lucid, not the Freda of her prime years. The realization that she was alive but that I would never meet her saddened me, especially because she would never know that I was writing about her. I had to develop other ways to get to "know" her. My extensive research in her manuscript collections and the papers of her family, *The Nation* colleagues, ideological friends, and enemies; in *The Nation*, the *New Republic,* and other journals; and in oral history interviews are all reflected in pages of footnotes that document *Freda Kirchwey: A Woman of "The Nation."*[2] But as I conducted my research and interviewed friends and family, I needed to go to some of her beloved haunts to get a feeling for how she experienced life. I visited *The Nation*'s offices in New York City. I walked in some of her neighborhoods in New York and into her former residence at 37 Washington Square West. I could not imagine Freda Kirchwey preening in front of the enormous mirrors on the ground floor. I went to her favorite restaurant, Ye Waverly Inn, and sat in a booth eating the chicken pot pie she always ordered there. I felt the coziness of the place and was convinced that this quality was what Freda must have liked about this unpretentious restaurant. I visited Ardnamurchan, the Clark family vacation home in Nova Scotia. I even convinced a dubious Michael Clark to row me out into the cold Nova Scotia waters so that I could swim where Freda had mostly floated. I tried writing with a pad and pencil, as she had done, but I compose better at the typewriter, so had to give that up. Once I sat down and retyped some of her key editorials verbatim, trying to get the feel of her writing, the flow of the words and ideas.

I also interviewed every person I could find who remembered Freda Kirchwey. I started with her sister, who had donated Freda's papers to the Schlesinger Library. Dorothy would often insist that I have a bowl of soup and some crackers before we got started with the interview.

As time went on and she discovered more papers, she would entrust them to me to bring to the library. One comment she made alerted me to the fact that the major collection had gone through a round of censorship. She said, "Look through them before you bring them in to make sure they are all right to give to the library."

Dorothy, active in the League of Women Voters, had been a friend of Eleanor Roosevelt's. Often she would divert the interview from information about Freda to chat about Eleanor Roosevelt or her other friends, Pauline and Josephine Goldmark, active reformers during the Progressive era. I wish I had taken notes on those diversions, but early on I was too fixated on my search for Freda and always tried to keep Dorothy on my subject. Dorothy was five years older than Freda, but her mind was still sharp. She provided much of the early history of the Kirchwey family. She also arranged an interview with Michael Clark, Freda's son, just two months after I had begun the project. Michael was in Boston visiting from his home in Switzerland.

Among the secrets of a good interview are the hours of preparation the researcher does beforehand. Despite several days of preparation, I knew that I had just scratched the surface of the vast Kirchwey collection. Although I was not ready to interview Michael Clark, I had to seize my chance to be in close proximity to him. This time less preparation proved helpful. I asked direct questions of Michael that would have been more difficult to ask even indirectly after I had read some of his letters to his mother. I asked him, for example, what kind of mother Freda was and how she blended her family with her career. Michael was sharply critical of her. I didn't want to hear his criticism; it didn't fit my expectation of the answers I wanted. But I recorded all of his remarks carefully, and in time, as I began to separate from Freda Kirchwey, I would integrate this information into my final analysis.

The oral histories I conducted with Michael and Dorothy, friends, former *Nation* colleagues, ideological friends and enemies all proved rich sources of information. I got better at these interviews as the years passed and as I learned to talk as little as possible and to listen to the answers to the open-ended questions I learned to ask. Always I prepared for several hours for each hour of an interview by complementing my manuscript research with extensive reading in secondary sources of the historical period. I want to share the sidelights of these interviews, moments of my search that had no place in the book but helped me connect with Freda Kirchwey, gave me new information and perspectives, and boosted my self-confidence, linking me to those who knew her, and so to Freda herself.

I interviewed Carey McWilliams for two hours at a New York restaurant. McWilliams succeeded Kirchwey as editor-in-chief at *The Nation* after she retired in 1955. After the interview we walked to his and his wife Iris's apartment, where he loaned me a typewriter. I began to type up all the information from the interview while it was still fresh in my mind and partly on my notepad and tape recorder. He finished writing an editorial for that week's edition of *The Nation*. Iris went out to do some errands and, on returning, remarked that neither Carey nor I had budged from our respective typewriters during her two-hour absence. I hand-carried his editorial to *The Nation* offices late that afternoon.

Another time I was ushered through the security check at the *New York Times* headquarters and into Robert Bendiner's office there. Feeling immediately comfortable after hearing his Pittsburgh accent (I was born there), I asked about his recollections as managing editor of *The Nation*. He told me that in those days, a government source would have been more responsive to his credentials as a *Nation* journalist than if he had been calling from the *New York Times*. He also told me that college men during his day used to carry *The Nation* and the *New Republic* in their back pockets to impress their dates.

During her interview, Freda's lifelong friend, Grace Epstein, related some of Freda's exploits in grade school through college. Once Freda convinced Grace to go out to a restaurant with her instead of studying at the library. Freda started to choke on some food and Grace (whose parents were fairly strict) screamed, "Freda stop that choking. You've got to stop that choking. If you die, it will be in all the papers, and my family will know that I was out in a restaurant with you." Grace Epstein provided much information about the early period of Freda's life and went over the yearbooks from their student days at Horace Mann School and Barnard College. She didn't remember much about Freda's mother, Dora, except that she was ill most of the time. I recall at the end of a series of questions about Dora, she said, "I'm afraid you'll have to settle with what you have so far on the mother." In fact, years later I was fortunate enough to find letters in Dorothy Kirchwey Brown's collection that detailed much more about Dora and her brave struggle to survive despite a long debilitating illness.

I will never forget the Washington, D.C., interview with the fiery journalist I. F. Stone, who had written for *The Nation*. He purposely arranged our first meeting in a coffee shop, where the music was so loud that I could not have recorded our conversation had I wanted to. He proceeded to interview *me* for most of the 1½ hours. Presumably I passed his test; he invited me to interview *him* the next day. Back in 1980 I was still identifying very strongly with Freda Kirchwey. I felt proud when Stone said, "The only thing in my life I regret is that I didn't get to be the editor of *The Nation*." Cheered on by my discoveries and by the support of people like I. F. Stone, I was also gaining more self-confidence. I will always treasure the words of encouragement he inscribed on two of his books, *The Truman Era* and *Underground to Palestine,* which he gave to me at the end of our last interview.

By 1983 I had put some distance between Freda Kirchwey and me, but I was no less dedicated to putting her ideas into the context of the times, and in so doing, finding the real Kirchwey. I had moved far beyond my original treatment of her as a new woman of the 1920s for my doctoral dissertation, in which I had given only a cursory glance at the latter part of her life. When I made a commitment to write a full-scale biography of Kirchwey, I knew I must reflect her interests, not mine. Her controversial positions on communism and the Soviet Union in the 1930s, 1940s, and 1950s had drawn ideological foes.

During that period critics often attacked Freda Kirchwey for being too sympathetic toward the Soviet Union, which she believed had every right to coexist with the United States as a major world power. No matter how repressive any particular actions of the Soviets were, Kirchwey never let go of her early dream that communism would survive what she considered its painful transitional phases. She believed Soviet leaders would make good their promises to create a just society. Perhaps because she was never a communist, Freda Kirchwey did not experience the disillusionment of former party members Arthur Koestler, Ignazio Silone, and others who wrote of communism as the "God That Failed."

I had not only to document Kirchwey's stands but also to understand those of her adversaries. I had read many of their books and articles and had studied secondary sources about the time period and its various ideological battles. That summer I also conducted interviews both in person or by phone with many of her ideological opponents. Some of the most important of these were with Daniel Bell, Irving Howe, Arthur Schlesinger, Jr., Sidney Hook, and Diana Trilling. I felt fortunate that

I was able to establish a good rapport with several of Kirchwey's ideological enemies as well as with those who had agreed with her.

I came away from my meeting with Diana Trilling with a better understanding of her belief that Kirchwey's faith in the Soviet Union had been misplaced, naive, and even dangerous, given the influence she wielded as an opinion maker of an influential liberal journal. Sidney Hook spent much of a several-hour interview at his home giving me quite a different point of view of circumstances surrounding some specific written exchanges between him and Kirchwey. He also sent me away with a list of sources for later use. The trail from Hook's charming home in South Wardsboro, Vermont, led around curve after curve. I was driving carefully but noticed I did not have my seat belt fastened. With no space to pull over, I decided to be that much more careful. Behind me came a car honking and honking, and in front of me were endless turns of the road. When the car behind me became more insistent, I became increasingly more frightened. Finally, I found a small place to pull over, expecting some crazy person to alight from the car. Instead, there was the kindly face of Sidney Hook, who was still casually dressed, wearing rubber flip-flops, and dangling my handbag from his hand. "You know what they say about people who leave things behind? They want to come back," he chuckled.

I remember the long entrance way off Orchard Drive in Cos Cob, Connecticut, the hot summer day when I found Barbara Tuchman's lovely home. The Pulitzer Prize–winning author's very first job was on *The Nation*. We shared lots of talk about Freda Kirchwey. At lunchtime she fixed a peanut butter sandwich for her grandchild, and one for me, too. She also sent me to my next interview carrying an inscribed copy of her *Practicing History*.

At another point that summer I reached a peaceful residence in Lenox, Massachusetts. I knocked at the door, before seeing the "come in" sign on it. I entered an outside study, with yet another door. I knocked on it but received no answer. I must have waited over an hour out there, and suddenly I heard a voice inside, talking on the phone. My next knock was much louder. A slightly hard of hearing William Shirer came out wondering just how long I had been there. We spent our time discussing Freda Kirchwey's lifelong commitment to reinstating a democratic Spain.

Aside from interviews with Michael Clark, my longest continuous visit took place earlier that summer with Caroline Whiting, who had worked for Freda Kirchwey at *The Nation* for twenty-five years. Caroline Whiting greeted me at the door, leaning on her walker, and asked whom I had interviewed the day before. When I told her, she grabbed my shoulder with one hand. "Tell me, does he still look like a rabbit?" So began three delightful days. I took pages of notes and filled several tapes with priceless stories and details. Although she was eighty-seven, her memory was still sharp; she even corrected a date I had jotted down incorrectly. In her cozy home in Winsted, Connecticut, I read the quote from the bottom of page one of *The Traveler's Journal,* which I dated July 11, 1983: " 'Good company in a journey makes the way seem the shorter,' Izaak Walton (1593–1683) English biographer." I wrote in the journal: "How true and I've been having wonderful company—delightful people who knew Freda—each so individual, each so special in his or her own way—each open, to a point, to share about her." All these interviews helped me fill out my picture of Freda Kirchwey. Some challenged my previous assessments; others confirmed judgments; still others gave me research leads for the future. They also reassured me that all this work to find Freda Kirchwey was worthwhile to others too.

During the summer of 1983, I interspersed interviewing with travel to various manuscript collections, including those of several of Kirchwey's ideological adversaries. Reading their own words helped me to experience the strength of their convictions, based on positions as intellectually and emotionally charged as Kirchwey's opposing views. I was able to put Kirchwey's beliefs in perspective and to recreate a fuller context for a number of key incidents.

Using Louis Fischer's manuscript papers at Yale, I documented his noisy resignation from *The Nation* in 1945 over the communism issue. In the Dwight MacDonald papers, also at Yale, I uncovered some intriguing information about Kirchwey, who had been an original member of the American Committee for the Defense of Leon Trotsky. Although unwilling to choose sides in the Stalin/Trotsky rift, she had joined the committee that was seeking asylum for Trotsky. She was to have received endorsements for the committee. Instead, after the committee issued pro-Trotsky statements without her knowledge, she resigned from what she decided had become a partisan group. Tracing this incident in Dwight MacDonald's manuscripts, as well as in her own papers, yielded a fuller critique of Freda Kirchwey—as did my treatment of her firing of Margaret Marshall as literary editor in 1953.

Kirchwey eliminated *The Nation*'s literary section, thereby abolishing Marshall's position. Marshall, a staunch anticommunist who had served on *The Nation* for twenty-four years, and as literary editor for fifteen years, charged Kirchwey with political motivation. Marshall had been given freedom to select books and book reviewers for the literary section. In the post–World War II years, that section had been as anticommunist in tone as the editorial pages had been sympathetic to communism and the Soviet Union. Marshall charged that she had been fired to bring the book reviews in line with the editorial views of the journal. Kirchwey vigorously denied any such intent. I struggled with my interpretation of this important incident for some time. Separate from Kirchwey, I assessed the evidence from each side and concluded that Kirchwey believed that the decision she made was strictly financial. I, however, included a caveat that no one can be certain of Kirchwey's unconscious motivation for this particular decision.

At some point in the middle of that summer's research trip I had a dream that encouraged me. In it Freda Kirchwey appeared in the black dress that she wore for the photograph cover of a 1944 Tribute Dinner Booklet. (The photo of her in this dress also accompanies this essay.) As Freda walked toward a friend and me, I exclaimed, "There's Freda Kirchwey. How young she looks. You would never believe that she is fifty years old, would you?" She approached me, carrying a black shoulder strap briefcase like the one I carried everywhere. Hers was made of leather but, like mine, had lots of zippered compartments. When she reached me, she said, "I've been mugged, but I don't have to worry about that anymore because"—she unzipped one compartment after another until she came up with a very small zipped sack—"because, I keep my valuables here." After showing me her valuables, she replaced them, zipped up the several compartments, put the strap back on her shoulder, turned around, and walked away. I awoke from this dream feeling elated. I interpreted the dream to mean that I had "mugged" Freda my first time writing about her, but that on this trip she was "showing me her valuables" and that I need not worry about mugging her again. Now I was on the right track to discovering a more accurate picture of Freda Kirchwey.

Maybe it was because Kirchwey showed me her valuables, or maybe I had simply moved beyond my original interests to understand hers. Perhaps it was my quest to understand the other side of that political worldview that had left her so isolated from so many previous political allies. Most of all, it may have been that I had matured as a person and as a scholar over many years. Whatever the reasons, I began to feel that I was getting closer to knowing the truth about Freda Kirchwey.

Difficulties

As my research and writing progressed, I faced several difficulties. At the outset was the mixed review I received for choosing to write about her in the first place. In the early years of women's history, scholars were determined not to write that history using male models of success and accomplishment. Uncovering the real history of women by tapping life among the anonymous women at home, at the workplace, and at schools seemed more important then. When I delivered a paper on Freda Kirchwey during the session called "The Invisibility of Prominent Women" at the Berkshire Conference on the History of Women in 1976, criticism focused on my writing about a white Anglo-Saxon Protestant woman who supposedly reflected a male model of importance. But I was convinced, and remain so, that while Freda Kirchwey was important enough by traditional standards to merit a biography, understanding her also helped me understand more about women of her times. Her influential career on *The Nation,* her creative stand against fascism, and her advocacy of civil liberties and the peaceful use of atomic power established her importance in twentieth-century liberalism. Attention to her private, as well as public, life in my questions of the sources I uncovered moved my study beyond an intellectual biography into women's history. Certainly the availability of sources for a prominent woman makes an in-depth private/public study possible and complements equally important work on anonymous women.

Other anxieties occurred during the final course of writing the book. Would the life story I revealed meet the expectations of readers? Not too long ago a friend asked me if her daughters should read my book on Freda Kirchwey. "Will Freda be a good role model for them?" she asked. The question struck at one of my most pressing concerns. Although modern women want role models, the problem is that the life stories of our presumed heroines don't always provide them. I, too, had begun my study of Freda Kirchwey to find a role model. I hoped that the Kirchwey/Clark couple had found answers to their dual-career marriage. I wished that Freda had paid more attention to her son Michael. As a feminist, there were times when I wanted the story to come out differently. As a historian I had to tell what I found. Although there are lots of lessons in the book, my book is not a "how to do it all" guide for modern superwomen. Freda did not live her life to be a role model for future women. She was a human being who did the best she could.

A related concern involved readers' judgments of Kirchwey after reading my biography of her. The temptation for a sympathetic biographer is to make the story come out right. The task of a scholar, however, is to tell the truth, no matter how damaging. This meant that I had to present her full story, of the effects of her parenting on her son Michael. I pointed out the irony of her reliance on child experts of the day to deal with Michael's obvious need for greater closeness. At the beginning of my search for Freda, I remember telling a senior colleague that Freda's son had expressed quite a bit of resentment against his mother. I later found letters corroborating this point of view. "Forget about Michael" the scholar said. "This is a story about Freda." But I couldn't forget about Michael. Not to include the relationship between mother and son would have been ahistorical and would have created a gap in her story. I had enough gaps in other parts of her life without purposefully creating one.

These gaps presented other problems. I found few personal letters written after 1930. The voluminous correspondence that I did find was much more politically than personally oriented. After the death of her son Jeffrey, when Kirchwey finally came back to work at *The Nation,* she seemed to merge her personal life into the journal itself. Early concerns dealing with women's issues all but disappeared as her personal struggle was subsumed in the working of the journal. For this reason, Kirchwey's personal life receded during the second half of the book. But what else is a scholar to do? We cannot make up sources where none exist. The book divides into two parts: chapters one through four contain detailed personal information; chapters five through eight contain little personal information. In hindsight I should have been more insistent that I prepare the reader more adequately for the book's abrupt shift in recounting Kirchwey's life and life focus.

A different kind of dilemma involved whether I could ethically include certain information. Being a good scholar was always my foremost concern, but there were grey areas where I realized how my scholarship might affect a living person. Over the course of writing the biography Michael Clark had been most helpful uncovering more papers, successfully getting his mother's Federal Bureau of Investigation files released when my efforts had failed, and reading for accuracy revision after revision of the manuscript. I decided that my portrayal of the death of Freda's son Jeffrey was wrenching enough, so that I need not use Freda's quotes telling the reader that Jeffrey was her favorite child. Out of sensitivity to Michael's feelings, I deleted the passage. Michael, who had read each word of the many revisions of the final book, noticed the missing quotes and wrote to me that I owed the reader this information. I put it back in.

My decision to write of Freda Kirchwey's and her husband Clark's open extramarital relationships involved similar concerns. I considered it necessary to reveal the fact of their relationships but hurtful to disclose the names of the other parties involved. To identify these people would pander to sensationalism and, more important, might have been an invasion of their right to privacy. Much to the disappointment of some reviewers, this biography does not scandalously name names!

Permissions

Tracking down permissions to quote in the book proved the final research task for me. While undergoing the last revisions, I also began the arduous permissions process. Harvard University Press wanted a "permission to quote" form signed for any extensive quotations from published journals and each direct quote from an unpublished source. This included every phrase quoted from a letter to Kirchwey or by her.

When I began note taking, I had thought that permission to use a collection at any given library actually gave the researcher permission to quote from any sources there in the published work. Nothing could be further from the truth. The person who holds the literary rights for the person quoted has the power to permit or deny the publication of any direct quote. That person can demand sums of money for this permission or a copy of the published book (or photocopies of chapters of the book). In my most extreme case, a son of a notable person originally asked me to pay him five hundred dollars for the privilege of quoting one of his mother's phrases. He eventually agreed to fifty. Thank goodness for the good working relationship I had developed with Michael Clark. He was the literary heir for his mother, father, aunt, grandfather, grandmother, and, of course, for himself, and he readily gave me permission to quote from family materials. Other permissions were harder to acquire.

There was also the matter of finding the person who possessed the literary rights. Many were deceased. Sometimes the person had disappeared without a trace. Occasionally a given library was helpful in having an address for the person in charge of the collection. But this was rare. I became a detective, tracing the missing person by a phone or letter search of colleagues or friends, from information that I found in an obituary (i.e., place of death, names of survivors), and through telephone books. Occasionally I tracked down a literary heir through the publisher of one of the deceased person's books or the journal with which he or she was associated. I had an excellent "find" record— with a few exceptions. Once I wrote to the Chilean government to obtain permission to quote a former Chilean ambassador. A package full of beautiful tourist booklets of Chile arrived; I never found the ambassador!

End of the Search

I was once told that to write a biography you must either love or hate your subject; you cannot remain neutral. I would put it slightly differently. My initial step in writing a biography of Freda Kirchwey was to identify with her. To complete that biography, however, I had to separate from her. The journey from identification to separation was long, but I had to travel it to produce a good biography.

The commitment to tell Freda's story became so strong that at times people had trouble separating us. Friends, wanting to know how I was, often asked, "How are you doing, Freda?" My son, barely three when I started my original project was at home with me at age seven when a visitor asked, "Josh, do you have any brothers or sisters?"

"Yes."

"Josh, it's not nice to lie."

"Mommy, I'm not lying. I have a sister."

"Joshua, you do *not* have a sister."

"Yes, I do; I'll show her to you."

He promptly jumped off the couch and brought over a bound dissertation, which he held out to the incredulous visitor, explaining, "This is my sister, Freda Kirchwey!"

Nor did the attachment disappear with time as I conducted research for a full-scale biography. I continued to trace every possible clue that came my way whether a colleague from Australia had sent it or whether I had found another manuscript collection to check out. Intent upon writing as much about Kirchwey's life as I could possibly find, I talked about her incessantly. The man I was involved with during the final preparation of a book on Freda Kirchwey once moaned, "I feel like I'm dating two women and one of them is dead!"

But there was also a gradual separation from her over several years. Immersion in the ideas and papers of some of Kirchwey's ideological adversaries was especially helpful. So too was the process of revising the manuscript to meet my reevaluations of her life and the rigorous demands of my editors at Harvard University Press. I was able to place Kirchwey more into the context of her times and to see other points of view that differed sharply from hers, resulting in some major reinterpretations of her positions. While I brought to life her admirable fight against fascism, her early determined exposé of Hitler and the Holocaust, her support for the establishment of Israel, and her resolute stand against McCarthyism, I also described how during her last years on the journal she became dogmatic, a quality that she despised. No longer was she "the invisible prominent woman" I would rescue for history. She stood as a human being restored to the proper place she once occupied in history, not a heroine, not a scoundrel, but a courageous woman who cared about causes with an amazing intensity.

Despite my intellectual separation from her, I retained an emotional link. Writing about those final years was painful. The epilogue seemed to take forever. Freda Kirchwey's tragic worsening mental and physical state got to me each time I rewrote the ending, and with every revision I cried. It was hard to say goodbye.

NOTES

The photo of Freda Kirchwey at her desk at *The Nation* in 1944 appears courtesy of the late Marion Hess. I am grateful to Charlotte Berkowitz and Elsie Kersten for their helpful comments on an earlier version of this essay.

1. Freda Kirchwey, ed., *Our Changing Morality* (1924; reprint, New York: Arno Press and the New York Times, 1972), viii–ix.

2. Sara Alpern, *Freda Kirchwey: A Woman of "The Nation"* (Cambridge, Mass.: Harvard University Press, 1987).

Pursuing the Life of a Star:
Helen Gahagan Douglas

HELEN GAHAGAN DOUGLAS (1900–1980) was born on November 25, 1900, the middle child in Lillian and Walter Gahagan's family of five. Lillian, a former schoolteacher, had grown up in Wisconsin; Walter, an engineer trained at MIT, in Ohio. The Gahagans moved to Brooklyn in 1897. Walter's engineering business prospered, and Lillian busied herself with raising children and participating in community activities. They lived in Brooklyn's posh Park Slope.

From a young age, Helen showed intense interest in the theater. She disliked school and did not apply herself academically. After failing most courses her sophomore year at Berkeley Institute, she transferred to another preparatory school for women, the Capen School in Northampton, Massachusetts. In 1920 Helen entered Barnard College, concentrating her energies on theatrical activities. Two years later she received a contract for starring roles on Broadway. Despite her father's opposition, she accepted the contract.

Although successful as an actress, Helen grew restless. In 1928 she began intensive voice lessons in preparation for operatic roles. She sang in Europe two summers but in 1930 returned to the stage in a David Belasco production. She married her leading man, Melvyn Douglas, and the two moved to California in 1931. In the 1930s, Melvyn became a well-paid leading man in Hollywood, but Helen had only sporadic opportunities to perform. Two children, Peter and Mary Helen, born in 1933 and 1938, added parenting responsibilities.

Both Douglases became involved in the Hollywood Anti-Nazi League in 1937. Helen then became interested in migrant worker problems. Aubrey Williams, director of the National Youth Authority, a New Deal agency, introduced the Douglases to President Franklin D. Roosevelt and his wife Eleanor in the fall of 1939. A friendship developed between the two couples that drew Helen into Democratic politics. She rose quickly in the party structure. Within six months of meeting the Roosevelts, Douglas became California's Democratic national committeewoman and director of the party's Women's Division in the state. She became well acquainted with high-ranking New Dealers and southern California's Democratic members of Congress and laid a political base for herself among California Democrats.

In 1944 Helen Douglas ran successfully for Congress from an inner-city Los Angeles district with a large black population. As her reputation as a leading liberal grew, she was reelected in 1946 and 1948 by increasing majorities. She fought for low-cost housing, price controls, and civil rights and worked diligently on the Foreign Affairs Committee to help shape President Harry S Truman's foreign policy program. She coauthored the Atomic Energy Act (1946), her principal legislative accomplishment, and Truman appointed her an alternate delegate to the 1946 United Nations General Assembly. In her third term Douglas challenged the incumbent conservative Democratic senator, Sheridan Downey. She lost the race to the Republican congressman Richard M. Nixon in a celebrated red-smear campaign.

Following Helen's defeat, the Douglases moved back to New York. Helen spoke widely, particularly on disarmament, joined the boards of liberal organizations, and campaigned for Democratic candidates. She spent time with her children, hoping to make up for long periods of separation in the 1940s. The Watergate hearings renewed interest in Douglas's political legacy. She died June 28, 1980. Her autobiography, *A Full Life,* was published in 1982.

In the 1940s, Helen Gahagan Douglas, the first actor and Hollywood figure ever to move successfully into national electoral politics, became a widely respected liberal member of Congress. By 1948, when she ran for her third term, she ranked at the top of blacks' and labor's list of critically valuable politicians on Capitol Hill, played an active role in refining postwar foreign policy as a member of the House Foreign Affairs Committee, and bravely stood out as one of few members of Congress willing to oppose legislation curtailing civil liberties as the cold war developed. A tall, stunning woman who presented herself in a dignified and fashionable style, Douglas's vivacious, warm, magnetic, self-confident manner motivated people to political action and created loyal staff members and friends.

In my biography on Douglas, I place her life into the context of early twentieth-century upper-class Brooklyn society, commercial Broadway theater in the 1920s, the Hollywood social and political milieu of the 1930s, female volunteerism in politics during World War II, and postwar liberalism. I look at how a female member of Congress with unusual credentials and wealth became powerful as a member of the second generation of postsuffrage women. I redefine congressional power, taking gender differences into account. I argue that the skills of a mature and talented actor can serve as excellent preparation for American-style politics. I also address questions arising from Douglas's determination to carve out her own professional directions while at the same time coping with her complicated home life as a wife and mother. This personal/public conflict shaped her professional style and choices.[1]

My investigation into the life of Helen Gahagan Douglas began in 1968 and was ending as I completed this essay. At the start, I was a twenty-five-year-old history graduate student at the University of Wisconsin, Madison, specializing in twentieth-century social and political history. I was also a new bride and a stepmother of two preschoolers. I held traditional notions about what historians did and how they acted. My father, Oscar O. Winther, was a well-known United States western

history specialist and my thirty-seven-year-old husband, James R. Scobie, a noted Latin Americanist.

The story of my Douglas biography follows the contours of my
changing life—to professional historian and mother of four, to widowhood, and finally into my first tenure-track job with the challenge
of single-parenting four children. The adventure also follows my evolution from a traditionally trained historian to a self-taught women's
historian. While it seems a long time to have had a book brewing, this
span of years of living with this project has profoundly affected both
my life and my view of Douglas.

As I wrote about Helen Douglas's life, changes in my own life
affected my interpretation of Douglas and vice versa. My work on the
book also influenced the perception I had of myself as a woman and
a professional. I grew increasingly aware, during the twenty-plus years
I worked on the project, of the difficulties women face in trying to
combine a professional life with marriage and child rearing. My historical vision of women also matured, as did my sensitivity to women's
issues, particularly as a teacher at a women's university and as a parent.
Second, I discovered the advantages and disadvantages of working on
a person who is still alive. Frankly, as a biographer, I consider it fortunate that I was able to spend time with Douglas, but I also am relieved
that both she and her husband, Melvyn, are no longer living. The
thought that she might eventually read my book made me uncomfortable. These feelings were complicated by the fact that she never
let me forget that I was writing about a star. Third, I found that I
changed the interpretive framework as I grew to understand Douglas
better as a professional and a woman. I also gained access to extensive
materials about her private life; I had to figure out how to combine
this new information with my conceptualization of her public life.

When I first became acquainted with Douglas, I had no interest in
writing her biography. I was working on my dissertation, which dealt
with anticommunist legislation in California in the 1940s, particularly
the activities of the state Un-American Activities Committee and its
chair, Jack B. Tenney. In the process of my research, at the insistence
of my thesis advisor, I gathered materials about the 1950 U.S. Senate
race in California between Douglas and Richard M. Nixon from the
Douglas papers housed in the Western History Collection at the University of Oklahoma. As they contained little information related to

my thesis topic, I stored the materials away. I do remember thinking it strange to be working on a California figure in Oklahoma. Apparently a university archivist who was in Washington, D.C., to collect papers from defeated Oklahoma members of the House of Representatives passed by her office door and offered his condolences about her Senate defeat to Nixon. In the course of the conversation, he learned she had no plans for depositing her papers in an archive and asked her if she would be interested in considering Oklahoma. She was flattered by the interest and agreed immediately.

Two years later, in 1970, I completed my Ph.D. and worked for three years as the assistant executive secretary to the Organization of American Historians (OAH). These were the infant years of the new field of women's history. I held this new marginal field at arm's length. Women historians had also begun working together for equal treatment within departments and professional associations as well as demanding services such as day-care centers at the annual convention. But I felt little kinship with these women. I had a supportive husband who helped cook, wash dishes, and take care of our children; I had little sympathy (and no firsthand acquaintance) with women less fortunate than I in terms of home support needs or professional position.

I did identify strongly with Anne Firor Scott and Willie Lee Rose, members of the OAH Executive Council, a group with which I worked closely. Both women offered me hope that I, too, could blossom with a first book in my forties and still be respected within the profession. (I made it—I turned forty-nine as my book was published.) I liked their style. It fit the professional mode in which I had grown up. They worked with men for women's goals, not angrily against them. They dressed like I did. The only noted "protesting" historian I even met during these three years with the OAH was Gerda Lerner, and I sat in complete awe of her. My only personal encounter with her was in the executive secretary's suite at an OAH convention. Her spiked hair complemented her huge purple sunglasses, mini-skirt, and wild gesturing. She had come to complain that it was not her fault that her membership had expired, making her ineligible to obtain a ballot for voting at the annual meeting; she had lost her renewal slip. (I have had, for some time, very deep respect and love for Gerda. We have chuckled over her early 1970s image.)

During these three years with the OAH, I concentrated on my mar-

riage, raising my two young stepchildren and our new baby, my challenging job, and some research and writing. Only later did I look back
and realize my naivete about gender issues in academe, including my
own professional life, my complete insensitivity to other women's
struggles, and my lack of awareness of what a "balanced marriage"
for a professional couple really meant.

My first positive response to women's history came in 1973. I received a letter asking me if I could present a paper for the Western
History Association annual meetings on a western woman (anyone, it
did not matter) for a session on women (no specific topic). I jumped
at the chance; I was still at the stage where I received few invitations
to give papers. I had those materials on the 1950 Douglas-Nixon campaign. As I prepared my paper, I realized that I did not care where
women's history stood in the profession; I found my study fascinating.
The issue of Nixon running against a woman became an important
theme. My paper was well received at the 1973 Fort Worth meetings.
By chance, I received considerable press attention because President
Richard Nixon's vice president, Spiro Agnew, had resigned that morning. I happened to be four months' pregnant and found myself mystified
when the photographer for the *Fort Worth Star-Telegram* took a very
close-up shot. When I asked him why, he indicated that the paper
would not publish photographs of pregnant professional women. I was
really taken aback, and a bit angry. I associate my interest in women's
history and equal treatment of women beginning with this paper and
the convention.

After the meetings I returned to the University of Oklahoma to
work in the Douglas papers to prepare my piece for publication.[2] As
I rummaged through Douglas's theater scrapbooks, opera programs,
and political speeches, I got hooked. Though I admit to the allure of
writing about a glamorous public woman married to a celebrated movie
star, what most intrigued me was the question of how a wealthy actress-
opera singer from Hollywood managed to get elected to three congressional terms from an inner-city Los Angeles district in which she had
never set foot prior to campaigning, and then nominated as the Democratic candidate for the U.S. Senate in 1950. The fact that in 1973
Helen and Melvyn, both in their early seventies, lived in New York
was important; I possibly could interview them. When I discovered a
group of over three hundred unidentified photographs in her papers,
I thought myself quite clever when I suggested to the Oklahoma staff

that I could take the photos to New York and work with Douglas identifying the individuals, the setting, and the date. The archivists were delighted with this offer of free scholarly assistance, despite the fact that I would be removing materials from the manuscript collection.

Douglas realized the importance of making the photographs more useful to researchers. She agreed to work with me, and in December 1973 we spent two days, occasionally with Melvyn, pouring over the photographs. Helen frequently asked Melvyn his opinion of who an individual might be in a photograph, but she generally argued with his reaction and rarely agreed with him. I gained my first insights into their relationship by listening to them interact.

I had a horrible experience on my way to Douglas's apartment, located at 50 Riverside Drive on the corner of Seventy-seventh Street, two blocks west of Broadway. I was by then six months' pregnant. I had donned a pants suit for the cold and rainy day. I felt self-confident and excited. My arms were loaded—a heavy suitcase with the photographs in one arm, a briefcase with books, tape recorder, and various supplies in the other, and an umbrella wedged in somehow. It did not occur to me to take a cab; I always used the subway, particularly for long distances. After battling crowds, I emerged at the Seventy-ninth Street and Broadway exit with a sigh of relief—only four more blocks. But I soon realized my new maternity pantyhose were gradually slipping down over my enlarged belly, carrying my slacks with them. With no restaurant in sight, I finally stopped in the secluded entrance of what turned out to be a synagogue. As I began pulling myself together, an elderly man approached the door. He only wanted to enter the building, but I became terrified and left immediately, still disheveled. When I arrived at the Douglas apartment, I was completely undone. I barely greeted the famous woman I had come to see, asking only for the bathroom. It was Douglas, not me, who played the role of putting the other at ease. After a cup of hot tea and a quick rundown about my husband and children, I had calmed down.

No matter the number of times I tell my students how *not* to arrive for a first interview, I am convinced that the humiliating incident affected my visit, and in turn our relationship, in positive ways. The situation could, of course, have resulted in quite opposite consequences. Unexpectedly we met as private, not public, women. While we changed roles back to public women as we began to talk about the photographs and many other subjects, a bond had formed. A second incident during that visit reinforced that bond. I received an unexpected phone call from my husband telling me he would shortly have to undergo a heart catheterization in New York for what appeared to be a very serious condition. After a helpful discussion about the situation with Douglas, we both shifted back to our professional roles. We did not have to say what we both knew; combining private and public lives was difficult but possible.

Throughout this intensive two-day stretch, we worked well together on the photograph project. I also spoke at length with her about various questions relating to her acting and political experiences. When I left, I sensed that she liked me personally; she was pleased to have a professional historian, not a journalist, take an interest in her life, and she trusted me not to misuse information she had given me. I parted with the comment that some day, when I emerged from child rearing, I planned to write her biography. She smiled but said nothing.

The Douglas project sat for four years, until 1977. But I began to grow as a novice historian of women. Probably the most intense changes occurred in 1975 when I held a Fulbright professorship in Buenos Aires. I taught women's history for the first time. This experience provided me with a new vision of historical interpretation and women's issues as they affected my students. I also became acutely aware that my husband and I did not share parenting and household chores in as well-balanced a fashion as I had thought. I remember telling him that since our careers were of equal importance, he should be shouldering half of the home-front responsibilities. He answered, "That doesn't make any sense; I earn three times as much as you do." During these months and subsequent years, after many discussions, Jim gradually diminished his professional load and became increasingly supportive at home; I in turn came to define my professional goals more clearly.

In 1977 we moved from Indiana University to the University of California, San Diego (UCSD). We left for two reasons: Jim felt he would have a less pressured job and thus could spend more time with the family, and I had been offered a token teaching position, three courses over a two-year period. Thus began another segment of four years, from 1977 to 1981, during which I once again became quite active professionally despite being knee-deep in children, aged three to fifteen. Jim and I also enjoyed a very intense but positive time in our marriage; we balanced our professional-spouse-parenting roles in a more equitable and mutually satisfying way.

In addition to my teaching, I also had the opportunity to explore Douglas's life once again. The Regional Oral History Office at the Bancroft Library, University of California, Berkeley, was working on a substantial project with Douglas and twenty-six of her friends and colleagues. I was asked to help edit and conduct interviews. My growing perspective on women's lives influenced the structure of my questions. I wanted to explore gender relations and issues in Congress and in political campaigns; how Douglas's personal and professional lives shaped each other and where the children "fit"; the structure of Douglas's daily life; and how various Washington women viewed Douglas— not just as a woman but a Hollywood "star."

In the fall of 1979, as my teaching responsibilities ended, I began serious work on the Douglas book. I traveled first to Fairlee, Vermont, where the Douglas family summered.[3] Douglas had agreed to see me briefly in September. My goal was to gain access to her private papers, which covered primarily her activities after the 1950 campaign. I was nervous. She did not feel well; breast cancer that developed in 1972 had recurred in 1976, spreading to her bones. She had scheduled hip replacement surgery for October. But as we began talking, she became increasingly open and friendly. After lunch she suddenly suggested that, since I was going to be reading all her personal letters, I might as well start with her summer correspondence while she napped. I was surprised but obviously delighted. I covered her frail body on the dayroom couch, closed the door, and began to read, mainly letters from longtime political friends. Before I left late that afternoon, she had invited me to stay with her in New York in December to go through her papers with the understanding that I would not interview her. She was working diligently to complete her autobiography and had limited energy.

The New York visit provided essential research materials for the post-campaign years, offered insights into Douglas's private life, and proved emotionally exhausting. I arrived in early December at supper-time and set my bags in Melvyn's bedroom, which I was to use while he was on location in San Francisco filming *Tell Me a Riddle*. (It took me about twenty-four hours to get over the excitement of sleeping in a movie star's bed with an Oscar, an Emmy, and other awards two feet away.) We sat down to a leftover pot roast dinner—complete with china, crystal, and silver—in front of the television to watch a meeting of the

United Nations Security Council. Mary Helen, the Douglases' daughter, aged forty-one and single, ate with us; she was living at the apartment to help care for her mother.

Douglas's days, unlike during the hectic pace of years past, followed a simple routine. She rose about 9:30 A.M., ate breakfast in bed, consulted with the elderly maid who had worked for the family for years, and then turned to her writing. Three unemployed actors helped out— one typed the hand-written pages of Helen's manuscript and two others alternated cooking dinner. Helen generally rested in the afternoon, worked a bit more on her book, and often concluded the day dictating correspondence to Nan Stevens, her longtime secretary. If Helen had not invited company for dinner, she, I, and sometimes Mary Helen dined and then watched television, played cards, or chatted.

Helen and Melvyn telephoned each other frequently to check on each other's health and to share the day's events. Occasionally a friend dropped by the apartment; several times one or a few guests were invited to dinner—extended family or close friends. Helen left the apartment only for brief walks. She included me in her conversations with visitors, and I often accompanied her on walks, moments I found delightful.

Other than these few diversions, my daytime work pattern was varied only by occasional errands I did for Douglas, episodes that offered clues to her temperament. Despite my careful adherence to a detailed grocery list when I shopped, for example, Douglas never failed to chastise me for spending too much money, a reflection of years of concern, often unwarranted, about lack of sufficient funds. The execution of one errand helped explain the remarkable devotion of certain female friends and staff, which I had never understood. In this instance, I offered to track down some bedroom slippers that Douglas needed. I proceeded down Fifth Avenue, which was overflowing with shoppers and slick with falling snow. I stopped in every major department store, starting at Sixty-fifth Street, each time without success. The temperature dropped as the sun gradually went down. I suddenly wondered, why am I doing this? Something kept me going, a need to please her beyond any reasonable expectations. I knew that Douglas could make people want to please her to the point of creating a dependency relationship; I had fallen into that trap. I finally found the right slippers, and I hurried back to Riverside Drive. I felt frightened; I realized that I had become too involved. I knew I had to back off, to distance myself to maintain detachment and scholarly integrity. A similar situation occurred again in the spring when she asked me to help her complete her autobiography. While I did a few simple research tasks that seemed overwhelming to her, I turned down the opportunity to become substantively involved. I had learned my lesson.

Another result of my visit turned out to be an awareness of family tensions, particularly between Helen and her children. Helen and Mary Helen often lapsed into sharp verbal exchanges, futile attempts to control each other. They argued about Helen's medical needs, Mary's dressing and eating habits, interpretation of the news, the "facts" of a family anecdote, how long to cook food, Mary washing her hair too often. Mary Helen was too old for the mothering she felt she had been denied as a child. She wanted to help her dying mother, to reverse roles. Helen felt somehow responsible for her daughter's unhappiness. Helen also had a fiery independence and disliked pampering from family members. All this resulted in constant bickering. The Douglases' son Peter, forty-six, had long since distanced himself emotionally and physically from his parents. Although he lived only a few blocks away with his wife, Janie, and three sons, he rarely visited. Helen kept in touch with the family's news by phone, principally through Janie. Helen's stepson, Gregory, in his mid-fifties, who lived in Connecticut, was not close to the family either.

The chance to spend substantial time with Douglas offered me as a biographer a most unusual opportunity. While I could only imagine what she was like in her younger years, the experience provided something concrete for my imagination. But while personal contact enriched interpretation, it decreased objectivity. As I have already mentioned, I was constantly aware of a fine line over which I knew I could not cross. When I inadvertently crossed the line (as in the case of the slippers), I knew immediately it was necessary to pull back. Helen, too, had her own line, but it was less defined. Sometimes she would open up about her feelings concerning Melvyn or the children—even ask my advice about Mary Helen. I also realized I was learning far more than I could eventually include in my book.

While I have suggestions for scholars who find themselves in the same position, I recognize that each relationship is different. The critical caveat is to know when you are in compromising territory. I believe the biographer should never get into a position of owing anything to her subject in the way of interpretation. Access should never be traded for detachment. Never become your subject's confidante. I do not recommend offering your interpretations, even if asked. You might change your interpretation about a question at a later date and, even more disastrous, lose your entrée through too much honesty. Your subject must know you respect her but that the interpretive realm is your province. Douglas never asked me what I thought about her, and I never questioned her about information I came across. I also opted not to interview family members outside of the primary unit despite their eagerness to tell me "marvelous Helen stories" because I did not want to get entangled in the Gahagan family network.

Six months later, during the summer of 1980, I took my family to Oklahoma for the summer. This research trip had been preceded by several shorter trips to Oklahoma and lengthy stays at the Franklin D. Roosevelt Library to probe the relationship of Douglas to the Roosevelts and the New Deal political activists Molly Dewson and Lorena Hickok; at the New York Public Library at Lincoln Center to delve into the Broadway years; and at several California libraries to look up papers of Helen's colleagues and friends. This trip was different, however, because I needed a full summer in Oklahoma, and I wanted my family with me. In theory, my husband Jim seemed most amiable about the idea; but when it became clear we were actually going, he found it hard to accept. He made only one negative comment, but it hurt. "My research takes us to Buenos Aires, which is fun for you; what does Norman offer me?" That very hot summer of 1980, it offered very little. I knew that I had to be relieved of most child-care and housekeeping responsibilities—who knew if I could ever come back for a long stretch? Initially I developed headaches, my research process was inefficient, and I felt guilty for wanting to have the family with me. When I was a child, my mother had played the supportive role when the family went west summers so my historian father could do research; as a wife I had done the same for Jim. I had no model for role reversal. Once again, Jim and I dealt with the "balance" issue, and eventually my time became productive.

That summer experience clarified new issues in my marriage, my understanding of women in general, and of Douglas specifically. I remembered the women to whom I had been exposed in the early seventies and felt new compassion. While Douglas spent considerable time away from her children, she, like I, had assumed the principal responsibility for making decisions regarding the children. Also, another shift in my perspective occurred that summer; Helen died shortly after I arrived in Norman. While I felt a degree of sadness, the overriding emotion was relief. When Melvyn died a year later, I really felt emotionally and intellectually liberated.

That summer I knew I needed an interpretive framework to shape my research. While I found the theatrical side of this famous, glamorous couple fascinating, I decided that a biography that dealt principally with Helen's political life, the public side, was a justifiable historical venture. It seemed logical to place Douglas within the framework of California history in the late 1930s and 1940s, minimizing her years before 1938 and after 1950. I planned to argue that she represented major themes in California's social and political history during this period. This regional structure served as the basis for an application for a grant from the Research Division of State, Local, and Regional Studies at the National Endowment for the Humanities.

The next year's research proved productive. Our marriage had reached a new level of love and sharing. In the spring of 1981 I received a research appointment at UCSD after learning of the success of my NEH grant application. I was completing a paper for the 1981 Berkshire Conference on Women's History. But on June 4, that world fell apart. With no warning signs, Jim collapsed; he died immediately. The eventual explanation, "probable cardiac arrhythmia." At the hospital, as dozens gathered, the fear that I could never finish my book frequently dominated my wide-ranging feelings and thoughts. The project had become an intimate part of me; yet at the same time I remained reliant on my intellectual and emotional relationship with Jim.

I knew I had to move away to progress in my career. As long as I lived in San Diego, I lived in Jim's shadow as his widow. Nine months later, I accepted a tenure-track position in women's history at Texas Woman's University in Denton, Texas, near Dallas. Living in Texas, teaching full-time, and raising four children (now aged eight to nineteen) away from anything or anyone familiar proved challenging and exciting as well as sad and lonely. But my life had silver linings. I eventually learned that I could finish the book without Jim by my side and raise children well without a husband/father. I lived in a state intimately linked to Douglas's closest congressional friend, Lyndon B. Johnson. Texas also had a network of politically savvy women of which I became a small part. These women, including Sarah Weddington and Ann Richards, brought some reality into my analytical perception of political women. Liz Carpenter also provided insights into Douglas (she was a young Texas journalist on the Hill during the 1940s) and into widowhood. I also became involved in community theater in Denton, rekindling an old interest. Although my family commitments would not permit the time required for acting, I combined my past theater experience with artistic training as a child and in college and began working with costumes, eventually designing for numerous productions and even winning awards. These new realities in my life heightened my understanding of Douglas.

During this transition period, I changed my interpretive framework in two ways. My Berkshire paper dealt with Douglas's relationship with Eleanor Roosevelt within the context of second-generation postsuffrage political women.[4] The regional framework I had established proved inadequate. Douglas was more than a California political figure; she had gained national stature as a politician. I also realized that to understand Douglas I needed to extend my study to a full-scale biography and interrelate private and public lives.

Developing a new, broader analytical structure proved frustrating initially. When viewed separately and through traditional evaluative frameworks, her careers as an actress, singer, and politician seemed to have no major significance. Although she was one of the leading Broadway stars of the 1920s, her name faded because she was only on the New York stage regularly for six years. She had a lovely voice, but not one adequate to gain her entrance into the best American opera companies. Despite national visibility as a politician, she served only three terms in Congress, and during the last one she spent much of her time running for the Senate. A new member of Congress, male or female, had little opportunity to make a legislative mark, the standard measure for congressional power. The growing body of analytical literature on political women legislators did not help. Irwin N. Gertzog in his book *Congressional Women: Their Recruitment, Treatment, and Behavior* (1984) offered for the first time a contextual framework for looking at female access to the male-defined congressional power structure. But he too left me wondering, where did Douglas fit? She was elected on her own, not as a widow; she had always moved quickly to center stage—she did not "pay her dues" in theater, opera, or politics.

My feeling of discomfort about Douglas as a viable subject for biography had another dimension. Biographies of women were not in vogue in the 1970s. While I had a growing understanding of the gender issues I needed to address, Douglas did not seem to measure up to current definitions of a feminist. My concern about this had initially developed in 1979 when the women's studies director at a nearby university invited me to deliver a paper on Douglas. The scholar wanted to make sure, however, that Douglas fit her view of feminism. I indicated that while Douglas worked for women's political involvement, the extension of social security to include jobs dominated by women, and equal pay legislation, she, like most 1940s liberals, opposed the Equal Rights Amendment and worked to preserve special interest legislation for women workers. She certainly did not think of herself as a "feminist" in terms of fighting for equal roles in rearing children, running a household, or in the labor force. I suddenly found the invitation to speak withdrawn. I kept going, but the doubts lingered. Eventually the intellectual climate changed.

My first conceptual breakthrough was a realization that Douglas's professional life could not be analyzed as three separate careers—acting, singing, and politics; it was an integrated whole. Douglas was an actress accustomed to success and attention throughout her lifetime. As she moved to different arenas for acting, only her stage and audience changed. Not all actors can move from the theatrical to the political stage, but Douglas could.

The growing literature of the postsuffrage generation of women reformers and the question of dual-career marriages also helped me understand Douglas. Historians began, for example, to recreate the female world that shaped Eleanor Roosevelt, who in turn helped define a new political milieu for women. Although Douglas's background did not parallel any pattern of political female participation, she did excel within the preexisting female-defined structure in her Women's Division work. She also came of age during a time when the discussion abounded about the possibility of continuing a career, marrying, and raising children. Helen's relationship with Melvyn and her children reveals her struggle to pursue her career and to take responsibility for the domestic health of their private life. The story of their relationship suggests the difficulty of maintaining a healthy dual-career marriage and helps explain certain professional decisions.

Another breakthrough occurred as I read in the political science literature on congressional power. While this literature dealt exclusively with men, I found I could apply certain assumptions and models to

Douglas. When she entered Congress, she discovered quickly that to have any sort of impact, she would have to play a nontraditional role. The first basic rule of legislative success—to specialize—did not interest Douglas. She considered herself a generalist fighting for an overarching plan for postwar America. Douglas saw political issues in terms of right and wrong. She had faith that government, run for and by the American people, should be improved through the power of the voter. She had little inclination to learn the intricacies of legislation. In her campaign manager Ed Lybeck's words, "Helen could not have gotten a bill passed making December 25th a holiday" even if she tried. He added, however, that "she was a light in the window for liberals at a time when things were very dark." House Speaker Sam Rayburn's dictum that new members should "go along to get along" did not fit her style. She had no intention of ingratiating herself with her colleagues. She got along with those who thought about issues as she did; she viewed the rest as her enemies or as simply incompetent.

The role that did work for Douglas was that of a self-appointed whip.[5] She had a distinctive flair that set her apart from her colleagues, yet her style was not a role unknown to the House or Senate. Political scientists have variously typed these legislators as outsiders, mavericks, crusaders, and agitators. Generally the fewer rules that such legislators followed, the faster they became cast in this nonconformist role. Ralph K. Huitt and Robert L. Peabody wrote in *Congress: Two Decades of Analysis* (1969) that outsiders feel "impelled to stand for principle absolutely, preferring defeat on those items to half-a-loaf." They like "to tell people what they should and frequently do not want to hear." These types take themselves very seriously, often lacking a sense of humor. While I had to add a gender component, these conceptual models fit Douglas well.

Materials to understand her private life—her self-perceptions as a young woman, her frustrations, once married, in carrying alone household and child-care responsibilities, carving out a satisfying professional life, and keeping alive a marriage punctuated with long separations—came from various sources, including interviews, her autobiography, letters, and insights gained from my personal contact with Douglas, her family, and her friends. This information made it clear that Helen's relationship with her family in the 1920s and, after 1931, with Melvyn and their two children played a significant role in defining her professional choices. On the one hand, Douglas could take risks that were not possible for most women. As a young actress she could be choosy about acting roles because she did not have to make her living from her salary; her wealthy father supported her. With Melvyn's income as a prominent Hollywood leading man she could continue to make choices about acting and singing opportunities. As California's Democratic national committeewoman, a volunteer position, she had the resources, unlike most others in a similar post, to set up an office, hire a staff, and fly all over the country to speak. She worked and socialized easily with Washington politicians. With her children in boarding schools and a secretary, maid, gardener, and cook, her time became increasingly her own, once Melvyn joined the army in 1942.

But her home life had its downside. Her decision to move to Los Angeles in 1931 when Melvyn had a movie offer decreased her acting opportunities. She did not want to act or sing for long periods of time in New York and Europe because that would take her away from home. Los Angeles provided few stage opportunities. For various reasons Helen Douglas did not have a film career. Eventually politics offered her a new stage, but after her Senate defeat she lost her political base when she agreed to move back to New York so that Melvyn could pursue a stage career. She also promised that she would shoulder full responsibility for their teenaged children. Over the course of her life, it is clear that she was torn between her professional interests and her deep sense of obligation to keep her marriage intact and to raise her children as best she knew how.

I was glad to dot the last "i" in this story. A biography is a never-ending project; at some point, one has to come to a halt. I finally reached that stage. My life helped define my perception of Helen Gahagan Douglas. And my work has, in turn, changed my professional and personal identity. So while in one sense my long venture is near a close, in another it will continue to play an important part in shaping my life. In the course of this project I became a part of those who consider themselves women's historians. I combined my research skills and my understanding of theater to become an active participant in theater production. Furthermore, for the last eight years, I have raised a daughter deeply involved in the theater. Every day at Texas Woman's University I work with women of all ages who are seeking, often desperately, to expand their lives as future professionals as they cope with children, current or past husbands, extended family commitments, and growing self-esteem. Questions about modern women and how they shape their lives will always affect who I am and my future research.

NOTES

The photograph of Helen Gahagan Douglas campaigning for Congress in 1944 appears courtesy of the Carl Albert Congressional Research and Studies Center, University of Oklahoma. Portions of the material in this essay have appeared in *Center Stage: Helen Gahagan Douglas, a Life*, © 1992 by Ingrid Winther Scobie, used by permission of Oxford University Press. I have been influenced by numerous historians, and I am indebted to those who read my manuscript closely. I mention only a few—Susan Ware, James T. Patterson, and Gerda Lerner.

1. My article "Helen Gahagan Douglas: Broadway Star as California Politician," *California History* 66 (December 1987): 242–61, 310–14, examines Douglas's public life. I overview her Broadway career in "Helen Gahagan Douglas," *Notable Women in the American Theatre: A Biographical Dictionary*, ed. Alice M. Robinson (New York: Greenwood Press, 1989), 218–22.

2. These initial findings were published as "Helen Gahagan Douglas and Her 1950 Senate Race with Richard M. Nixon" in the *Southern California Historical Quarterly* 58 (Spring 1976): 113–26.

3. See Scobie, "Helen and Melvyn Douglas: Two Lives in Vermont," *Vermont Life* 36 (Summer 1982): 35–37, for the importance of Vermont to the Douglases.

4. See Scobie, "Helen Gahagan Douglas and the Roosevelt Connection," in *Without Precedent: The Life and Career of Eleanor Roosevelt*, ed. Marjorie Lightman and Joan Hoff Wilson (Bloomington: Indiana University Press, 1984), 153–75.

5. Richard F. Fenno, Jr., *Home Style: House Members in Their District* (Boston: Little, Brown, 1978) proved particularly useful.

Notes on Contributors

SARA ALPERN is associate professor of history at Texas A&M University, where she teaches courses on the history of U.S. women. She received a Ph.D. in history from the University of Maryland. Alpern is the author of *Freda Kirchwey: A Woman of The Nation* (Harvard University Press, 1987). She has also written on the effects of woman suffrage, women in banking, and the history of women in management. Currently she is working on a book-length manuscript on the history of women in business.

JOYCE ANTLER is associate professor of American studies at Brandeis University and former director of its Women's Studies Program. In addition to her biography of Lucy Sprague Mitchell, she is the author of *The Educated Woman and Professionalization: The Struggle for a New Feminine Identity, 1890–1920* (Garland, 1987) and, with Elinor Fuchs, of *Year One of the Empire: A Play of American War, Politics, and Protest* (Houghton Mifflin, 1973). She has edited *America and I: Short Stories of American Jewish Women Writers* (Beacon Press, 1991) and, with Sari Biklen, *Changing Education: Women as Radicals and Conservators* (State University of New York Press, 1990).

DEE GARRISON is professor of history at Rutgers University, with a specialty in American women's history and radical history. Among her publications are *Apostles of Culture: The Public Librarian and American Society, 1876–1920* (Macmillan, 1979) and *Mary Heaton Vorse:*

The Life of an American Insurgent (Temple University Press, 1989). Current research is focused on the late 1950s protest movement against civil defense air raid drills.

JACQUELYN DOWD HALL is director of the Southern Oral History Program and Julia Cherry Spruill Professor of History at the University of North Carolina at Chapel Hill. She is the author of *Revolt against Chivalry: Jessie Daniel Ames and the Women's Campaign against Lynching* (Columbia University Press, 1979) and coauthor of *Like a Family: The Making of a Southern Cotton Mill World* (University of North Carolina Press, 1987; Norton, 1989). Her current research focuses on class, race, and sexuality in the turn-of-the-century South.

ELISABETH ISRAELS PERRY is associate professor of history at Vanderbilt University, where she teaches U.S. women's history. She is the author of *From Theology to History: French Religious Controversy and the Revocation of the Edict of Nantes* (Martinus Nijhoff, 1973) and *Belle Moskowitz: Feminine Politics and the Exercise of Power in the Age of Alfred E. Smith* (Oxford University Press, 1987; Routledge, 1992). Her present research is on the civic life of postsuffrage women in twentieth-century New York City.

LOIS RUDNICK is associate professor of English and director of the American Studies Program at the University of Massachusetts/Boston. She has coedited *1915: The Cultural Moment* (Rutgers University Press, 1991) and written *Mabel Dodge Luhan: New Woman, New Worlds* (University of New Mexico Press, 1984, 1987). She is now writing a history of the Mabel Dodge Luhan House in Taos, New Mexico, as "creative space."

INGRID WINTHER SCOBIE is associate professor of history at Texas Woman's University and specializes in American twentieth-century social and political history, the history of California, and women's history. She has published a variety of articles in these areas as well as in oral history and is the author of *Center Stage: Helen Gahagan Douglas, a Life* (Oxford University Press, 1992).

KATHRYN KISH SKLAR is Distinguished Professor of History at the State University of New York, Binghamton. She is the author of *Ca-*

tharine Beecher: A Study in American Domesticity (Yale University Press, 1973; Norton, 1976) and of numerous articles in women's history. Her book *Doing the Nation's Work: Florence Kelley and Women's Political Culture, 1830–1930* is scheduled for publication by Yale University Press in 1994.

SUSAN WARE, associate professor of history at New York University, is the author of several books on women in the 1930s, including *Beyond Suffrage: Women in the New Deal* (Harvard University Press, 1981) and *Partner and I: Molly Dewson, Feminism, and New Deal Politics* (Yale University Press, 1987). She is currently writing a book on popular heroines in the 1930s that focuses on Amelia Earhart.

ALICE WEXLER earned a B.A. in Latin American studies at Stanford University and then spent a year as a Fulbright Scholar in Venezuela. She has returned there several times to pursue research on Huntington's disease. After receiving her Ph.D. in history from Indiana University, she taught history and women's studies at Sonoma State University and the University of California at Riverside. She is the author of *Emma Goldman in America* (Beacon Press, 1984) and *Emma Goldman in Exile* (Beacon Press, 1989). Her book on Huntington's disease will be published by Times Books/Random House.

Index

Books in the Series
Women in American History

Women Doctors in Gilded-Age Washington:
Race, Gender, and Professionalization
Gloria Moldow

Friends and Sisters: Letters between Lucy Stone
and Antoinette Brown Blackwell, 1846–93
Edited by Carol Lasser and Marlene Deahl Merrill

Reform, Labor, and Feminism: Margaret Dreier Robins
and the Women's Trade Union League
Elizabeth Anne Payne

Private Matters: American Attitudes toward Childbearing
and Infant Nurture in the Urban North, 1800–1860
Sylvia D. Hoffert

Civil Wars: Women and the Crisis
of Southern Nationalism
George C. Rable

I Came a Stranger: The Story of a Hull-House Girl
Hilda Satt Polacheck
Edited by Dena J. Polacheck Epstein

Labor's Flaming Youth: Telephone Operators
and Worker Militancy, 1878–1923
Stephen H. Norwood

Winter Friends: Women Growing Old
in the New Republic, 1785–1835
Terri L. Premo

Better Than Second Best:
Love and Work in the Life of Helen Magill
Glenn C. Altschuler

Dishing It Out: Waitresses and Their Unions
in the Twentieth Century
Dorothy Sue Cobble